CLEP-3   COLLEGE-LEVEL EXAMINATION
         PROGRAM SERIES

This is your
PASSBOOK for...

American Literature

Test Preparation Study Guide
Questions & Answers

COPYRIGHT NOTICE

This book is SOLELY intended for, is sold ONLY to, and its use is RESTRICTED to individual, bona fide applicants or candidates who qualify by virtue of having seriously filed applications for appropriate license, certificate, professional and/or promotional advancement, higher school matriculation, scholarship, or other legitimate requirements of education and/or governmental authorities.

This book is NOT intended for use, class instruction, tutoring, training, duplication, copying, reprinting, excerption, or adaptation, etc., by:

1) Other publishers
2) Proprietors and/or Instructors of "Coaching" and/or Preparatory Courses
3) Personnel and/or Training Divisions of commercial, industrial, and governmental organizations
4) Schools, colleges, or universities and/or their departments and staffs, including teachers and other personnel
5) Testing Agencies or Bureaus
6) Study groups which seek by the purchase of a single volume to copy and/or duplicate and/or adapt this material for use by the group as a whole without having purchased individual volumes for each of the members of the group
7) Et al.

Such persons would be in violation of appropriate Federal and State statutes.

PROVISION OF LICENSING AGREEMENTS – Recognized educational, commercial, industrial, and governmental institutions and organizations, and others legitimately engaged in educational pursuits, including training, testing, and measurement activities, may address request for a licensing agreement to the copyright owners, who will determine whether, and under what conditions, including fees and charges, the materials in this book may be used them. In other words, a licensing facility exists for the legitimate use of the material in this book on other than an individual basis. However, it is asseverated and affirmed here that the material in this book CANNOT be used without the receipt of the express permission of such a licensing agreement from the Publishers. Inquiries re licensing should be addressed to the company, attention rights and permissions department.

All rights reserved, including the right of reproduction in whole or in part, in any form or by any means, electronic or mechanical, including photocopying, recording, or by any information storage and retrieval system, without permission in writing from the Publisher.

Copyright © 2025 by

National Learning Corporation

212 Michael Drive, Syosset, NY 11791
(516) 921-8888 • www.passbooks.com
E-mail: info@passbooks.com

PASSBOOK® SERIES

THE *PASSBOOK® SERIES* has been created to prepare applicants and candidates for the ultimate academic battlefield – the examination room.

At some time in our lives, each and every one of us may be required to take an examination – for validation, matriculation, admission, qualification, registration, certification, or licensure.

Based on the assumption that every applicant or candidate has met the basic formal educational standards, has taken the required number of courses, and read the necessary texts, the *PASSBOOK® SERIES* furnishes the one special preparation which may assure passing with confidence, instead of failing with insecurity. Examination questions – together with answers – are furnished as the basic vehicle for study so that the mysteries of the examination and its compounding difficulties may be eliminated or diminished by a sure method.

This book is meant to help you pass your examination provided that you qualify and are serious in your objective.

The entire field is reviewed through the huge store of content information which is succinctly presented through a provocative and challenging approach – the question-and-answer method.

A climate of success is established by furnishing the correct answers at the end of each test.

You soon learn to recognize types of questions, forms of questions, and patterns of questioning. You may even begin to anticipate expected outcomes.

You perceive that many questions are repeated or adapted so that you can gain acute insights, which may enable you to score many sure points.

You learn how to confront new questions, or types of questions, and to attack them confidently and work out the correct answers.

You note objectives and emphases, and recognize pitfalls and dangers, so that you may make positive educational adjustments.

Moreover, you are kept fully informed in relation to new concepts, methods, practices, and directions in the field.

You discover that you are actually taking the examination all the time: you are preparing for the examination by "taking" an examination, not by reading extraneous and/or supererogatory textbooks.

In short, this PASSBOOK®, used directedly, should be an important factor in helping you to pass your test.

NONTRADITIONAL EDUCATION

Students returning to school as adults bring more varied experience to their studies than do the teenagers who begin college shortly after graduating from high school. As a result, there are numerous programs for students with nontraditional learning curves. Hundreds of colleges and universities grant degrees to people who cannot attend classes at a regular campus or have already learned what the college is supposed to teach.

You can earn nontraditional education credits in many ways:
- Passing standardized exams
- Demonstrating knowledge gained through experience
- Completing campus-based coursework, and
- Taking courses off campus

Some methods of assessing learning for credit are objective, such as standardized tests. Others are more subjective, such as a review of life experiences.

With some help from four hypothetical characters – Alice, Vin, Lynette, and Jorge – this article describes nontraditional ways of earning educational credit. It begins by describing programs in which you can earn a high school diploma without spending 4 years in a classroom. The college picture is more complicated, so it is presented in two parts: one on gaining credit for what you know through course work or experience, and a second on college degree programs. The final section lists resources for locating more information.

Earning High School Credit

People who were prevented from finishing high school as teenagers have several options if they want to do so as adults. Some major cities have back-to-school programs that allow adults to attend high school classes with current students. But the more practical alternatives for most adults are to take the General Educational Development (GED) tests or to earn a high school diploma by demonstrating their skills or taking correspondence classes.

Of course, these options do not match the experience of staying in high school and graduating with one's friends. But they are viable alternatives for adult learners committed to meeting and, often, continuing their educational goals.

GED Program

Alice quit high school her sophomore year and took a job to help support herself, her younger brother, and their newly widowed mother. Now an adult, she wants to earn her high school diploma – and then go on to college. Because her job as head cook and her family responsibilities keep her busy during the day, she plans to get a high school equivalency diploma. She will study for, and take, the GED tests. Every year, about half a million adults earn their high school credentials this way. A GED diploma is accepted in lieu of a high school one by more than 90 percent of employers, colleges, and universities, so it is a good choice for someone like Alice.

The GED testing program is sponsored by the American Council on Education and State and local education departments. It consists of examinations in five subject areas: Writing, science, mathematics, social studies, and literature and the arts. The tests also measure skills such as analytical ability, problem solving, reading comprehension, and ability to understand and apply information. Most of the questions are multiple choice; the writing test includes an essay section on a topic of general interest.

Eligibility rules for taking the exams vary, but some states require that you must be at least 18. Tests are given in English, Spanish, and French. In addition to standard print, versions in large print, Braille, and audiocassette are also available. Total time allotted for the tests is 7 1/2 hours.

The GED tests are not easy. About one-fourth of those who complete the exams every year do not pass. Passing scores are established by administering the tests to a sample of graduating high school seniors. The minimum standard score is set so that about one-third of graduating seniors would not pass the tests if they took them.

Because of the difficulty of the tests, people need to prepare themselves to take them. Often, they start by taking the Official GED Practice Tests, usually available through a local adult education center. Centers are listed in your phone book's blue pages under "Adult Education," "Continuing Education," or "GED." Adult education centers also have information about GED preparation classes and self-study materials. Classes are generally arranged to accommodate adults' work schedules. National Learning Corporation publishes several study guides that aim to thoroughly prepare test-takers for the GED.

School districts, colleges, adult education centers, and community organizations have information about GED testing schedules and practice tests. For more information, contact them, your nearest GED testing center, or:

GED Testing Service
One Dupont Circle, NW, Suite 250
Washington, DC 20036-1163
1(800) 62-MY GED (626-9433)
(202) 939-9490

Skills Demonstration

Adults who have acquired high school level skills through experience might be eligible for the National External Diploma Program. This alternative to the GED does not involve any direct instruction. Instead, adults seeking a high school diploma must demonstrate mastery of 65 competencies in 8 general areas: Communication; computation; occupational preparedness; and self, social, consumer, scientific, and technological awareness.

Mastery is shown through the completion of the tasks. For example, a participant could prove competency in computation by measuring a room for carpeting, figuring out the amount of carpet needed, and computing the cost.

Before being accepted for the program, adults undergo an evaluation. Tests taken at one of the program's offices measure reading, writing, and mathematics abilities. A take-home segment includes a self-assessment of current skills, an individual skill evaluation, and an occupational interest and aptitude test.

Adults accepted for the program have weekly meetings with an assessor. At the meeting, the assessor reviews the participant's work from the previous week. If the task has not been completed properly, the assessor explains the mistake. Participants continue to correct their errors until they master each competency. A high school diploma is awarded upon proven mastery of all 65 competencies.

Fourteen States and the District of Columbia now offer the External Diploma Program. For more information, contact:

External Diploma Program
One Dupont Circle, NW, Suite 250
Washington, DC 20036-1193
(202) 939-9475

Correspondence and Distance Study
Vin dropped out of high school during his junior year because his family's frequent moves made it difficult for him to continue his studies. He promised himself at the time he dropped out that he would someday finish the courses needed for his diploma. For people like Vin, who prefer to earn a traditional diploma in a nontraditional way, there are about a dozen accredited courses of study for earning a high school diploma by correspondence, or distance study. The programs are either privately run, affiliated with a university, or administered by a State education department.

Distance study diploma programs have no residency requirements, allowing students to continue their studies from almost any location. Depending on the course of study, students need not be enrolled full time and usually have more flexible schedules for finishing their work. Selection of courses ranges from vo-tech to college prep, and some programs place different emphasis on the types of diplomas offered. University affiliated schools, for example, allow qualified students to take college courses along with their high school ones. Students can then apply the college credits toward a degree at that university or transfer them to another institution.

Taking courses by distance study is often more challenging and time consuming than attending classes, especially for adults who have other obligations. Success depends on each student's motivation. Students usually do reading assignments on their own. Written exercises, which they complete and send to an instructor for grading, supplement their reading material.

A list of some accredited high schools that offer diplomas by distance study is available free from the Distance Education and Training Council, formerly known as the National Home Study Council. Request the "DETC Directory of Accredited Institutions" from:

The Distance Education and Training Council
1601 18th Street, NW.
Washington, DC 20009-2529
(202) 234-5100

Some publications profiling nontraditional college programs include addresses and descriptions of several high school correspondence ones. See the Resources section at the end of this article for more information.

Getting College Credit For What You Know
Adults can receive college credit for prior coursework, by passing examinations, and documenting experiential learning. With help from a college advisor, nontraditional students should assess their skills, establish their educational goals, and determine the number of college credits they might be eligible for.

Even before you meet with a college advisor, you should collect all your school and training records. Then, make a list of all knowledge and abilities acquired through experience, no matter how irrelevant they seem to your chosen field. Next, determine your educational goals: What specific field do you wish to study? What kind of a degree do you want? Finally, determine how your past work fits into the field of study. Later on, you will evaluate educational programs to find one that's right for you.

People who have complex educational or experiential learning histories might want to have their learning evaluated by the Regents Credit Bank. The Credit Bank, operated by Regents College of the University of the State of New York, allows people to consolidate credits earned through college, experience, or other methods. Special assessments are available for Regents College enrollees whose knowledge in a specific field cannot be adequately evaluated by standardized exams. For more information, contact the Regents Credit Bank at:

Regents College
7 Columbia Circle
Albany, NY 12203-5159
(518) 464-8500

Credit For Prior College Coursework

When Lynette was in college during the 1970s, she attended several different schools and took a variety of courses. She did well in some classes and poorly in others. Now that she is a successful business owner and has more focus, Lynette thinks she should forget about her previous coursework and start from scratch. Instead, she should start from where she is.

Lynette should have all her transcripts sent to the colleges or universities of her choice and let an admissions officer determine which classes are applicable toward a degree. A few credits here and there may not seem like much, but they add up. Even if the subjects do not seem relevant to any major, they might be counted as elective credits toward a degree. And comparing the cost of transcripts with the cost of college courses, it makes sense to spend a few dollars per transcript for a chance to save hundreds, and perhaps thousands, of dollars in books and tuition.

Rules for transferring credits apply to all prior coursework at accredited colleges and universities, whether done on campus or off. Courses completed off campus, often called extended learning, include those available to students through independent study and correspondence. Many schools have extended learning programs; Brigham Young University, for example, offers more than 300 courses through its Department of Independent Study. One type of extended learning is distance learning, a form of correspondence study by technological means such as television, video and audio, CD-ROM, electronic mail, and computer tutorials. See the Resources section at the end of this article for more information about publications available from the National University Continuing Education Association.

Any previously earned college credits should be considered for transfer, no matter what the subject or the grade received. Many schools do not accept the transfer of courses graded below a C or ones taken more than a designated number of years ago. Some colleges and universities also have limits on the number of credits that can be transferred and applied toward a degree. But not all do. For example, Thomas Edison State College, New Jersey's State college for adults, accepts the transfer of all 120 hours of credit required for a baccalaureate degree – provided all the credits are transferred from regionally accredited schools, no more than 80 are at the junior college level, and the student's grades overall and in the field of study average out to C.

To assign credit for prior coursework, most schools require original transcripts. This means you must complete a form or send a written, signed request to have your transcripts released directly to a college or university. Once you have chosen the schools you want to apply to, contact the schools you attended before. Find out how much each transcript costs, and ask them to send your transcripts to the ones you are applying to. Write a letter that includes your name (and names used during attendance, if different) and dates of attendance, along with the names and addresses of the schools to which your transcripts should be sent. Include payment and mail to the registrar at the schools you have attended. The registrar's office will process your request and send an official transcript of your coursework to the colleges or universities you have designated.

Credit For Noncollege Courses

Colleges and universities are not the only ones that offer classes. Volunteer organizations and employers often provide formal training worth college credit. The American Council on Education has two programs that assess thousands of specific courses and make recommendations on the amount of college credit they are worth. Colleges and universities accept the recommendations or use them as guidelines.

One program evaluates educational courses sponsored by government agencies, business and industry, labor unions, and professional and voluntary organizations. It is the Program on Noncollegiate Sponsored Instruction (PONSI). Some of the training seminars Alice has participated in covered topics such as food preparation, kitchen safety, and nutrition. Although she has not yet earned her GED, Alice can earn college credit because of her completion of these formal job-training seminars. The number of credits each seminar is worth does not hinge on Alice's current eligibility for college enrollment.

The other program evaluates courses offered by the Army, Navy, Air Force, Marines, Coast Guard, and Department of Defense. It is the Military Evaluations Program. Jorge has never attended college, but the engineering technology classes he completed as part of his military training are worth college credit. And as an Army veteran, Jorge is eligible for a service that takes the evaluations one step further. The Army/American Council on Education Registry Transcript System (AARTS) will provide Jorge with an individualized transcript of American Council on Education credit recommendations for all courses he completed, the military occupational specialties (MOS's) he held, and examinations he passed while in the Army. All Army and National Guard enlisted personnel and veterans who enlisted after October 1981 are eligible for the transcript. Similar services are being considered by the Navy and Marine Corps.

To obtain a free transcript, see your Army Education Center for a 5454R transcript request form. Include your name, Social Security number, basic active service date, and complete address where you want the transcript sent. Mail your request to:
AARTS Operations Center
415 McPherson Ave.
Fort Leavenworth, KS 66027-1373

Recommendations for PONSI are published in *The National Guide to Educational Credit for Training Programs;* military program recommendations are in *The Guide to the Evaluation of Educational Experiences in the Armed Forces.* See the Resources section at the end of this article for more information about these publications.

Former military personnel who took a foreign language course through the Defense Language Institute may request course transcripts by sending their name, Social Security number, course title, duration of the course, and graduation date to:

Commandant, Defense Language Institute
Attn: ATFL-DAA-AR
Transcripts
Presidio of Monterey
Monterey, CA 93944-5006

Not all of Jorge's and Alice's courses have been assessed by the American Council on Education. Training courses that have no Council credit recommendation should still be assessed by an advisor at the schools they want to attend. Course descriptions, class notes, test scores, and other documentation may be helpful for comparing training courses to their college equivalents. An oral examination or other demonstration of competency might also be required.

There is no guarantee you will receive all the credits you are seeking – but you certainly won't if you make no attempt.

Credit By Examination

Standardized tests are the best-known method of receiving college credit without taking courses. These exams are often taken by high school students seeking advanced placement for college, but they are also available to adult learners. Testing programs and colleges and universities offer exams in a number of subjects. Two U.S. Government institutes have foreign language exams for employees that also may be worth college credit.

It is important to understand that receiving a passing score on these exams does not mean you get college credit automatically. Each school determines which test results it will accept, minimum scores required, how scores are converted for credit, and the amount of credit, if any, to be assigned. Most colleges and universities accept the American Council on Education credit recommendations, published every other year in the 250-page *Guide to Educational Credit by Examination*. For more information, contact:

The American Council on Education
Credit by Examination Program
One Dupont Circle, Suite 250
Washington, DC 20036-1193
(202) 939-9434

Testing programs:

You might know some of the five national testing programs by their acronyms or initials: CLEP, ACT PEP: RCE, DANTES, AP, and NOCTI. (The meanings of these initialisms are explained below.) There is some overlap among programs; for example, four of them have introductory accounting exams. Since you will not be awarded credit more than once for a specific subject, you should carefully evaluate each program for the subject exams you wish to take. And before taking an exam, make sure you will be awarded credit by the college or university you plan to attend.

CLEP (College-Level Examination Program), administered by the College Board, is the most widely accepted of the national testing programs; more than 2,800 accredited schools award credit for passing exam scores. Each test covers material taught in basic undergraduate courses. There are five general exams – English composition, humanities, college mathematics, natural sciences, and social sciences and history – and many subject exams. Most exams are entirely multiple-choice, but English composition exams may include an essay section. For more information, contact:

    CLEP
    P.O. Box 6600
    Princeton, NJ 08541-6600
    (609) 771-7865

ACT PEP: RCE (American College Testing Proficiency Exam Program: Regents College Examinations) tests are given in 38 subjects within arts and sciences, business, education, and nursing. Each exam is recommended for either lower- or upper-level credit. Exams contain either objective or extended response questions, and are graded according to a standard score, letter grade, or pass/fail. Fees vary, depending on the subject and type of exam. For more information or to request free study guides, contact:

    ACT PEP: Regents College Examinations
    P.O. Box 4014
    Iowa City, IA 52243
    (319) 337-1387
    (New York State residents must contact Regents College directly.)

DANTES (Defense Activity for Nontraditional Education Support) standardized tests are developed by the Educational Testing Service for the Department of Defense. Originally administered only to military personnel, the exams have been available to the public since 1983. About 50 subject tests cover business, mathematics, social science, physical science, humanities, foreign languages, and applied technology. Most of the tests consist entirely of multiple-choice questions. Schools determine their own administering fees and testing schedules. For more information or to request free study sheets, contact:

    DANTES Program Office
    Mail Stop 31-X
    Educational Testing Service
    Princeton, NJ 08541
    1(800) 257-9484

The AP (Advanced Placement) Program is a cooperative effort between secondary schools and colleges and universities. AP exams are developed each year by committees of college and high school faculty appointed by the College Board and assisted by consultants from the Educational Testing Service. Subjects include arts and languages, natural sciences, computer science, social sciences, history, and mathematics. Most tests are 2 or 3 hours long and include both multiple-choice and essay questions. AP courses are available to help students prepare for exams, which are offered in the spring. For more information about the Advanced Placement Program, contact:

    Advanced Placement Services
    P.O. Box 6671
    Princeton, NJ 08541-6671
    (609) 771-7300

NOCTI (National Occupational Competency Testing Institute) assessments are designed for people like Alice, who have vocational-technical skills that cannot be evaluated by other tests. NOCTI assesses competency at two levels: Student/job ready and teacher/experienced worker. Standardized evaluations are available for occupations such as auto-body repair, electronics, mechanical drafting, quantity food preparation, and upholstering. The tests consist of multiple-choice questions and a performance component. Other services include workshops, customized assessments, and pre-testing. For more information, contact:

NOCTI
500 N. Bronson Ave.
Ferris State University
Big Rapids, MI 49307
(616) 796-4699

Colleges and universities:

Many colleges and universities have credit-by-exam programs, through which students earn credit by passing a comprehensive exam for a course offered by the institution. Among the most widely recognized are the programs at Ohio University, the University of North Carolina, Thomas Edison State College, and New York University.

Ohio University offers about 150 examinations for credit. In addition, you may sometimes arrange to take special examinations in non-laboratory courses offered at Ohio University. To take a test for credit, you must enroll in the course. If you plan to transfer the credit earned, you also need written permission from an official at your school. Books and study materials are available, for a cost, through the university. Exams must be taken within 6 months of the enrollment date; most last 3 hours. You may arrange to take the exam off campus if you do not live near the university.

Ohio University is on the quarter-hour system; most courses are worth 4 quarter hours, the equivalent of 3 semester hours. For more information, contact:

Independent Study
Tupper Hall 302
Ohio University
Athens, OH 45701-2979
1(800) 444-2910
(614) 593-2910

The University of North Carolina offers a credit-by-examination option for 140 independent study (correspondence) courses in foreign languages, humanities, social sciences, mathematics, business administration, education, electrical and computer engineering, health administration, and natural sciences. To take an exam, you must request and receive approval from both the course instructor and the independent studies department. Exams must be taken within six months of enrollment, and you may register for no more than two at a time. If you are not near the University's Chapel Hill campus, you may take your exam under supervision at an accredited college, university, community college, or technical institute. For more information, contact:

Independent Studies
CB #1020, The Friday Center
UNC-Chapel Hill
Chapel Hill, NC 27599-1020
1(800) 862-5669 / (919) 962-1134

The Thomas Edison College Examination Program offers more than 50 exams in liberal arts, business, and professional areas. Thomas Edison State College administers tests twice a month in Trenton, New Jersey; however, students may arrange to take their tests with a proctor at any accredited American college or university or U.S. military base. Most of the tests are multiple choice; some also include short answer or essay questions. Time limits range from 90 minutes to 4 hours, depending on the exam. For more information, contact:

Thomas Edison State College
TECEP, Office of Testing and Assessment
101 W. State Street
Trenton, NJ 08608-1176
(609) 633-2844

New York University's Foreign Language Program offers proficiency exams in more than 40 languages, from Albanian to Yiddish. Two exams are available in each language: The 12-point test is equivalent to 4 undergraduate semesters, and the 16-point exam may lead to upper level credit. The tests are given at the university's Foreign Language Department throughout the year.

Proof of foreign language proficiency does not guarantee college credit. Some colleges and universities accept transcripts only for languages commonly taught, such as French and Spanish. Nontraditional programs are more likely than traditional ones to grant credit for proficiency in other languages.

For an informational brochure and registration form for NYU's foreign language proficiency exams, contact:

New York University
Foreign Language Department
48 Cooper Square, Room 107
New York, NY 10003
(212) 998-7030

Government institutes:

The Defense Language Institute and Foreign Service Institute administer foreign language proficiency exams for personnel stationed abroad. Usually, the tests are given at the end of intensive language courses or upon completion of service overseas. But some people – like Jorge, who knows Spanish – speak another language fluently and may be allowed to take a proficiency exam in that language before completing their tour of duty. Contact one of the offices listed below to obtain transcripts of those scores. Proof of proficiency does not guarantee college credit, however, as discussed above.

To request score reports from the Defense Language Institute for Defense Language Proficiency Tests, send your name, Social Security number, language for which you were tested, and, most importantly, when and where you took the exam to:

Commandant, Defense Language Institute
Attn: ATFL-ES-T
DLPT Score Report Request
Presidio of Monterey
Monterey, CA 93944-5006

To request transcripts of scores for Foreign Service Institute exams, send your name, Social Security number, language for which you were tested, and dates or year of exams to:

Foreign Service Institute
Arlington Hall
4020 Arlington Boulevard
Rosslyn, VA 22204-1500
Attn: Testing Office (Send your request to the attention of the testing office of the foreign language in which you were tested)

Credit For Experience

Experiential learning credit may be given for knowledge gained through job responsibilities, personal hobbies, volunteer opportunities, homemaking, and other experiences. Colleges and universities base credit awards on the knowledge you have attained, not for the experience alone. In addition, the knowledge must be college level; not just any learning will do. Throwing horseshoes as a hobby is not likely to be worth college credit. But if you've done research on how and where the sport originated, visited blacksmiths, organized tournaments, and written a column for a trade journal – well, that's a horseshoe of a different color.

Adults attempting to get credit for their experience should be forewarned: Having your experience evaluated for college credit is time-consuming, tedious work – not an easy shortcut for people who want quick-fix college credits. And not all experience, no matter how valuable, is the equivalent of college courses.

Requesting college credit for your experiential learning can be tricky. You should get assistance from a credit evaluations officer at the school you plan to attend, but you should also have a general idea of what your knowledge is worth. A common method for converting knowledge into credit is to use a college catalog. Find course titles and descriptions that match what you have learned through experience, and request the number of credits offered for those courses.

Once you know what credit to ask for, you must usually present your case in writing to officials at the college you plan to attend. The most common form of presenting experiential learning for credit is the portfolio. A portfolio is a written record of your knowledge along with a request for equivalent college credit. It includes an identification and description of the knowledge for which you are requesting credit, an explanatory essay of how the knowledge was gained and how it fits into your educational plans, documentation that you have acquired such knowledge, and a request for college credit. Required elements of a portfolio vary by schools but generally follow those guidelines.

In identifying knowledge you have gained, be specific about exactly what you have learned. For example, it is not enough for Lynette to say she runs a business. She must identify the knowledge she has gained from running it, such as personnel management, tax law, marketing strategy, and inventory review. She must also include brief descriptions about her knowledge of each to support her claims of having those skills.

The essay gives you a chance to relay something about who you are. It should address your educational goals, include relevant autobiographical details, and be well organized, neat, and convey confidence. In his essay, Jorge might first state his goal of becoming an engineer. Then he would explain why he joined the Army, where he got hands-on training and experience in developing and servicing electronic equipment.

This, he would say, led to his hobby of creating remote-controlled model cars, of which he has built 20. His conclusion would highlight his accomplishments and tie them to his desire to become an electronic engineer.

Documentation is evidence that you've learned what you claim to have learned. You can show proof of knowledge in a variety of ways, including audio or video recordings, letters from current or former employers describing your specific duties and job performance, blueprints, photographs or artwork, and transcripts of certifying exams for professional licenses and certification – such as Alice's certification from the American Culinary Federation. Although documentation can take many forms, written proof alone is not always enough. If it is impossible to document your knowledge in writing, find out if your experiential learning can be assessed through supplemental oral exams by a faculty expert.

Earning a College Degree

Nontraditional students often have work, family, and financial obligations that prevent them from quitting their jobs to attend school full time. Can they still meet their educational goals? Yes.

More than 150 accredited colleges and universities have nontraditional bachelor's degree programs that require students to spend little or no time on campus; over 300 others have nontraditional campus-based degree programs. Some of those schools, as well as most junior and community colleges, offer associate's degrees nontraditionally. Each school with a nontraditional course of study determines its own rules for awarding credit for prior coursework, exams, or experience, as discussed previously. Most have charges on top of tuition for providing these special services.

Several publications profile nontraditional degree programs; see the Resources section at the end of this article for more information. To determine which school best fits your academic profile and educational goals, first list your criteria. Then, evaluate nontraditional programs based on their accreditation, features, residency requirements, and expenses. Once you have chosen several schools to explore further, write to them for more information. Detailed explanations of school policies should help you decide which ones you want to apply to.

Get beyond the printed word – especially the glowing words each school writes about itself. Check out the schools you are considering with higher education authorities, alumni, employers, family members, and friends. If possible, visit the campus to talk to students and instructors and sit in on a few classes, even if you will be completing most or all of your work off campus. Ask school officials questions about such things as enrollment numbers, graduation rate, faculty qualifications, and confusing details about the application process or academic policies. After you have thoroughly investigated each prospective college or university, you can make an informed decision about which is right for you.

Accreditation

Accreditation is a process colleges and universities submit to voluntarily for getting their credentials. An accredited school has been investigated and visited by teams of observers and has periodic inspections by a private accrediting agency. The initial review can take two years or more.

Regional agencies accredit entire schools, and professional agencies accredit either specialized schools or departments within schools. Although there are no national accrediting standards, not just any accreditation will do. Countless "accreditation associations" have been invented by schools, many of which have no academic programs and sell phony degrees, to accredit themselves. But 6 regional and about 80 professional accrediting associations in the United States are recognized by the U.S. Department of Education or the Commission on Recognition of Postsecondary Accreditation. When checking accreditation, these are the names to look for. For more information about accreditation and accrediting agencies, contact:

Institutional Participation Oversight Service Accreditation and State Liaison Division
U.S. Department of Education
ROB 3, Room 3915
600 Independence Ave., SW
Washington, DC 20202-5244
(202) 708-7417

Because accreditation is not mandatory, lack of accreditation does not necessarily mean a school or program is bad. Some schools choose not to apply for accreditation, are in the process of applying, or have educational methods too unconventional for an accrediting association's standards. For the nontraditional student, however, earning a degree from a college or university with recognized accreditation is an especially important consideration. Although nontraditional education is becoming more widely accepted, it is not yet mainstream. Employers skeptical of a degree earned in a nontraditional manner are likely to be even less accepting of one from an unaccredited school.

Program Features

Because nontraditional students have diverse educational objectives, nontraditional schools are diverse in what they offer. Some programs are geared toward helping students organize their scattered educational credits to get a degree as quickly as possible. Others cater to those who may have specific credits or experience but need assistance in completing requirements. Whatever your educational profile, you should look for a program that works with you in obtaining your educational goals.

A few nontraditional programs have special admissions policies for adult learners like Alice, who plan to earn their GEDs but want to enroll in college in the meantime. Other features of nontraditional programs include individualized learning agreements, intensive academic counseling, cooperative learning and internship placement, and waiver of some prerequisites or other requirements – as well as college credit for prior coursework, examinations, and experiential learning, all discussed previously.

Lynette, whose primary goal is to finish her degree, wants to earn maximum credits for her business experience. She will look for programs that do not limit the number of credits awarded for equivalency exams and experiential learning. And since well-documented proof of knowledge is essential for earning experiential learning credits, Lynette should make sure the program she chooses provides assistance to students submitting a portfolio.

Jorge, on the other hand, has more credits than he needs in certain areas and is willing to forego some. To become an engineer, he must have a bachelor's degree; but because he is accustomed to hands-on learning, Jorge is interested in getting experience as he gains more technical skills. He will concentrate on finding schools with strong cooperative education, supervised fieldwork, or internship programs.

Residency Requirements

Programs are sometimes deemed nontraditional because of their residency requirements. Many people think of residency for colleges and universities in terms of tuition, with in-state students paying less than out-of-state ones. Residency also may refer to where a student lives, either on or off campus, while attending school.

But in nontraditional education, residency usually refers to how much time students must spend on campus, regardless of whether they attend classes there. In some nontraditional programs, students need not ever step foot on campus. Others require only a very short residency, such as one day or a few weeks. Many schools have standard residency requirements of several semesters but schedule classes for evenings or weekends to accommodate working adults.

Lynette, who previously took courses by independent study, prefers to earn credits by distance study. She will focus on schools that have no residency requirement. Several colleges and universities have nonresident degree completion programs for adults with some college credit. Under the direction of a faculty advisor, students devise a plan for earning their remaining credits. Methods for earning credits include independent study, distance learning, seminars, supervised fieldwork, and group study at arranged sites. Students may have to earn a certain number of credits through the degree-granting institution. But many programs allow students to take courses at accredited schools of their choice for transfer toward their degree.

Alice wants to attend lectures but has an unpredictable schedule. Her best course of action will be to seek out short residency programs that require students to attend seminars once or twice a semester. She can take courses that are televised and videotape them to watch when her schedule permits, with the seminars helping to ensure that she properly completes her coursework. Many colleges and universities with short residency requirements also permit students to earn some credits elsewhere, by whatever means the student chooses.

Some fields of study require classroom instruction. As Jorge will discover, few colleges and universities allow students to earn a bachelor's degree in engineering entirely through independent study. Nontraditional residency programs are designed to accommodate adults' daytime work schedules. Jorge should look for programs offering evening, weekend, summer, and accelerated courses.

Tuition and Other Expenses

The final decisions about which schools Alice, Jorge, and Lynette attend may hinge in large part on a single issue: Cost. And rising tuition is only part of the equation. Beginning with application fees and continuing through graduation fees, college expenses add up.

Traditional and nontraditional students have some expenses in common, such as the cost of books and other materials. Tuition might even be the same for some courses, especially for colleges and universities offering standard ones at unusual times. But for nontraditional programs, students may also pay fees for services such as credit or transcript review, evaluation, advisement, and portfolio assessment.

Students are also responsible for postage and handling or setup expenses for independent study courses, as well as for all examination and transcript fees for transferring credits. Usually, the more nontraditional the program, the more detailed the fees. Some schools charge a yearly enrollment fee rather than tuition for degree completion candidates who want their files to remain active.

Although tuition and fees might seem expensive, most educators tell you not to let money come between you and your educational goals. Talk to someone in the financial aid department of the school you plan to attend or check your library for publications about financial aid sources. The U.S. Department of Education publishes a guide to Federal aid programs such as Pell Grants, student loans, and work-study. To order the free 74-page booklet, *The Student Guide: Financial Aid from the U.S. Department of Education,* contact:

Federal Student Aid Information Center
P.O. Box 84
Washington, DC 20044
1 (800) 4FED-AID (433-3243)

Resources

Information on how to earn a high school diploma or college degree without following the usual routes is available from several organizations and in numerous publications. Information on nontraditional graduate degree programs, available for master's through doctoral level, though not discussed in this article, can usually be obtained from the same resources that detail bachelor's degree programs.

National Learning Corporation publishes study guides for all of these exams, for both general examinations and tests in specific subject areas. To order study guides, or to browse their catalog featuring more than 5,000 titles, visit NLC online at www.passbooks.com, or contact them by phone at (800) 632-8888.

Organizations

Adult learners should always contact their local school system, community college, or university to learn about programs that are readily available. The following national organizations can also supply information:

American Council on Education
One Dupont Circle
Washington, DC 20036-1193
(202) 939-9300

Within the American Council on Education, the Center for Adult Learning and Educational Credentials administers the National External Diploma Program, the GED Program, the Program on Noncollegiate Sponsored Instruction, the Credit by Examination Program, and the Military Evaluations Program.

College-Level Examination Program (CLEP)

1. WHAT IS CLEP?

CLEP stands for the College-Level Examination Program, sponsored by the College Board. It is a national program of credit-by-examination that offers you the opportunity to obtain recognition for college-level achievement. No matter when, where, or how you have learned – by means of formal or informal study – you can take CLEP tests. If the results are acceptable to your college, you can receive credit.

You may not realize it, but you probably know more than your academic record reveals. Each day you, like most people, have an opportunity to learn. In private industry and business, as well as at all levels of government, learning opportunities continually occur. If you read widely or intensively in a particular field, think about what you read, discuss it with your family and friends, you are learning. Or you may be learning on a more formal basis by taking a correspondence course, a television or radio course, a course recorded on tape or cassettes, a course assembled into programmed tests, or a course taught in your community adult school or high school.

No matter how, where, or when you gained your knowledge, you may have the opportunity to receive academic credit for your achievement that can be counted toward an undergraduate degree. The College-Level Examination Program (CLEP) enables colleges to evaluate your achievement and give you credit. A wide range of college-level examinations are offered by CLEP to anyone who wishes to take them. Scores on the tests are reported to you and, if you wish, to a college, employer, or individual.

2. WHAT ARE THE PURPOSES OF THE COLLEGE-LEVEL EXAMINATION PROGRAM?

The basic purpose of the College-Level Examination Program is to enable individuals who have acquired their education in nontraditional ways to demonstrate their academic achievement. It is also intended for use by those in higher education, business, industry, government, and other fields who need a reliable method of assessing a person's educational level.

Recognizing that the real issue is not how a person has acquired his education but what education he has, the College Level Examination Program has been designed to serve a variety of purposes. The basic purpose, as listed above, is to enable those who have reached the college level of education in nontraditional ways to assess the level of their achievement and to use the test results in seeking college credit or placement.

In addition, scores on the tests can be used to validate educational experience obtained at a nonaccredited institution or through noncredit college courses.

Some colleges and universities may use the tests to measure the level of educational achievement of their students, and for various institutional research purposes.

Other colleges and universities may wish to use the tests in the admission, placement, and guidance of students who wish to transfer from one institution to another.

Businesses, industries, governmental agencies, and professional groups now accept the results of these tests as a basis for advancement, eligibility for further training, or professional or semi-professional certification.

Many people are interested in the examination simply to assess their own educational progress and attainment.

The college, university, business, industry, or government agency that adopts the tests in the College-Level Examination Program makes its own decision about how it will use and interpret the test scores. The College Board will provide the tests, score them, and report the results either to the individuals who took the tests or the college or agency that administered them. It does NOT, and cannot, award college credit, certify college equivalency, or make recommendations regarding the standards these institutions should establish for the use of the test results.

Therefore, if you are taking the tests to secure credit from an institution, you should FIRST ascertain whether the college or agency involved will accept the scores. Each institution determines which CLEP tests it will accept for credit and the amount of credit it will award. If you want to take tests for college credit, first call, write, or visit the college you wish to attend to inquire about its policy on CLEP scores, as well as its other admission requirements.

The services of the program are also available to people who have been requested to take the tests by an employer, a professional licensing agency, a certifying agency, or by other groups that recognize college equivalency on the basis of satisfactory CLEP scores. You may, of course, take the tests SOLELY for your own information. If you do, your scores will be reported only to you.

While neither CLEP nor the College Board can evaluate previous credentials or award college credit, you will receive, with your scores, basic information to help you interpret your performance on the tests you have taken.

3. WHAT ARE THE COLLEGE-LEVEL EXAMINATIONS?

In order to meet different kinds of curricular organization and testing needs at colleges and universities, the College-Level Examination Program offers 35 different subject tests falling under five separate general categories: Composition and Literature, Foreign Languages, History and Social Sciences, Science and Mathematics, and Business.

4. WHAT ARE THE SUBJECT EXAMINATIONS?

The 35 CLEP tests offered by the College Board are listed below:

COMPOSITION AND LITERATURE:
- American Literature
- Analyzing and Interpreting Literature
- English Composition
- English Composition with Essay
- English Literature
- Freshman College Composition
- Humanities

FOREIGN LANGUAGES
- French
- German
- Spanish

HISTORY AND SOCIAL SCIENCES
- American Government
- Introduction to Educational Psychology
- History of the United States I: Early Colonization to 1877
- History of the United States II: 1865 to the Present
- Human Growth and Development
- Principles of Macroeconomics
- Principles of Microeconomics
- Introductory Psychology
- Social Sciences and History
- Introductory Sociology
- Western Civilization I: Ancient Near East to 1648
- Western Civilization II: 1648 to the Present

SCIENCE AND MATHEMATICS
- College Algebra
- College Algebra-Trigonometry
- Biology
- Calculus
- Chemistry
- College Mathematics
- Natural Sciences
- Trigonometry
- Precalculus

BUSINESS
- Financial Accounting
- Introductory Business Law
- Information Systems and Computer Applications
- Principles of Management
- Principles of Marketing

CLEP Examinations cover material taught in courses that most students take as requirements in the first two years of college. A college usually grants the same amount of credit to students earning satisfactory scores on the CLEP examination as it grants to students successfully completing the equivalent course.

Many examinations are designed to correspond to one-semester courses; some, however, correspond to full-year or two-year courses.

Each exam is 90 minutes long and, except for English Composition with Essay, is made up primarily of multiple-choice questions. Some tests have several other types of questions besides multiple choice. To see a more detailed description of a particular CLEP exam, visit www.collegeboard.com/clep.

The English Composition with Essay exam is the only exam that includes a required essay. This essay is scored by college English faculty designated by CLEP and does not require an additional fee. However, other Composition and Literature tests offer optional essays, which some college and universities require and some do not. These essays are graded by faculty at the individual institutions that require them and require an additional $10 fee. Contact the particular institution to ask about essay requirements, and check with your test center for further details.

All 35 CLEP examinations are administered on computer. If you are unfamiliar with taking a test on a computer, consult the CLEP Sampler online at www.collegeboard.com/clep. The Sampler contains the same tutorials as the actual exams and helps familiarize you with navigation and how to answer different types of questions.

Points are not deducted for wrong or skipped answers – you receive one point for every correct answer. Therefore it is best that an answer is supplied for each exam question, whether it is a guess or not. The number of correct answers is then converted to a formula score. This formula, or "scaled," score is determined by a statistical process called *equating*, which adjusts for slight differences in difficulty between test forms and ensures that your score does not depend on the specific test form you took or how well others did on the same form. The scaled scores range from 20 to 80 – this is the number that will appear on your score report.

To ensure that you complete all questions in the time allotted, you would probably be wise to skip the more difficult or perplexing questions and return to them later. Although the multiple-choice items in these tests are carefully designed so as not to be tricky, misleading, or ambiguous, on the other hand, they are not all direct questions of factual information. They attempt, in their way, to elicit a response that indicates your knowledge or lack of knowledge of the material in question or your ability or inability to use or interpret a fact or idea. Thus, you should concentrate on answering the questions as they appear to be without attempting to out-guess the testmakers.

5. WHAT ARE THE FEES?

The fee for all CLEP examinations is $55. Optional essays required by some institutions are an additional $10.

6. WHEN ARE THE TESTS GIVEN?

CLEP tests are administered year-round. Consult the CLEP website (www.collegeboard.com/clep) and individual test centers for specific information.

7. WHERE ARE THE TESTS GIVEN?

More than 1,300 test centers are located on college and university campuses throughout the country, and additional centers are being established to meet increased needs. Any accredited collegiate institution with an explicit and publicly available policy of credit by examination can become a CLEP test center. To obtain a list of these centers, visit the CLEP website at www.collegeboard.com/clep.

8. HOW DO I REGISTER FOR THE COLLEGE-LEVEL EXAMINATION PROGRAM?

Contact an individual test center for information regarding registration, scheduling and fees. Registration/admission forms can also be obtained on the CLEP website.

9. MAY I REPEAT THE COLLEGE-LEVEL EXAMINATIONS?

You may repeat any examination providing at least six months have passed since you were last administered this test. If you repeat a test within a period of time less than six months, your scores will be cancelled and your fees forfeited. To repeat a test, check the appropriate space on the registration form.

10. WHEN MAY I EXPECT MY SCORE REPORTS?

With the exception of the English Composition with Essay exam, you should receive your score report instantly once the test is complete.

11. HOW SHOULD I PREPARE FOR THE COLLEGE-LEVEL EXAMINATIONS?

This book has been specifically designed to prepare candidates for these examinations. It will help you to consider, study, and review important content, principles, practices, procedures, problems, and techniques in the form of varied and concrete applications.

12. QUESTIONS AND ANSWERS APPEARING IN THIS PUBLICATION

The College-Level Examinations are offered by the College Board. Since copies of past examinations have not been made available, we have used equivalent materials, including questions and answers, which are highly recommended by us as an appropriate means of preparing for these examinations.

If you need additional information about CLEP Examinations, visit www.collegeboard.com/clep.

THE COLLEGE-LEVEL EXAMINATION PROGRAM

How The Program Works

CLEP examinations are administered at many colleges and universities across the country, and most institutions award college credit to those who do well on them. The examinations provide people who have acquired knowledge outside the usual educational settings the opportunity to show that they have learned college-level material without taking certain college courses.

The CLEP examinations cover material that is taught in introductory-level courses at many colleges and universities. Faculties at individual colleges review the tests to ensure that they cover the important material taught in their courses. Colleges differ in the examinations they accept; some colleges accept only two or three of the examinations while others accept nearly all of them.

Although CLEP is sponsored by the College Board and the examinations are scored by Educational Testing Service (ETS), neither of these organizations can award college credit. Only accredited colleges may grant credit toward a degree. When you take a CLEP examination, you may request that a copy of your score report be sent to the college you are attending or plan to attend. After evaluating your scores, the college will decide whether or not to award you credit for a certain course or courses, or to exempt you from them. If the college gives you credit, it will record the number of credits on your permanent record, thereby indicating that you have completed work equivalent to a course in that subject. If the college decides to grant exemption without giving you credit for a course, you will be permitted to omit a course that would normally be required of you and to take a course of your choice instead.

What the Examinations Are Like

The examinations consist mostly of multiple-choice questions to be answered within a 90-minute time limit. Additional information about each CLEP examination is given in the examination guide and on the CLEP website.

Where To Take the Examinations

CLEP examinations are administered throughout the year at the test centers of approximately 1,300 colleges and universities. On the CLEP website, you will find a list of institutions that award credit for satisfactory scores on CLEP examinations. Some colleges administer CLEP examinations to their own students only. Other institutions administer the tests to anyone who registers to take them. If your college does not administer the tests, contact the test centers in your area for information about its testing schedule.

Once you have been tested, your score report will be available instantly. CLEP scores are kept on file at ETS for 20 years; and during this period, for a small fee, you may have your transcript sent to another college or to anyone else you specify. (Your scores will never be sent to anyone without your approval.)

APPROACHING A COLLEGE ABOUT CLEP

The following sections provide a step-by-step approach to learning about the CLEP policy at a particular college or university. The person or office that can best assist students desiring CLEP credit may have a different title at each institution, but the following guidelines will lead you to information about CLEP at any institution.

Adults returning to college often benefit from special assistance when they approach a college. Opportunities for adults to return to formal learning in the classroom are now widespread, and colleges and universities have worked hard to make this a smooth process for older students. Many colleges have established special service offices that are staffed with trained professionals who understand the kinds of problems facing adults returning to college. If you think you might benefit from such assistance, be sure to find out whether these services are available at your college.

How to Apply for College Credit

STEP 1. Obtain the General Information Catalog and a copy of the CLEP policy from the colleges you are considering. If you have not yet applied for admission, ask for an admissions application form too.

Information about admissions and CLEP policies can be obtained by contacting college admissions offices or finding admissions information on the school websites. Tell the admissions officer that you are a prospective student and that you are interested in applying for admission and CLEP credit. Ask for a copy of the publication in which the college's complete CLEP policy is explained. Also get the name and the telephone number of the person to contact in case you have further questions about CLEP.

At this step, you may wish to obtain information from external degree colleges. Many adults find that such colleges suit their needs exceptionally well.

STEP 2. If you have not already been admitted to the college you are considering, look at its admission requirements for undergraduate students to see if you can qualify.

This is an important step because if you can't get into college, you can't get college credit for CLEP. Nearly all colleges require students to be admitted and to enroll in one or more courses before granting the students CLEP credit.

Virtually all public community colleges and a number of four-year state colleges have open admission policies for in-state students. This usually means that they admit anyone who has graduated from high school or has earned a high school equivalency diploma.

If you think you do not meet the admission requirements, contact the admissions office for an interview with a counselor. Colleges do sometimes make exceptions, particularly for adult applicants. State why you want the interview and ask what documents you should bring with you or send in advance. (These materials may include a high school transcript, transcript of previous college work, completed application for admission, etc.) Make an extra effort to have all the information requested in time for the interview.

During the interview, relax and be yourself. Be prepared to state honestly why you think you are ready and able to do college work. If you have already taken CLEP examinations and scored high enough to earn credit, you have shown that you are able to do college work. Mention this achievement to the admissions counselor because it may increase your chances of being accepted. If you have not taken a CLEP examination, you can still improve your chances of being accepted by describing how your job training or independent study has helped prepare you for college-level work. Tell the counselor what you have learned from your work and personal experiences.

STEP 3. Evaluate the college's CLEP policy.

Typically, a college lists all its academic policies, including CLEP policies, in its general catalog. You will probably find the CLEP policy statement under a heading such as Credit-by-Examination, Advanced Standing, Advanced Placement, or External Degree Program. These sections can usually be found in the front of the catalog.

Many colleges publish their credit-by-examination policies in a separate brochure, which is distributed through the campus testing office, counseling center, admissions office, or registrar's office. If you find a very general policy statement in the college catalog, seek clarification from one of these offices.

Review the material in the section of this guide entitled Questions to Ask About a College's CLEP Policy. Use these guidelines to evaluate the college's CLEP policy. If you have not yet taken a CLEP examination, this evaluation will help you decide which examinations to take and whether or not to take the free-response or essay portion. Because individual colleges have different CLEP policies, a review of several policies may help you decide which college to attend.

STEP 4. If you have not yet applied for admission, do so early.

Most colleges expect you to apply for admission several months before you enroll, and it is essential that you meet the published application deadlines. It takes time to process your application for admission; and if you have yet to take a CLEP examination, it will be some time before the college receives and reviews your score report. You will probably want to take some, if not all, of the CLEP examinations you are interested in before you enroll so you know which courses you need not register for. In fact, some colleges require that all CLEP scores be submitted before a student registers.

Complete all forms and include all documents requested with your application(s) for admission. Normally, an admissions decision cannot be reached until all documents have been submitted and evaluated. Unless told to do so, do not send your CLEP scores until you have been officially admitted.

STEP 5. Arrange to take CLEP examination(s) or to submit your CLEP score(s).

You may want to wait to take your CLEP examinations until you know definitely which college you will be attending. Then you can make sure you are taking tests your college will accept for credit. You will also be able to request that your scores be sent to the college, free of charge, when you take the tests.

If you have already taken CLEP examinations, but did not have a copy of your score report sent to your college, you may request the College Board to send an official transcript at any time for a small fee. Use the Transcript Request Form that was sent to you with your score report. If you do not have the form, you may find it online at www.collegeboard.com/clep.

Your CLEP scores will be evaluated, probably by someone in the admissions office, and sent to the registrar's office to be posted on your permanent record once you are enrolled. Procedures vary from college to college, but the process usually begins in the admissions office.

STEP 6. Ask to receive a written notice of the credit you receive for your CLEP score(s).

A written notice may save you problems later, when you submit your degree plan or file for graduation. In the event that there is a question about whether or not you earned CLEP credit, you will have an official record of what credit was awarded. You may also need this verification of course credit if you go for academic counseling before the credit is posted on your permanent record.

STEP 7. Before you register for courses, seek academic counseling.

A discussion with your academic advisor can prevent you from taking unnecessary courses and can tell you specifically what your CLEP credit will mean to you. This step may be accomplished at the time you enroll. Most colleges have orientation sessions for new students prior to each enrollment period. During orientation, students are usually assigned an academic advisor who then gives them individual help in developing long-range plans and a course schedule for the next semester. In conjunction with this counseling, you may be asked to take some additional tests so that you can be placed at the proper course level.

External Degree Programs

If you have acquired a considerable amount of college-level knowledge through job experience, reading, or noncredit courses, if you have accumulated college credits at a variety of colleges over a period of years, or if you prefer studying on your own rather than in a classroom setting, you may want to investigate the possibility of enrolling in an external degree program. Many colleges offer external degree programs that allow you to earn a degree by passing examinations (including CLEP), transferring credit from other colleges, and demonstrating in other ways that you have satisfied the educational requirements. No classroom attendance is required, and the programs are open to out-of-state candidates as well as residents. Thomas A. Edison State College in New Jersey and Charter Oaks College in Connecticut are fully accredited independent state colleges; the New York program is part of the state university system and is also fully accredited. If you are interested in exploring an external degree, you can write for more information to:

Charter Oak College
The Exchange, Suite 171
270 Farmington Avenue
Farmington, CT 06032-1909

Regents External Degree Program
Cultural Education Center
Empire State Plaza
Albany, New York 12230

Thomas A. Edison State College
101 West State Street
Trenton, New Jersey 08608

Many other colleges also have external degree or weekend programs. While they often require that a number of courses be taken on campus, the external degree programs tend to be more flexible in transferring credit, granting credit-by-examination, and allowing independent study than other traditional programs. When applying to a college, you may wish to ask whether it has an external degree or weekend program.

Questions to Ask About a College's CLEP Policy

Before taking CLEP examinations for the purpose of earning college credit, try to find the answers to these questions:

1. Which CLEP examinations are accepted by this college?

A college may accept some CLEP examinations for credit and not others - possibly not the one you are considering. The English faculty may decide to grant college English credit based on the CLEP English Composition examination, but not on the Freshman College Composition examination. Or, the mathematics faculty may decide to grant credit based on the College Mathematics to non-mathematics majors only, requiring majors to take an examination in algebra, trigonometry, or calculus to earn credit. For these reasons, it is important that you know the specific CLEP tests for which you can receive credit.

2. Does the college require the optional free-response (essay) section as well as the objective portion of the CLEP examination you are considering?

Knowing the answer to this question ahead of time will permit you to schedule the optional essay examination when you register to take your CLEP examination.

3. Is credit granted for specific courses? If so, which ones?

You are likely to find that credit will be granted for specific courses and the course titles will be designated in the college's CLEP policy. It is not necessary, however, that credit be granted for a specific course in order for you to benefit from your CLEP credit. For instance, at many liberal arts colleges, all students must take certain types of courses; these courses may be labeled the core curriculum, general education requirements, distribution requirements, or liberal arts requirements. The requirements are often expressed in terms of credit hours. For example, all students may be required to take at least six hours of humanities, six hours of English, three hours of mathematics, six hours of natural science, and six hours of social science, with no particular courses in these disciplines specified. In these instances, CLEP credit may be given as 6 hrs. English credit or 3 hrs. Math credit without specifying for which English or mathematics courses credit has been awarded. In order to avoid possible disappointment, you should know before taking a CLEP examination what type of credit you can receive and whether you will only be exempted from a required course but receive no credit.

4. How much credit is granted for each examination you are considering, and does the college place a limit on the total amount of CLEP credit you can earn toward your degree?

Not all colleges that grant CLEP credit award the same amount for individual tests. Furthermore, some colleges place a limit on the total amount of credit you can earn through CLEP or other examinations. Other colleges may grant you exemption but no credit toward your degree. Knowing several colleges' policies concerning these issues may help you decide which college you will attend. If you think you are capable of passing a number of CLEP examinations, you may want to attend a college that will allow you to earn credit for all or most of them. For example, the state external degree programs grant credit for most CLEP examinations (and other tests as well).

5. What is the required score for earning CLEP credit for each test you are considering?

Most colleges publish the required scores or percentile ranks for earning CLEP credit in their general catalog or in a brochure. The required score may vary from test to test, so find out the required score for each test you are considering.

6. What is the college's policy regarding prior course work in the subject in which you are considering taking a CLEP test?

Some colleges will not grant credit for a CLEP test if the student has already attempted a college-level course closely aligned with that test. For example, if you successfully completed English 101 or a comparable course on another campus, you will probably not be permitted to receive CLEP credit in that subject, too. Some colleges will not permit you to earn CLEP credit for a course that you failed.

7. Does the college make additional stipulations before credit will be granted?

It is common practice for colleges to award CLEP credit only to their enrolled students. There are other stipulations, however, that vary from college to college. For example, does the college require you to formally apply for or accept CLEP credit by completing and signing a form? Or does the college require you to validate your CLEP score by successfully completing a more advanced course in the subject? Answers to these and other questions will help to smooth the process of earning college credit through CLEP.

The above questions and the discussions that follow them indicate some of the ways in which colleges' CLEP policies can vary. Find out as much as possible about the CLEP policies at the colleges you are interested in so you can choose a college with a policy that is compatible with your educational goals. Once you have selected the college you will attend, you can find out which CLEP examinations your college recognizes and the requirements for earning CLEP credit.

DECIDING WHICH EXAMINATIONS TO TAKE

If You're Taking the Examinations for College Credit or Career Advancement:

Most people who take CLEP examinations do so in order to earn credit for college courses. Others take the examinations in order to qualify for job promotions or for professional certification or licensing. It is vital to most candidates who are taking the tests for any of these reasons that they be well prepared for the tests they are taking so that they can advance as rapidly as possible toward their educational or career goals.

It is usually advisable that those who have limited knowledge in the subjects covered by the tests they are considering enroll in the college courses in which that material is taught. Those who are uncertain about whether or not they know enough about a subject to do well on a particular CLEP test will find the following guidelines helpful.

There is no way to predict if you will pass a particular CLEP examination, but answers to the questions under the seven headings below should give you an indication of whether or not you are likely to succeed.

1. Test Descriptions

Read the description of the test provided. Are you familiar with most of the topics and terminology in the outline?

2. Textbooks

Examine the suggested textbooks and other resource materials following the test descriptions in this guide. Have you recently read one or more of these books, or have you read similar college-level books on this subject? If you have not, read through one or more of the textbooks listed, or through the textbook used for this course at your college. Are you familiar with most of the topics and terminology in the book?

3. Sample Questions

The sample questions provided are intended to be typical of the content and difficulty of the questions on the test. Although they are not an exact miniature of the test, the proportion of the sample questions you can answer correctly should be a rough estimate of the proportion of questions you will be able to answer correctly on the test.

Answer as many of the sample questions for this test as you can. Check your answers against the correct answers. Did you answer more than half the questions correctly?

Because of variations in course content at different institutions, and because questions on CLEP tests vary from easy to difficult - with most being of moderate difficulty - the average student who passes a course in a subject can usually answer correctly about half the questions on the corresponding CLEP examination. Most colleges set their passing scores near this level, but some set them higher. If your college has set its required score above the level required by most colleges, you may need to answer a larger proportion of questions on the test correctly.

4. Previous Study

Have you taken noncredit courses in this subject offered by an adult school or a private school, through correspondence, or in connection with your job? Did you do exceptionally well in this subject in high school, or did you take an honors course in this subject?

5. Experience

Have you learned or used the knowledge or skills included in this test in your job or life experience? For example, if you lived in a Spanish-speaking country and spoke the language for a year or more, you might consider taking the Spanish examination. Or, if you have worked at a job in which you used accounting and finance skills, Principles of Accounting would be a likely test for you to take. Or, if you have read a considerable amount of literature and attended many art exhibits, concerts, and plays, you might expect to do well on the Humanities exam.

6. Other Examinations

Have you done well on other standardized tests in subjects related to the one you want to take? For example, did you score well above average on a portion of a college entrance examination covering similar skills, or did you obtain an exceptionally high score on a high school equivalency test or a licensing examination in this subject? Although such tests do not cover exactly the same material as the CLEP examinations and may be easier, persons who do well on these tests often do well on CLEP examinations, too.

7. Advice

Has a college counselor, professor, or some other professional person familiar with your ability advised you to take a CLEP examination?

If your answer was yes to questions under several of the above headings, you probably have a good chance of passing the CLEP examination you are considering. It is unlikely that you would have acquired sufficient background from experience alone. Learning gained through reading and study is essential, and you will probably find some additional study helpful before taking a CLEP examination.

If You're Taking the Examinations to Prepare for College

Many people entering college, particularly adults returning to college after several years away from formal education, are uncertain about their ability to compete with other college students. They wonder whether they have sufficient background for college study, and those who have been away from formal study for some time wonder whether they have forgotten how to study, how to take tests, and how to write papers. Such people may wish to improve their test-taking and study skills prior to enrolling in courses.

One way to assess your ability to perform at the college level and to improve your test-taking and study skills at the same time is to prepare for and take one or more CLEP examinations. You need not be enrolled in a college to take a CLEP examination, and you may have your scores sent only to yourself and later request that a transcript be sent to a college if you then decide to apply for credit. By reviewing the test descriptions and sample questions, you may find one or several subject areas in which you think you have substantial knowledge. Select one examination, or more if you like, and carefully read at least one of the textbooks listed in the bibliography for the test. By doing this, you will get a better idea of how much you know of what is usually taught in a college-level course in that subject. Study as much material as you can, until you think you have a good grasp of the subject matter. Then take the test at a college in your area. It will be several weeks before you receive your results, and you may wish to begin reviewing for another test in the meantime.

To find out if you are eligible for credit for your CLEP score, you must compare your score with the score required by the college you plan to attend. If you are not yet sure which college you will attend, or whether you will enroll in college at all, you should begin to follow the steps outlined. It is best that you do this before taking a CLEP test, but if you are taking the test only for the experience and to familiarize yourself with college-level material and requirements, you might take the test before you approach a college. Even if the college you decide to attend does not accept the test you took, the experience of taking such a test will enable you to meet with greater confidence the requirements of courses you will take.

You will find information about how to interpret your scores in WHAT YOUR SCORES MEAN, which you will receive with your score report, and which can also be found online at the CLEP website. Many colleges follow the recommendations of the American Council on Education (ACE) for setting their required scores, so you can use this information as a guide in determining how well you did. The ACE recommendations are included in the booklet.

If you do not do well enough on the test to earn college credit, don't be discouraged. Usually, it is the best college students who are exempted from courses or receive credit-by-examination. The fact that you cannot get credit for your score means that you should probably enroll in a college course to learn the material. However, if your score was close to the required score, or if you feel you could do better on a second try or after some additional study, you may retake the test after six months. Do not take it sooner or your score will not be reported and your fee will be forfeited.

If you do earn the score required to earn credit, you will have demonstrated that you already have some college-level knowledge. You will also have a better idea whether you should take additional CLEP examinations. And, what is most important, you can enroll in college with confidence, knowing that you do have the ability to succeed.

PREPARING TO TAKE CLEP EXAMINATIONS

Having made the decision to take one or more CLEP examinations, most people then want to know if it is worthwhile to prepare for them - how much, how long, when, and how should they go about it? The precise answers to these questions vary greatly from individual to individual. However, most candidates find that some type of test preparation is helpful.

Most people who take CLEP examinations do so to show that they have already learned the important material that is taught in a college course. Many of them need only a quick review to assure themselves that they have not forgotten some of what they once studied, and to fill in some of the gaps in their knowledge of the subject. Others feel that they need a thorough review and spend several weeks studying for a test. A few wish to take a CLEP examination as a kind of final examination for independent study of a subject instead of the college course. This last group requires significantly more study than those who only need to review, and they may need some guidance from professors of the subjects they are studying.

The key to how you prepare for CLEP examinations often lies in locating those skills and areas of prior learning in which you are strong and deciding where to focus your energies. Some people may know a great deal about a certain subject area, but may not test well. These individuals would probably be just as concerned about strengthening their test-taking skills as they are about studying for a specific test. Many mental and physical skills are used in preparing for a test. It is important not only to review or study for the examinations, but to make certain that you are alert, relatively free of anxiety, and aware of how to approach standardized tests. Suggestions on developing test-taking skills and preparing psychologically and physically for a test are given. The following section suggests ways of assessing your knowledge of the content of a test and then reviewing and studying the material.

Using This Study Guide

Begin by carefully reading the test description and outline of knowledge and skills required for the examination, if given. As you read through the topics listed there, ask yourself how much you know about each one. Also note the terms, names, and symbols that are mentioned, and ask yourself whether you are familiar with them. This will give you a quick overview of how much you know about the subject. If you are familiar with nearly all the material, you will probably need a minimum of review; however, if less than half of it is familiar, you will probably require substantial study to do well on the test.

If, after reviewing the test description, you find that you need extensive review, delay answering the sample question until you have done some reading in the subject. If you complete them before reviewing the material, you will probably look for the answers as you study, and then they will not be a good assessment of your ability at a later date.

If you think you are familiar with most of the test material, try to answer the sample questions.

Apply the test-taking strategies given. Keeping within the time limit suggested will give you a rough idea of how quickly you should work in order to complete the actual test.

Check your answers against the answer key. If you answered nearly all the questions correctly, you probably do not need to study the subject extensively. If you got about half the questions correct, you ought o review at least one textbook or other suggested materials on the subject. If you answered less than half the questions correctly, you will probably benefit from more extensive reading in the subject and thorough study of one or more textbooks. The textbooks listed are used at many colleges but they are not the only good texts. You will find helpful almost any standard text available to you., such as the textbook used at your college, or earlier editions of texts listed. For some examinations, topic outlines and textbooks may not be available. Take the sample tests in this book and check your answers at the end of each test. Check wrong answers.

Suggestions for Studying

The following suggestions have been gathered from people who have prepared for CLEP examinations or other college-level tests.

1. Define your goals and locate study materials

First, determine your study goals. Set aside a block of time to review the material provided in this book, and then decide which test(s) you will take. Using the suggestions, locate suitable resource materials. If a preparation course is offered by an adult school or college in your area, you might find it helpful to enroll.

2. Find a good place to study

To determine what kind of place you need for studying, ask yourself questions such as: Do I need a quiet place? Does the telephone distract me? Do objects I see in this place remind me of things I should do? Is it too warm? Is it well lit? Am I too comfortable here? Do I have space to spread out my materials? You may find the library more conducive to studying than your home. If you decide to study at home, you might prevent interruptions by other household members by putting a sign on the door of your study room to indicate when you will be available.

3. Schedule time to study

To help you determine where studying best fits into your schedule, try this exercise: Make a list of your daily activities (for example, sleeping, working, and eating) and estimate how many hours per day you spend on each activity. Now, rate all the activities on your list in order of their importance and evaluate your use of time. Often people are astonished at how an average day appears from this perspective. They may discover that they were unaware how large portions of time are spent, or they learn their time can be scheduled in alternative ways. For example, they can remove the least important activities from their day and devote that time to studying or another important activity.

4. Establish a study routine and a set of goals

In order to study effectively, you should establish specific goals and a schedule for accomplishing them. Some people find it helpful to write out a weekly schedule and cross out each study period when it is completed. Others maintain their concentration better by writing down the time when they expect to complete a study task. Most people find short periods of intense study more productive than long stretches of time. For example, they may follow a regular schedule of several 20- or 30-minute study periods with short breaks between them. Some people like to allow themselves rewards as they complete each study goal. It is not essential that you accomplish every goal exactly within your schedule; the point is to be committed to your task.

5. Learn how to take an active role in studying.

If you have not done much studying for some time, you may find it difficult to concentrate at first. Try a method of studying, such as the one outlined below, that will help you concentrate on and remember what you read.

    a. First, read the chapter summary and the introduction. Then you will know what to look for in your reading.

    b. Next, convert the section or paragraph headlines into questions. For example, if you are reading a section entitled, The Causes of the American Revolution, ask yourself: *What were the causes of the American Revolution?* Compose the answer as you read the paragraph. Reading and answering questions aloud will help you understand and remember the material.

c. Take notes on key ideas or concepts as you read. Writing will also help you fix concepts more firmly in your mind. Underlining key ideas or writing notes in your book can be helpful and will be useful for review. Underline only important points. If you underline more than a third of each paragraph, you are probably underlining too much.

d. If there are questions or problems at the end of a chapter, answer or solve them on paper as if you were asked to do them for homework. Mathematics textbooks (and some other books) sometimes include answers to some or all of the exercises. If you have such a book, write your answers before looking at the ones given. When problem-solving is involved, work enough problems to master the required methods and concepts. If you have difficulty with problems, review any sample problems or explanations in the chapter.

e. To retain knowledge, most people have to review the material periodically. If you are preparing for a test over an extended period of time, review key concepts and notes each week or so. Do not wait for weeks to review the material or you will need to relearn much of it.

Psychological and Physical Preparation

Most people feel at least some nervousness before taking a test. Adults who are returning to college may not have taken a test in many years or they may have had little experience with standardized tests. Some younger students, as well, are uncomfortable with testing situations. People who received their education in countries outside the United States may find that many tests given in this country are quite different from the ones they are accustomed to taking.

Not only might candidates find the types of tests and the kinds of questions on them unfamiliar, but other aspects of the testing environment may be strange as well. The physical and mental stress that results from meeting this new experience can hinder a candidate's ability to demonstrate his or her true degree of knowledge in the subject area being tested. For this reason, it is important to go to the test center well prepared, both mentally and physically, for taking the test. You may find the following suggestions helpful.

1. Familiarize yourself, as much as possible, with the test and the test situation before the day of the examination. It will be helpful for you to know ahead of time:

a. How much time will be allowed for the test and whether there are timed subsections.

b. What types of questions and directions appear on the examination.

c. How your test score will be computed.

d. How to properly answer the questions on the computer (See the CLEP Sample on the CLEP website)

e. In which building and room the examination will be administered. If you don't know where the building is, locate it or get directions ahead of time.

f. The time of the test administration. You might wish to confirm this information a day or two before the examination and find out what time the building and room will be open so that you can plan to arrive early.

g. Where to park your car or, if you wish to take public transportation, which bus or train to take and the location of the nearest stop.

h. Whether smoking will be permitted during the test.

i. Whether there will be a break between examinations (if you will be taking more than one on the same day), and whether there is a place nearby where you can get something to eat or drink.

2. Go to the test situation relaxed and alert. In order to prepare for the test:

a. Get a good night's sleep. Last minute cramming, particularly late the night before, is usually counterproductive.

b. Eat normally. It is usually not wise to skip breakfast or lunch on the day of the test or to eat a big meal just before the test.

c. Avoid tranquilizers and stimulants. If you follow the other directions in this book, you won't need artificial aids. It's better to be a little tense than to be drowsy, but stimulants such as coffee and cola can make you nervous and interfere with your concentration.

d. Don't drink a lot of liquids before the test. Having to leave the room during the test will disturb your concentration and take valuable time away from the test.

e. If you are inclined to be nervous or tense, learn some relaxation exercises and use them before and perhaps during the test.

3. Arrive for the test early and prepared. Be sure to:

a. Arrive early enough so that you can find a parking place, locate the test center, and get settled comfortably before testing begins. Allow some extra time in case you are delayed unexpectedly.

b. Take the following with you:

- Your completed Registration/Admission Form
- Two forms of identification – one being a government-issued photo ID with signature, such as a driver's license or passport
- Non-mechanical pencil
- A watch so that you can time your progress (digital watches are prohibited)
- Your glasses if you need them for reading or seeing the chalkboard or wall clock

    c. Leave all books, papers, and notes outside the test center. You will not be permitted to use your own scratch paper; it will be provided. Also prohibited are calculators, cell phones, beepers, pagers, photo/copy devices, radios, headphones, food, beverages, and several other items.

    d. Be prepared for any temperature in the testing room. Wear layers of clothing that can be removed if the room is too hot but will keep you warm if it is too cold.

4. When you enter the test room:

    a. Sit in a seat that provides a maximum of comfort and freedom from distraction.

    b. Read directions carefully, and listen to all instructions given by the test administrator. If you don't understand the directions, ask for help before test timing begins. If you must ask a question after the test has begun, raise your hand and a proctor will assist you. The proctor can answer certain kinds of questions but cannot help you with the test.

    c. Know your rights as a test taker. You can expect to be given the full working time allowed for the test(s) and a reasonably quiet and comfortable place in which to work. If a poor test situation is preventing you from doing your best, ask if the situation can be remedied. If bad test conditions cannot be remedied, ask the person in charge to report the problem in the Irregularity Report that will be sent to ETS with the answer sheets. You may also wish to contact CLEP. Describe the exact circumstances as completely as you can. Be sure to include the test date and name(s) of the test(s) you took. ETS will investigate the problem to make sure it does not happen again, and, if the problem is serious enough, may arrange for you to retake the test without charge.

TAKING THE EXAMINATIONS

A person may know a great deal about the subject being tested, but not do as well as he or she is capable of on the test. Knowing how to approach a test is an important part of the testing process. While a command of test-taking skills cannot substitute for knowledge of the subject matter, it can be a significant factor in successful testing.

Test-taking skills enable a person to use all available information to earn a score that truly reflects his or her ability. There are different strategies for approaching different kinds of test questions. For example, free-response questions require a very different tack than do multiple-choice questions. Other factors, such as how the test will be graded, may also influence your approach to the test and your use of test time. Thus, your preparation for a test should include finding out all you can about the test so that you can use the most effective test-taking strategies.

Before taking a test, you should know approximately how many questions are on the test, how much time you will be allowed, how the test will be scored or graded, what types of questions and directions are on the test, and how you will be required to record your answers.

Taking Multiple-Choice Tests

1. Listen carefully to the instructions given by the test administrator and read carefully all directions before you begin to answer the questions.

2. Note the time that the test administrator starts timing the test. As you proceed, make sure that you are not working too slowly. You should have answered at least half the questions in a section when half the time for that section has passed. If you have not reached that point in the section, speed up your pace on the remaining questions.

3. Before answering a question, read the entire question, including all the answer choices. Don't think that because the first or second answer choice looks good to you, it isn't necessary to read the remaining options. Instructions usually tell you to select the best answer. Sometimes one answer choice is partially correct, but another option is better; therefore, it is usually a good idea to read all the answers before you choose one.

4. Read and consider every question. Questions that look complicated at first glance may not actually be so difficult once you have read them carefully.

5. Do not puzzle too long over any one question. If you don't know the answer after you've considered it briefly, go on to the next question. Make sure you return to the question later.

6. Make sure you record your response properly.

7. In trying to determine the correct answer, you may find it helpful to cross out those options that you know are incorrect, and to make marks next to those you think might be correct. If you decide to skip the question and come back to it later, you will save yourself the time of reconsidering all the options.

8. Watch for the following key words in test questions:

all	generally	never	perhaps
always	however	none	rarely
but	may	not	seldom
except	must	often	sometimes
every	necessary	only	usually

When a question or answer option contains words such as always, every, only, never, and none, there can be no exceptions to the answer you choose. Use of words such as often, rarely, sometimes, and generally indicates that there may be some exceptions to the answer.

9. Do not waste your time looking for clues to right answers based on flaws in question wording or patterns in correct answers. Professionals at the College Board and ETS put

a great deal of effort into developing valid, reliable, fair tests. CLEP test development committees are composed of college faculty who are experts in the subject covered by the test and are appointed by the College Board to write test questions and to scrutinize each question that is included on a CLEP test. Committee members make every effort to ensure that the questions are not ambiguous, that they have only one correct answer, and that they cover college-level topics. These committees do not intentionally include trick questions. If you think a question is flawed, ask the test administrator to report it, or contact CLEP immediately.

Taking Free-Response or Essay Tests

If your college requires the optional free-response or essay portion of a CLEP Composition and Literature exams, you should do some additional preparation for your CLEP test. Taking an essay test is very different from taking a multiple-choice test, so you will need to use some other strategies.

The essay written as part of the English Composition and Essay exam is graded by English professors from a variety of colleges and universities. A process called holistic scoring is used to rate your writing ability.

The optional free-response essays, on the other hand, are graded by the faculty of the college you designate as a score recipient. Guidelines and criteria for grading essays are not specified by the College Board or ETS. You may find it helpful, therefore, to talk with someone at your college to find out what criteria will be used to determine whether you will get credit. If the test requires essay responses, ask how much emphasis will be placed on your writing ability and your ability to organize your thoughts as opposed to your knowledge of subject matter. Find out how much weight will be given to your multiple-choice test score in comparison with your free-response grade in determining whether you will get credit. This will give you an idea where you should expend the greatest effort in preparing for and taking the test.

Here are some strategies you will find useful in taking any essay test:

1. Before you begin to write, read all questions carefully and take a few minutes to jot down some ideas you might include in each answer.

2. If you are given a choice of questions to answer, choose the questions you think you can answer most clearly and knowledgeably.

3. Determine in what order you will answer the questions. Answer those you find the easiest first so that any extra time can be spent on the more difficult questions.

4. When you know which questions you will answer and in what order, determine how much testing time remains and estimate how many minutes you will devote to each question. Unless suggested times are given for the questions or one question appears to require more or less time than the others, allot an equal amount of time to each question.

5. Before answering each question, indicate the number of the question as it is given in the test book. You need not copy the entire question from the question sheet, but it will be helpful to you and to the person grading your test if you indicate briefly the topic you are addressing – particularly if you are not answering the questions in the order in which they appear on the test.

6. Before answering each question, read it again carefully to make sure you are interpreting it correctly. Underline key words, such as those listed below, that often appear in free-response questions. Be sure you know the exact meaning of these words before taking the test.

analyze	demonstrate	enumerate	list
apply	derive	explain	outline
assess	describe	generalize	prove
compare	determine	illustrate	rank
contrast	discuss	interpret	show
define	distinguish	justify	summarize

If a question asks you to outline, define, or summarize, do not write a detailed explanation; if a question asks you to analyze, explain, illustrate, interpret, or show, you must do more than briefly describe the topic.

For a current listing of CLEP Colleges

where you can get credit and be tested, write:

CLEP, P.O. Box 6600, Princeton, NJ 08541-6600

Or e-mail: clep@ets.org, or call: (609) 771-7865

AMERICAN LITERATURE

Description of the Examination

The American Literature examination covers material that is usually taught in a two-semester survey course (or the equivalent) at the college level. It deals with the prose and poetry written in the United States from colonial times to the present. It is primarily a test of knowledge about literary works—their content, their background, and their authors—but also requires an ability to interpret poetry, fiction, and nonfiction prose, as well as a familiarity with the terminology used by literary critics and historians. The examination emphasizes fiction and poetry and deals to a lesser degree with the essay, drama, and autobiography.

In both coverage and approach, the examination resembles the chronologically organized survey of American literature offered by many colleges. It assumes that candidates have read widely and developed an appreciation of American literature, know the basic literary periods, and have a sense of the historical development of American literature.

The test contains approximately 100 questions to be answered in 90 minutes. Some of these are pretest questions that will not be scored. Any time candidates spend on tutorials and providing personal information is in addition to the actual testing time.

An optional essay section can be taken in addition to the multiple-choice test. The essay section requires that two essays be written during a total time of 90 minutes. For the first essay, a common theme in American literature and a list of major American authors are provided. Candidates are asked to write a well-organized essay discussing the way that theme is handled in works by any two of those authors. For the second essay, candidates are asked to respond to one of two topics—one requiring analysis of a poem, the other requiring analysis of a prose excerpt. In each case, the specific poem or prose excerpt is provided and questions are offered for guidance.

Candidates are expected to write well-organized essays in clear and precise prose. The essay section is graded by faculty at the institution that requests it and is still administered in paper-and-pencil format. There is an additional fee for taking this section, payable to the institution that administers the exam.

Knowledge and Skills Required

Questions on the American Literature examination require candidates to demonstrate one or more of the following abilities in the approximate proportions indicated.

- Knowledge of particular literary works—their authors, characters, plots, style, setting, themes, etc. (about 45 to 60 percent of the examination)
- Ability to understand and interpret short poems or excerpts from long poems and prose works presented in the test (about 25 to 40 percent of the examination)
- Knowledge of the historical and social settings of specific works, their relations to other literary works and to literary traditions, and the influences on their authors (about 10 to 15 percent of the examination)
- Familiarity with critical terms, verse forms, and literary devices (about 5 to 10 percent of the examination)

The subject matter of the American Literature examination is drawn from the following chronological periods. The percentages indicate the approximate percentage of exam questions from each period.

15%	the Colonial and Early National Period (Beginnings-1830)
25%	The Romantic Period (1830-1870)
20%	The Period of Realism and Naturalism (1870-1910)
25%	The Modernist Period (1910-1945)
15%	The Contemporary Period (1945-Present)

For instructional purposes from the official announcement © CEEB

HOW TO TAKE A TEST

You have studied long, hard and conscientiously.

With your official admission card in hand, and your heart pounding, you have been admitted to the examination room.

You note that there are several hundred other applicants in the examination room waiting to take the same test.

They all appear to be equally well prepared.

You know that nothing but your best effort will suffice. The "moment of truth" is at hand: you now have to demonstrate objectively, in writing, your knowledge of content and your understanding of subject matter.

You are fighting the most important battle of your life—to pass and/or score high on an examination which will determine your career and provide the economic basis for your livelihood.

What extra, special things should you know and should you do in taking the examination?

I. YOU MUST PASS AN EXAMINATION

A. WHAT EVERY CANDIDATE SHOULD KNOW
Examination applicants often ask us for help in preparing for the written test. What can I study in advance? What kinds of questions will be asked? How will the test be given? How will the papers be graded?

B. HOW ARE EXAMS DEVELOPED?
Examinations are carefully written by trained technicians who are specialists in the field known as "psychological measurement," in consultation with recognized authorities in the field of work that the test will cover. These experts recommend the subject matter areas or skills to be tested; only those knowledges or skills important to your success on the job are included. The most reliable books and source materials available are used as references. Together, the experts and technicians judge the difficulty level of the questions.
Test technicians know how to phrase questions so that the problem is clearly stated. Their ethics do not permit "trick" or "catch" questions. Questions may have been tried out on sample groups, or subjected to statistical analysis, to determine their usefulness.
Written tests are often used in combination with performance tests, ratings of training and experience, and oral interviews. All of these measures combine to form the best-known means of finding the right person for the right job.

II. HOW TO PASS THE WRITTEN TEST

A. BASIC STEPS

1) Study the announcement

How, then, can you know what subjects to study? Our best answer is: "Learn as much as possible about the class of positions for which you've applied." The exam will test the knowledge, skills and abilities needed to do the work.

Your most valuable source of information about the position you want is the official exam announcement. This announcement lists the training and experience qualifications. Check these standards and apply only if you come reasonably close to meeting them. Many jurisdictions preview the written test in the exam announcement by including a section called "Knowledge and Abilities Required," "Scope of the Examination," or some similar heading. Here you will find out specifically what fields will be tested.

2) Choose appropriate study materials

If the position for which you are applying is technical or advanced, you will read more advanced, specialized material. If you are already familiar with the basic principles of your field, elementary textbooks would waste your time. Concentrate on advanced textbooks and technical periodicals. Think through the concepts and review difficult problems in your field.

These are all general sources. You can get more ideas on your own initiative, following these leads. For example, training manuals and publications of the government agency which employs workers in your field can be useful, particularly for technical and professional positions. A letter or visit to the government department involved may result in more specific study suggestions, and certainly will provide you with a more definite idea of the exact nature of the position you are seeking.

3) Study this book!

III. KINDS OF TESTS

Tests are used for purposes other than measuring knowledge and ability to perform specified duties. For some positions, it is equally important to test ability to make adjustments to new situations or to profit from training. In others, basic mental abilities not dependent on information are essential. Questions which test these things may not appear as pertinent to the duties of the position as those which test for knowledge and information. Yet they are often highly important parts of a fair examination. For very general questions, it is almost impossible to help you direct your study efforts. What we can do is to point out some of the more common of these general abilities needed in public service positions and describe some typical questions.

1) General information

Broad, general information has been found useful for predicting job success in some kinds of work. This is tested in a variety of ways, from vocabulary lists to questions about current events. Basic background in some field of work, such as sociology or economics, may be sampled in a group of questions. Often these are principles which have become familiar to most persons through exposure rather than through formal training. It is difficult to advise you how to study for these questions; being alert to the world around you is our best suggestion.

2) Verbal ability

An example of an ability needed in many positions is verbal or language ability. Verbal ability is, in brief, the ability to use and understand words. Vocabulary and grammar tests are typical measures of this ability. Reading comprehension or paragraph interpretation questions are common in many kinds of civil service tests. You are given a paragraph of written material and asked to find its central meaning.

IV. KINDS OF QUESTIONS

1. Multiple-choice Questions

Most popular of the short-answer questions is the "multiple choice" or "best answer" question. It can be used, for example, to test for factual knowledge, ability to solve problems or judgment in meeting situations found at work.

A multiple-choice question is normally one of three types:
- It can begin with an incomplete statement followed by several possible endings. You are to find the one ending which best completes the statement, although some of the others may not be entirely wrong.
- It can also be a complete statement in the form of a question which is answered by choosing one of the statements listed.
- It can be in the form of a problem – again you select the best answer.

Here is an example of a multiple-choice question with a discussion which should give you some clues as to the method for choosing the right answer:

When an employee has a complaint about his assignment, the action which will best help him overcome his difficulty is to
- A. discuss his difficulty with his coworkers
- B. take the problem to the head of the organization
- C. take the problem to the person who gave him the assignment
- D. say nothing to anyone about his complaint

In answering this question, you should study each of the choices to find which is best. Consider choice "A" – Certainly an employee may discuss his complaint with fellow employees, but no change or improvement can result, and the complaint remains unresolved. Choice "B" is a poor choice since the head of the organization probably does not know what assignment you have been given, and taking your problem to him is known as "going over the head" of the supervisor. The supervisor, or person who made the assignment, is the person who can clarify it or correct any injustice. Choice "C" is, therefore, correct. To say nothing, as in choice "D," is unwise. Supervisors have and interest in knowing the problems employees are facing, and the employee is seeking a solution to his problem.

2. True/False

3. Matching Questions

Matching an answer from a column of choices within another column.

V. RECORDING YOUR ANSWERS

Computer terminals are used more and more today for many different kinds of exams.

For an examination with very few applicants, you may be told to record your answers in the test booklet itself. Separate answer sheets are much more common. If this separate answer sheet is to be scored by machine – and this is often the case – it is highly important that you mark your answers correctly in order to get credit.

VI. BEFORE THE TEST

YOUR PHYSICAL CONDITION IS IMPORTANT

If you are not well, you can't do your best work on tests. If you are half asleep, you can't do your best either. Here are some tips:

1) Get about the same amount of sleep you usually get. Don't stay up all night before the test, either partying or worrying—DON'T DO IT!
2) If you wear glasses, be sure to wear them when you go to take the test. This goes for hearing aids, too.
3) If you have any physical problems that may keep you from doing your best, be sure to tell the person giving the test. If you are sick or in poor health, you relay cannot do your best on any test. You can always come back and take the test some other time.

Common sense will help you find procedures to follow to get ready for an examination. Too many of us, however, overlook these sensible measures. Indeed, nervousness and fatigue have been found to be the most serious reasons why applicants fail to do their best on civil service tests. Here is a list of reminders:

- Begin your preparation early – Don't wait until the last minute to go scurrying around for books and materials or to find out what the position is all about.
- Prepare continuously – An hour a night for a week is better than an all-night cram session. This has been definitely established. What is more, a night a week for a month will return better dividends than crowding your study into a shorter period of time.
- Locate the place of the exam – You have been sent a notice telling you when and where to report for the examination. If the location is in a different town or otherwise unfamiliar to you, it would be well to inquire the best route and learn something about the building.
- Relax the night before the test – Allow your mind to rest. Do not study at all that night. Plan some mild recreation or diversion; then go to bed early and get a good night's sleep.
- Get up early enough to make a leisurely trip to the place for the test – This way unforeseen events, traffic snarls, unfamiliar buildings, etc. will not upset you.
- Dress comfortably – A written test is not a fashion show. You will be known by number and not by name, so wear something comfortable.
- Leave excess paraphernalia at home – Shopping bags and odd bundles will get in your way. You need bring only the items mentioned in the official notice you received; usually everything you need is provided. Do not bring reference books to the exam. They will only confuse those last minutes and be taken away from you when in the test room.

- Arrive somewhat ahead of time – If because of transportation schedules you must get there very early, bring a newspaper or magazine to take your mind off yourself while waiting.
- Locate the examination room – When you have found the proper room, you will be directed to the seat or part of the room where you will sit. Sometimes you are given a sheet of instructions to read while you are waiting. Do not fill out any forms until you are told to do so; just read them and be prepared.
- Relax and prepare to listen to the instructions
- If you have any physical problem that may keep you from doing your best, be sure to tell the test administrator. If you are sick or in poor health, you really cannot do your best on the exam. You can come back and take the test some other time.

VII. AT THE TEST

The day of the test is here and you have the test booklet in your hand. The temptation to get going is very strong. Caution! There is more to success than knowing the right answers. You must know how to identify your papers and understand variations in the type of short-answer question used in this particular examination. Follow these suggestions for maximum results from your efforts:

1) Cooperate with the monitor

The test administrator has a duty to create a situation in which you can be as much at ease as possible. He will give instructions, tell you when to begin, check to see that you are marking your answer sheet correctly, and so on. He is not there to guard you, although he will see that your competitors do not take unfair advantage. He wants to help you do your best.

2) Listen to all instructions

Don't jump the gun! Wait until you understand all directions. In most civil service tests you get more time than you need to answer the questions. So don't be in a hurry. Read each word of instructions until you clearly understand the meaning. Study the examples, listen to all announcements and follow directions. Ask questions if you do not understand what to do.

3) Identify your papers

Civil service exams are usually identified by number only. You will be assigned a number; you must not put your name on your test papers. Be sure to copy your number correctly. Since more than one exam may be given, copy your exact examination title.

4) Plan your time

Unless you are told that a test is a "speed" or "rate of work" test, speed itself is usually not important. Time enough to answer all the questions will be provided, but this does not mean that you have all day. An overall time limit has been set. Divide the total time (in minutes) by the number of questions to determine the approximate time you have for each question.

5) Do not linger over difficult questions

If you come across a difficult question, mark it with a paper clip (useful to have along) and come back to it when you have been through the booklet. One caution if you do this – be sure to skip a number on your answer sheet as well. Check often to be sure that you have not lost your place and that you are marking in the row numbered the same as the question you are answering.

6) Read the questions
Be sure you know what the question asks! Many capable people are unsuccessful because they failed to read the questions correctly.

7) Answer all questions
Unless you have been instructed that a penalty will be deducted for incorrect answers, it is better to guess than to omit a question.

8) Speed tests
It is often better NOT to guess on speed tests. It has been found that on timed tests people are tempted to spend the last few seconds before time is called in marking answers at random – without even reading them – in the hope of picking up a few extra points. To discourage this practice, the instructions may warn you that your score will be "corrected" for guessing. That is, a penalty will be applied. The incorrect answers will be deducted from the correct ones, or some other penalty formula will be used.

9) Review your answers
If you finish before time is called, go back to the questions you guessed or omitted to give them further thought. Review other answers if you have time.

10) Return your test materials
If you are ready to leave before others have finished or time is called, take ALL your materials to the monitor and leave quietly. Never take any test material with you. The monitor can discover whose papers are not complete, and taking a test booklet may be grounds for disqualification.

VIII. EXAMINATION TECHNIQUES

1) Read the general instructions carefully. These are usually printed on the first page of the exam booklet. As a rule, these instructions refer to the timing of the examination; the fact that you should not start work until the signal and must stop work at a signal, etc. If there are any special instructions, such as a choice of questions to be answered, make sure that you note this instruction carefully.

2) When you are ready to start work on the examination, that is as soon as the signal has been given, read the instructions to each question booklet, underline any key words or phrases, such as least, best, outline, describe and the like. In this way you will tend to answer as requested rather than discover on reviewing your paper that you listed without describing, that you selected the worst choice rather than the best choice, etc.

3) If the examination is of the objective or multiple-choice type – that is, each question will also give a series of possible answers: A, B, C or D, and you are called upon to select the best answer and write the letter next to that answer on your answer paper – it is advisable to start answering each question in turn. There may be anywhere from 50 to 100 such questions in the three or four hours allotted and you can see how much time would be taken if you read through all the questions before beginning to answer any. Furthermore, if you

come across a question or group of questions which you know would be difficult to answer, it would undoubtedly affect your handling of all the other questions.

4) If the examination is of the essay type and contains but a few questions, it is a moot point as to whether you should read all the questions before starting to answer any one. Of course, if you are given a choice – say five out of seven and the like – then it is essential to read all the questions so you can eliminate the two that are most difficult. If, however, you are asked to answer all the questions, there may be danger in trying to answer the easiest one first because you may find that you will spend too much time on it. The best technique is to answer the first question, then proceed to the second, etc.

5) Time your answers. Before the exam begins, write down the time it started, then add the time allowed for the examination and write down the time it must be completed, then divide the time available somewhat as follows:
    - If 3-1/2 hours are allowed, that would be 210 minutes. If you have 80 objective-type questions, that would be an average of 2-1/2 minutes per question. Allow yourself no more than 2 minutes per question, or a total of 160 minutes, which will permit about 50 minutes to review.
    - If for the time allotment of 210 minutes there are 7 essay questions to answer, that would average about 30 minutes a question. Give yourself only 25 minutes per question so that you have about 35 minutes to review.

6) The most important instruction is to read each question and make sure you know what is wanted. The second most important instruction is to time yourself properly so that you answer every question. The third most important instruction is to answer every question. Guess if you have to but include something for each question. Remember that you will receive no credit for a blank and will probably receive some credit if you write something in answer to an essay question. If you guess a letter – say "B" for a multiple-choice question – you may have guessed right. If you leave a blank as an answer to a multiple-choice question, the examiners may respect your feelings but it will not add a point to your score. Some exams may penalize you for wrong answers, so in such cases only, you may not want to guess unless you have some basis for your answer.

7) Suggestions
   a. Objective-type questions
      1. Examine the question booklet for proper sequence of pages and questions
      2. Read all instructions carefully
      3. Skip any question which seems too difficult; return to it after all other questions have been answered
      4. Apportion your time properly; do not spend too much time on any single question or group of questions
      5. Note and underline key words – all, most, fewest, least, best, worst, same, opposite, etc.
      6. Pay particular attention to negatives
      7. Note unusual option, e.g., unduly long, short, complex, different or similar in content to the body of the question
      8. Observe the use of "hedging" words – probably, may, most likely, etc.

9. Make sure that your answer is put next to the same number as the question
10. Do not second-guess unless you have good reason to believe the second answer is definitely more correct
11. Cross out original answer if you decide another answer is more accurate; do not erase until you are ready to hand your paper in
12. Answer all questions; guess unless instructed otherwise
13. Leave time for review

b. Essay questions
1. Read each question carefully
2. Determine exactly what is wanted. Underline key words or phrases.
3. Decide on outline or paragraph answer
4. Include many different points and elements unless asked to develop any one or two points or elements
5. Show impartiality by giving pros and cons unless directed to select one side only
6. Make and write down any assumptions you find necessary to answer the questions
7. Watch your English, grammar, punctuation and choice of words
8. Time your answers; don't crowd material

8) Answering the essay question

Most essay questions can be answered by framing the specific response around several key words or ideas. Here are a few such key words or ideas:

M's: manpower, materials, methods, money, management
P's: purpose, program, policy, plan, procedure, practice, problems, pitfalls, personnel, public relations

a. Six basic steps in handling problems:
1. Preliminary plan and background development
2. Collect information, data and facts
3. Analyze and interpret information, data and facts
4. Analyze and develop solutions as well as make recommendations
5. Prepare report and sell recommendations
6. Install recommendations and follow up effectiveness

b. Pitfalls to avoid
1. Taking things for granted – A statement of the situation does not necessarily imply that each of the elements is necessarily true; for example, a complaint may be invalid and biased so that all that can be taken for granted is that a complaint has been registered
2. Considering only one side of a situation – Wherever possible, indicate several alternatives and then point out the reasons you selected the best one
3. Failing to indicate follow up – Whenever your answer indicates action on your part, make certain that you will take proper follow-up action to see how successful your recommendations, procedures or actions turn out to be
4. Taking too long in answering any single question – Remember to time your answers properly

EXAMINATION SECTION

EXAMINATION SECTION
TEST 1

DIRECTIONS: Each question or incomplete statement is followed by several suggested answers or completions. Select the one that BEST answers the question or completes the statement. *PRINT THE LETTER OF THE CORRECT ANSWER IN THE SPACE AT THE RIGHT.*

1. The poetry of Philip Freneau was characterized by

    A. political support of the Federalists
    B. slavish imitation of English writers
    C. romantic, imaginative descriptions of nature
    D. emphasis on moral and religious themes

2. The most surprising peculiarity about him was the entire indifference with which he regarded all distinctions that did not depend on personal merit.
   This description by his creator BEST depicts the fictional character

    A. Roger Chillingworth   B. Natty Bumppo
    C. Huckleberry Finn   D. Martin Eden

3. Native prose fiction had little vogue in the American colonies MAINLY because of

    A. the preference for English novels
    B. a moral aversion to imaginative literature
    C. preoccupation with political discussion
    D. the tacit opposition of American printers

4. Each of the following writers treated the topic indicated EXCEPT

    A. William Bradford - a plea against religious intolerance
    B. John Winthrop - a history of New England
    C. Anne Bradstreet - poetry on nature and the seasons
    D. Michael Wigglesworth - poetry on religious themes

5. The style that he attained is probably more like Defoe's than Addison's, clear, direct, unemotional, lacking the imagination and urbanity of THE SPECTATOR, but possessing a humor of which Defoe was void, and graced with the ripeness of experience that a broad contact with men and affairs alone can give.
   The writer described in the above passage is

    A. Washington Irving   B. John Woolman
    C. Benjamin Franklin   D. Joel Barlow

6. The influence of the Gothic novelists can be discerned MOST strongly in the work of

    A. Charles Brockden Brown   B. Ralph Waldo Emerson
    C. James Fenimore Cooper   D. William Dean Howells

7. All of the following characters are paired CORRECTLY with the novel in which they appear EXCEPT

    A. Harvey Birch - THE SPY
    B. Long Tom Coffin - THE PILOT

C. Chingachgook - THE DEERSLAYER
D. Cora Munro - THE PATHFINDER

8. In OMOO, Herman Melville expresses the view that the Polynesians

   A. are happiest as unsophisticated but sincere pagans
   B. will eventually appreciate the influence of Western civilization
   C. represent the natural forces that civilized man cannot overcome
   D. are superior in intelligence to Western man

9. All of the following are true of Thoreau EXCEPT that he

   A. was born and died in Massachusetts
   B. wrote poetry as well as prose
   C. disliked slavery but opposed the abolitionist movement
   D. showed his strong disapproval of the Mexican War

10. The SALMAGUNDI PAPERS are

    A. humorous accounts of old Dutch legends in New York
    B. descriptions of the author's travels in England
    C. essays on European art and culture
    D. satires on New York life and society

11. The curse of Matthew Maule seemed to be carried out by the

    A. arrest and imprisonment of Clifford Pyncheon
    B. vengeance of the lodger, Mr. Holgrave
    C. death by apoplexy of Judge Pyncheon
    D. flight of Clifford and Hepzibah

12. A work in which Mark Twain's humor is clouded by bitterness and pessimism is

    A. THE MYSTERIOUS STRANGER   B. THE GILDED CAGE
    C. A CONNECTICUT YANKEE   D. THE INNOCENTS ABROAD

13. Though never a brilliant writer, he attempted to deal conscientiously with the everyday experiences of ordinary people. His novels are characterized chiefly by their moral atmosphere and authentic domestic realism.
    The novelist to whom the foregoing description applies wrote

    A. McTEAGUE   B. CHAD HANNA
    C. A MODERN INSTANCE   D. THE YEMASSEE

14. The short story of Hawthorne's in which the central character's face is covered to conceal the ravages of pestilence is

    A. ETHAN BRAND   B. RAPPACCINI'S DAUGHTER
    C. LADY ELEANORE'S MANTLE D. THE MINISTER'S BLACK VEIL

15. He was born and lived with a silver spoon in his mouth, and if a grudging posterity inclines to rate him and his little world somewhat lower than he rated them, what difference can that make to him? Tolerant himself, we should perhaps emulate his example and not insist too rudely that he is only a minor figure in American literature.
    The above passage applies to

A.	William Cullen Bryant	B.	John Greenleaf Whittier
C.	Henry Wadsworth Longfellow	D.	Oliver Wendell Holmes

16. Henry James describes the influence of European culture on Americans in all of the following works EXCEPT   16.____

    A. THE ALTAR OF THE DEAD   B. DAISY MILLER
    C. THE PORTRAIT OF A LADY   D. THE GOLDEN BOWL

17. Of the following descriptions of characters created by Willa Cather, the one that is CORRECT is: 17.____

    A. Marian Forrester - the understanding wife of an unhappy college professor
    B. Alexandra Bergson - an unhappily married woman in a midwestern town
    C. Antonia Shimerda - an immigrant girl who settles in Boston
    D. Thea Kronborg - a small-town girl who becomes a famous opera singer

18. The return of a Civil War soldier to his home and the cheating of a farmer by a usurer are two of the events narrated in   18.____

    A. HORSES AND MEN   B. OLD CREOLE DAYS
    C. MAIN-TRAVELLED ROADS   D. THE HEART OF THE WEST

19. As Theodore Dreiser presents the case, the downfall of Clyde Griffiths is MAINLY the result of   19.____

    A. the social and economic inequalities of American society
    B. the harsh fundamentalism of his religious-minded parents
    C. his inherent qualities of moral and emotional depravity
    D. his blundering attempts to meet the insistent demands of others

20. Each of the following novels by Upton Sinclair is paired CORRECTLY with a subject it describes EXCEPT   20.____

    A. BOSTON - the Sacco-Vanzetti case
    B. WIDE IS THE GATE - the rise of Nazism
    C. WORLD'S END - the outbreak of World War I
    D. THE BRASS CHECK - abuses by the railroads

21. A humorous short story in which a young man faces the consequences of a glorious drinking spree, on the morning after, is   21.____

    A. THAT'S WHAT HAPPENED TO ME   B. I'M IN A HURRY
    C. THE CATBIRD SEAT   D. YOU WERE PERFECTLY FINE

22. A common bond between the short stories HAIRCUT and CHAMPION is the   22.____

    A. antagonistic view of the sports world
    B. similarity in locale and theme
    C. cheerful acceptance of human failings
    D. savage dissection of despicable characters

23. Beneath its involved and difficult technique, it is a compelling study of the dissolution of an old Southern family gone to seed.   23.____
The novel MOST aptly described by the foregoing passage is

A. THE WEB AND THE ROCK
B. GONE WITH THE WIND
C. KNEEL TO THE RISING SUN
D. THE SOUND AND THE FURY

24. Each of the following novels is directly concerned with the problem or topic indicated EXCEPT

    A. BHOWANI JUNCTION - the modern Anglo-Indian
    B. THE CATCHER IN THE RYE - a maladjusted adolescent
    C. PICTURES FROM AN INSTITUTION - patients in a sanitarium
    D. THE FALL OF A TITAN - politics in Soviet Russia

25. A novelist whose sports stories have a wide appeal for adolescent boys is

    A. Clarence B. Kelland
    B. John R. Tunis
    C. Ray Bradbury
    D. Ira Levin

KEY (CORRECT ANSWERS)

1. C
2. B
3. B
4. A
5. C

6. A
7. D
8. A
9. C
10. D

11. C
12. A
13. C
14. C
15. D

16. A
17. D
18. C
19. A
20. D

21. D
22. D
23. D
24. C
25. B

TEST 2

DIRECTIONS: Each question or incomplete statement is followed by several suggested answers or completions. Select the one that BEST answers the question or completes the statement. *PRINT THE LETTER OF THE CORRECT ANSWER IN THE SPACE AT THE RIGHT.*

1. THE SONG OF THE CHATTAHOOCHEE is a poem about the

   A. injustice done to the Indian
   B. growth and expansion of the West
   C. necessity to respond to the call of duty
   D. worth of determination in great leaders

   1.____

2. "...Three fifths of him genius and two fifths sheer fudge ...Who has written some things quite the best of their kind, But the heart somehow seems all squeezed out by the mind."
   The above quotation from A FABLE FOR CRITICS refers to

   A. Oliver Wendell Holmes   B. Ralph Waldo Emerson
   C. Edgar Allan Poe   D. Henry Wadsworth Longfellow

   2.____

3. The collapse of Calvinistic theology in New England is described in a humorous allegorical poem written by

   A. James Russell Lowell   B. Oliver Wendell Holmes
   C. Henry David Thoreau   D. Ralph Waldo Emerson

   3.____

4. The author of the lines,
   "Were half the power, that fills the world with terror,
   Were half the wealth, bestowed on camps and courts,
   Given to redeem the human mind from error,
   There were no need of arsenals or forts,"
   also wrote a poem called

   A. SKIPPER IRESON'S RIDE   B. THE SKELETON IN ARMOR
   C. THE DEACON'S MASTERPIECE   D. THE VISION OF SIR LAUNFAL

   4.____

5. Of the following poems by Walt Whitman, the one that deals with a tragedy of the Civil War is

   A. COME UP FROM THE FIELDS, FATHER
   B. THE OX-TAMER
   C. OUT OF THE CRADLE ENDLESSLY ROCKING
   D. WHEN I PERUSE THE CONQUER'D FAME

   5.____

6. All of the following lines are from Ralph Waldo Emerson EXCEPT:

   A. "We sit here in the promised land
      That flows with Freedom's honey and milk."
   B. "I like a church; I like a cowl;
      I love a prophet of the soul."

   6.____

C. "Hast thou named all the birds without a gun;
. . O be my friend and teach me to be thine."
D. "'Twas one of the charmed days
When the genius of God doth flow."

7. A writer who was NOT born in the region about which he centers much of his work is

   A. James Farrell
   B. Sherwood Anderson
   C. Robert Frost
   D. Edwin Arlington Robinson

8. All of the following lines are from Emily Dickinson EXCEPT:

   A. "Success is counted sweetest
      By those who ne'er succeed."
   B. "Parting is all we know of heaven
      And all we need of hell."
   C. "The soul selects her own society,
      Then shuts the door."
   D. "Who is in love with loveliness
      Need not shake with cold."

9. PLAIN LANGUAGE FROM TRUTHFUL JAMES is a(n)

   A. tirade against the Mexican War
   B. humorous commentary on the shrewdness of the Chinese
   C. description of courting customs in New England
   D. attack on the poetasters of New England

10. Beyond her cunningly poised and polished syllables or her concerns with freezing silvers, frail china, and pearly monotones, she frequently achieves a quality of intensity and mysticism that gives her craftmanship the depth of memorable poetry.
    This passage would MOST aptly describe the poetry of

    A. Elinor Wylie
    B. Emily Dickinson
    C. Hilda Doolittle
    D. Marianne Moore

11. THE LOVE SONG OF J. ALFRED PRUFROCK is a portrait of a man who

    A. can recognize the sham of his superficial existence but lacks the courage to make any significant decisions
    B. regrets the fact that he has grown old without having realized the optimistic ambitions of his youth
    C. has a vague uneasiness about his status but does not really understand the fundamental nature of his mediocrity
    D. has become so imbued with romantic notions that he can no longer bring himself to face reality

12. Assume that you are planning a unit entitled, *"America - Its Peoples and Traditions."*
    Of the following poems, the one that would be LEAST appropriate in this unit is

    A. THE TUFT OF FLOWERS by Robert Frost
    B. YOU, ANDREW MARVELL by Archibald MacLeish
    C. THE EAGLE THAT IS FORGOTTEN by Vachel Lindsay
    D. THE MOUNTAIN WHIPPOORWILL by Stephen Vincent Benet

13. MINE THE HARVEST is the published posthumous work of a poet noted for   13.____

    A. powerful, pulsating rhythms and refrains
    B. a frank attitude toward romantic attachments
    C. intimate portrayals of small-town inhabitants
    D. haunting qualities of surrealism and fantasy

14. "O World, thou choosest not the better part!   14.____
    It is not wisdom to be only wise."
    "As a fond mother, when the day is o'er
    Leads by the hand her little child to bed..."
    "Enamored architect of airy rhyme,
    Build as thou wilt, heed not what each man says."
    The above quotations are the opening lines of sonnets by
        I. Thomas Bailey Aldrich
        II. Henry Wadsworth Longfellow
        III. George Santayana

    If these poets were arranged in order, as the authors of the above lines, the CORRECT order would be:

    A. III, I, II   B. I, II, III   C. II, III, I   D. III, II, I

15. All of the following are true of Parrington's MAIN CURRENTS IN AMERICAN THOUGHT   15.____
    EXCEPT that in it he

    A. shows the influence of economic thought on American literature
    B. discusses fully the Romantic revolution in nineteenth century American literature
    C. stresses aesthetic considerations in his analysis of each author
    D. shows the relationship between literature and the social background

16. In this drama, O'Neill is truly heroic in his anti-heroic reiteration that humanity leads a life   16.____
    so snarled by weaknesses and contradictions that it can subsist only on illusions. In most
    of the characters, regrets and anxieties war with their resignations and rationalized passivity.
    The play referred to in the foregoing passage is

    A. MOURNING BECOMES ELECTRA   B. ANNA CHRISTIE
    C. THE ICEMAN COMETH   D. BEYOND THE HORIZON

17. A characteristic of twentieth century drama illustrated strongly by the plays of Eugene   17.____
    O'Neill is

    A. concern with wartime problems
    B. increased use of social satire
    C. Freudian interpretation of character
    D. revival of poetic language

18. A pair of plays written by the same playwright are   18.____

    A. PICNIC and COME BACK LITTLE SHEBA
    B. THE CRUCIBLE and THE LIVING ROOM
    C. ONDINE and QUADRILLE
    D. THE LITTLE FOXES and THE TIME OF THE CUCKOO

19. Each of the following plays is CORRECTLY paired with the work from which it was derived EXCEPT

   A. THE WISTERIA TREES - THE CHERRY ORCHARD
   B. THE INNOCENTS - THE MARK OF THE BEAST
   C. THE KING AND I - ANNA AND THE KING OF SIAM
   D. LOST IN THE STARS - CRY, THE BELOVED COUNTRY

20. THE EDUCATION OF HENRY ADAMS is an autobiography which

   A. presents a vivid picture of people and events in the middle of the nineteenth century
   B. tells how the author was able to adjust himself successfully in a hostile, complex world
   C. emphasizes spiritual values rather than science in considering the future of civilization
   D. takes a fundamentally pessimistic view concerning the course of historical development

21. Each of the following men is matched correctly with a biographer EXCEPT

   A. Benjamin Franklin - Carl Van Doren
   B. Edgar Allan Poe - Harvey Allen
   C. Paul Revere - Esther Forbes
   D. F. Scott Fitzgerald - Francis O. Matthiessen

22. All of the following have written biographies of Mark Twain EXCEPT

   A. William Dean Howells
   B. Van Wyek Brooks
   C. Bernard De Voto
   D. Carl Van Doren

23. All of the following statements are true of Karl Shapiro EXCEPT that

   A. he is the editor of the magazine called POETRY
   B. he has won a Pulitzer Prize for his volume of poems, V-LETTER
   C. his ESSAY IN RHYME is an attempt to write poetic criticism in verse
   D. he re-evaluates some modern poets in his book POETRY AND THE AGE

24. T.S. Eliot has been instrumental in re-establishing the reputation of the

   A. Renaissance poets
   B. Metaphysical poets
   C. Romantic poets
   D. Imagists

25. "If I read a book and it makes my body so cold no fire can ever warm me, I know it is poetry. If I feel physically as if the top of my head were taken off, I know this is poetry. These are the only ways I know it."
   The above passage was written by

   A. Emily Dickinson
   B. Sidney Lanier
   C. Walt Whitman
   D. Edwin Markham

KEY (CORRECT ANSWERS)

1. C
2. C
3. B
4. B
5. A

6. A
7. C
8. D
9. B
10. A

11. A
12. B
13. B
14. D
15. C

16. C
17. C
18. A
19. B
20. D

21. D
22. D
23. D
24. B
25. A

TEST 3

DIRECTIONS: Each question or incomplete statement is followed by several suggested answers or completions. Select the one that BEST answers the question or completes the statement. *PRINT THE LETTER OF THE CORRECT ANSWER IN THE SPACE AT THE RIGHT.*

1. Robert Penn Warren, in his famous essay PURE AND IMPURE POETRY, objects to *pure* poetry because   1.____

    A. poetry must contain both texture and structure
    B. the philosophic message of a poem is paramount in importance
    C. *pure* poetry neglects imagery
    D. *pure* poetry is too traditional

2. Allan Tate builds his critical theory around the doctrine of *tension,* by which he means   2.____

    A. fusing the abstract idea and concrete image
    B. stirring the emotions of the reader
    C. expressing the conflicts of the society in which the poet lives
    D. making articulate the character's hidden inner drives

3. The NEW CRITICISM devotes LEAST attention to the   3.____

    A. imagery of a poem
    B. historical background of a poem
    C. relationship between the imagery and the poet's purpose
    D. structure of a poem

4. In THE MIKADO, it is decreed that all shall be beheaded who   4.____

    A. embezzle   B. write novels   C. flirt   D. flatter

5. Of the following plays, the one that could be appropriately used to illustrate the *questioning of established values* is   5.____

    A. STREET SCENE   B. DEATH OF A SALESMAN
    C. EVE OF ST. MARK   D. ABE LINCOLN IN ILLINOIS

6. Of the following plays, the one that would BEST fit the characterization of *revolt against previously neglected injustices* is   6.____

    A. MISTER ROBERTS   B. THE GLASS MENAGERIE
    C. THE TIME OF YOUR LIFE   D. DEAD END

7. Of the following twentieth century plays, the one that is LEAST concerned with questioning accepted values is   7.____

    A. WINTERSET   B. NATIVE SON
    C. OUR TOWN   D. AWAKE AND SING

8. Of the following poets, the one who worked MOST actively as an agitator for abolition of slavery was   8.____

    A. James Russell Lowell   B. Walt Whitman
    C. William Cullen Bryant   D. John Greenleaf Whittier

9. WALDEN is a

   A. poem about the beauty of New England
   B. statement of political and philosophical anarchism
   C. discussion of the meaning of friendship
   D. series of essays on an experiment in simple living

10. Practically, it was an assertion of the inalienable worth of man; theoretically, it was an assertion of the immanence of divinity in instinct, the transference of supernatural attributes to the natural constitution of mankind.
    The above statement is MOST true of

    A. Brahminism   B. Transcendentalism
    C. Unitarianism   D. Puritanism

11. The nobility of rough and uncouth characters is a major theme in the short stories of

    A. Henry James   B. Ambrose Bierce
    C. Bret Harte   D. Nathaniel Hawthorne

12. The technique of the modern detective story was FIRST developed by

    A. Mark Twain   B. Nathaniel Hawthorne
    C. Edgar Allan Poe   D. Bret Harte

13. Primitive cultures in the South Seas have been sympathetically described by

    A. William Gilmore Simms   B. Charles Brockden Brown
    C. Herman Melville   D. Hamlin Garland

14. The intrigues and financial deals of an unscrupulous Senator are described in

    A. THE AMBASSADORS   B. THE GILDED AGE
    C. THE RISE OF SILAS LAPHAM D. A SON OF THE MIDDLE BORDER

15. All of the following are Civil War songs EXCEPT

    A. BATTLE HYMN OF THE REPUBLIC
    B. MY OLD KENTUCKY HOME
    C. TENTING ON THE OLD CAMP GROUND
    D. MARYLAND! MY MARYLAND!

16. WHEN LILACS LAST IN THE DOORYARD BLOOM'D was written in memory of

    A. F.D. Roosevelt   B. Woodrow Wilson
    C. Abraham Lincoln   D. George Washington

17. *"A boy's will is the wind's will,*
    And the thoughts of youth are long, long thoughts"
    is a refrain that runs through a poem by

    A. Henry Wadsworth Longfellow   B. Bret Harte
    C. William Cullen Bryant   D. John Greenleaf Whittier

18. The poem which expressed a protest against Daniel Webster's Seventh of March Speech was

    A. THE LOST LEADER   B. ICHABOD
    C. THRENODY   D. THE PRESENT CRISIS

19. Of the following statements, the one BEST describing Emily Dickinson as a poet is that she

    A. was a bizarre teller of tales
    B. reflected the spirit of the frontier
    C. spoke out angrily against materialism
    D. delighted in epigram and paradox

20. All of the following are typical of O. Henry's short stories EXCEPT

    A. interest in ordinary people
    B. depth of social perception
    C. humor and sentiment
    D. the surprise ending

21. MINIVER CHEEVY and RICHARD CORY are poems that illustrate Edwin Arlington Robinson's

    A. strong sense of moral values
    B. gift for combining the lyric and dramatic
    C. ironic insight into spiritual frustration
    D. underlying faith in modern society

22. His style is simple, plain, and colloquial, often in the form of blank verse in which his Yankee farmers speak for themselves.
    The poet referred to in the above passage is

    A. Edgar Lee Masters   B. Vachel Lindsay
    C. Robinson Jeffers   D. Robert Frost

23. A writer noted for his poems in free verse celebrating industrial America is

    A. Edgar Lee Masters   B. Edwin Markham
    C. Robinson Jeffers   D. Carl Sandburg

24. Of the following lines, the one by Edna St. Vincent Millay is:

    A. "I have a rendezvous with Death"
    B. "There's a barrel organ caroling across a golden street"
    C. "How do I love thee? Let me count the ways"
    D. "Euclid alone has looked on beauty bare"

25. JOHN BROWN'S BODY by Stephen Vincent Benet is a

    A. short story about an American hero
    B. narrative poem dealing with the Civil War
    C. collection of essays on American martyrs
    D. novel which won the Pulitizer Prize

KEY (CORRECT ANSWERS)

1.	A	11.	C
2.	A	12.	C
3.	B	13.	C
4.	C	14.	B
5.	B	15.	B
6.	D	16.	C
7.	C	17.	A
8.	D	18.	B
9.	D	19.	D
10.	B	20.	B

21. C
22. D
23. D
24. D
25. B

TEST 4

DIRECTIONS: Each question or incomplete statement is followed by several suggested answers or completions. Select the one that BEST answers the question or completes the statement. *PRINT THE LETTER OF THE CORRECT ANSWER IN THE SPACE AT THE RIGHT.*

1. The biographer who used the term *psychograph* to describe his work is

    A. Gamaliel Bradford
    B. Marquis James
    C. Matthew Josephson
    D. Morris Robert Werner

    1._____

2. All of the following were closely associated with the Abolitionist movement EXCEPT

    A. Richard Henry Dana
    B. John Greenleaf Whittier
    C. Wendell Phillips
    D. Henry W. Longfellow

    2._____

3. Sherwood Anderson wrote all of the following EXCEPT

    A. DARK LAUGHTER
    B. WINESBURG, OHIO
    C. THE GRAIN OF DUST
    D. POOR WHITE

    3._____

4. The following have been closely associated with the publications noted EXCEPT

    A. E.B. White - THE NEW YORKER
    B. Norman Corwin - THE SATURDAY REVIEW OF LITERATURE
    C. Ellery Sedgwick - THE ATLANTIC MONTHLY
    D. Harriet Monroe - POETRY

    4._____

5. All of the following statements are true EXCEPT

    A. Hamlin Garland was born in Wisconsin in 1860
    B. His pioneering father took the family to Oregon
    C. Impressed by the hardships of pioneer life, Garland described these experiences in his writing
    D. He was a member of the realistic school of writers

    5._____

6. All of the following statements are true EXCEPT:

    A. Lafcadio Hearn was the son of an Irish father and a Greek mother
    B. He was fascinated by the color of New Orleans
    C. He settled in China and later married a Chinese woman
    D. For a time, he was a lecturer in English literature at the University of Tokyo

    6._____

7. Tilbury Town is an imaginary town created in the poems of

    A. William Rose Benet
    B. William Vaughn Moody
    C. Edwin Arlington Robinson
    D. Bliss Carman

    7._____

8. Henry Adams was an ardent student of the architecture of

    A. ancient Greece
    B. the Italian Renaissance
    C. medieval cathedrals
    D. Chinese pagodas

    8._____

9. All of the following have written stories occurring in the state indicated EXCEPT

    A. Georgia - Erskine Caldwell
    B. California - John Steinbeck
    C. Mississippi - William Faulkner
    D. Arizona - Glenway Westcott

10. The writer who should NOT be classified with the other three is

    A. John Burroughs
    B. James Truslow Adams
    C. William Beebe
    D. John Muir

11. Martin Eden, in Jack London's novel,

    A. committed suicide
    B. died of alcoholism
    C. was murdered by his rival
    D. lived a long, fruitful life

12. All of the following were used as librettos of operas EXCEPT

    A. THE KING'S HENCHMAN
    B. THE SONG OF THE LARK
    C. FOUR SAINTS IN THREE ACTS
    D. THE EMPEROR JONES

13. Washington Irving wrote all of the following EXCEPT

    A. THE SPECTRE BRIDEGROOM
    B. THE ALHAMBRA
    C. THE CONQUEST OF CANAAN
    D. LIFE OF WASHINGTON

14. The Lowell who is NOT known principally as a poet is _____ Lowell.

    A. Abbott Lawrence
    B. Amy
    C. James Russell
    D. Robert

15. THE ROAD TO XANADU, a study of the poetic art of Coleridge, was written by

    A. Amy Lowell
    B. John L. Lowes
    C. H.L. Mencken
    D. G.L. Kittredge

16. This American poet is known for his extreme individualism, his opposition to a mechanical and commercial civilization, and his attraction to strong physical types. His work, chiefly narrative and dramatic, shows the influence of Greek drama, is marked by tragedy and physical violence, employs symbolism and a loose, free verse style.
    The poet characterized is

    A. Robinson Jeffers
    B. Joaquin Miller
    C. Archibald MacLeish
    D. Robert Frost

17. This American novelist's most famous book is considered one of the great novels of American literature. His writing is marked by pessimism and symbolism, by realism, by rich and poetic prose, by the use of allegory, by an effort to express the philosophical and religious meaning the author felt he had found in life.
    The writer characterized is

    A. Mark Twain
    B. John Steinbeck
    C. Herman Melville
    D. Floyd Dell

18. This American poet is best known for his narrative poems and his objective, psychological portraits representing tragedy and frustration. His poems are usually in blank verse or the monologue form and use the simple imagery and rhythms of everyday speech. His works are marked by tragedy, moral conflict, and emphasis on the individual.
He evidences the influence of Browning, Hardy, and Tennyson.
The poet characterized is

    A. Robert Frost
    B. Ezra Pound
    C. Edgar Lee Masters
    D. Edwin Arlington Robinson

19. This American novelist and poet is considered one of the most original and important of twentieth century writers. He has engaged in stylistic and structural experimentation, employing both the stream-of-consciousness technique and poetic and staccato prose.
The writer characterized is

    A. Hervey Allen
    B. John Dos Passos
    C. William Faulkner
    D. Robert Penn Warren

20. This American novelist is considered one of the greatest figures in the history of the novel form. He is known for his realistic, psychological analysis, for his intricate and balanced prose style, and for his frequent use of the supernatural and melodrama for purposes of psychological symbolism. He found the materialistic spirit of the U.S. not conducive to his best work.
The novelist characterized is

    A. Herman Melville
    B. Nathaniel Hawthorne
    C. Henry James
    D. James Branch Cabell

21. THE WINE OF THE PURITANS is a

    A. book of poetry by Edna St. Vincent Millay
    B. novel by William Dean Howells
    C. book of essays by George Santayana
    D. book of criticism by Van Wyck Brooks

22. YOUTH AND THE BRIGHT MEDUSA is a

    A. novel by Henry James
    B. volume of poetry by Amy Lowell
    C. volume of poetry by Elinor Wylie
    D. volume of short stories by Willa Cather

23. Susan Glaspell's play, ALISON'S HOUSE, it is believed, tells a story based on incidents from the life of

    A. Emily Dickinson
    B. Elizabeth Barrett Browning
    C. Christina Rossetti
    D. Edna St. Vincent Millay

24. Of the following plays, the one based on the story of the Sacco-Venzetti case is

    A. THE PURE IN HEART
    B. WINTERSET
    C. PATHS OF GLORY
    D. BOTH YOUR HOUSES

25. The one of the following pairings which is INCORRECT is: 25.____
   A. William Dean Howells - ATLANTIC MONTHLY
   B. Richard W. Gilder - CENTURY MAGAZINE
   C. Edgar Allan Poe - SOUTHERN LITERARY MESSENGER
   D. Walt Whitman - NORTH AMERICAN REVIEW

KEY (CORRECT ANSWERS)

1.	A	11.	A
2.	D	12.	B
3.	C	13.	C
4.	B	14.	A
5.	B	15.	B
6.	C	16.	A
7.	C	17.	C
8.	C	18.	D
9.	D	19.	B
10.	B	20.	C

21. D
22. D
23. A
24. B
25. D

TEST 5

DIRECTIONS: Each question or incomplete statement is followed by several suggested answers or completions. Select the one that BEST answers the question or completes the statement. *PRINT THE LETTER OF THE CORRECT ANSWER IN THE SPACE AT THE RIGHT.*

1. He has sought the death pattern wherever it appeared, on the battlefield, in the bull ring, in the African jungle, in the individual consciousness, because only there could the full capacity of man's powers of survival be tested. The writer to whom the foregoing passage refers is

    A. Thomas Wolfe
    B. John Dos Passes
    C. Ernest Hemingway
    D. William Faulkner

    1.____

2. A Nobel Prize was awarded to the author of

    A. AH! WILDERNESS
    B. DEATH COMES FOR THE ARCHBISHOP
    C. HOLIDAY
    D. FRANK MERRIWELL

    2.____

3. Of the following, the one who has NOT written about Joan of Arc is

    A. Maxwell Anderson
    B. Mark Twain
    C. George Bernard Shaw
    D. Oliver Goldsmith

    3.____

4. Of the following authors, the one CORRECTLY described is:

    A. Archibald MacLeish - poet - former Librarian of Congress
    B. E.E. Cummings - novelist - editor of THE ATLANTIC
    C. John Milton - poet - member of Parliament under Charles I
    D. John Steinbeck - novelist - author of historical romances

    4.____

5. In his elegy on Lincoln, Whitman speaks of a trinity. All of the following are part of that trinity EXCEPT

    A. lilac blooming perennial
    B. live oak growing
    C. shy and hidden thrust
    D. drooping star in the west

    5.____

6. Van Wyck Brooks wrote all of the following EXCEPT

    A. THE ORDEAL OF MARK TWAIN
    B. THE PILGRIMAGE OF HENRY JAMES
    C. THE LAST PURITAN
    D. THE OPINIONS OF OLIVER ALLSTON

    6.____

7. In THE LEGEND OF SLEEPY HOLLOW by Irving, Ichabod eventually

    A. marries Katrina
    B. becomes the principal of his school
    C. leaves the neighborhood
    D. defeats his adversary, Brom Bones

    7.____

8. Of the following pairings, the one which is INCORRECT is:

    A. John Lothrop Motley - HISTORY OF THE DUTCH
    B. Francis Parkman - FRENCH AND INDIAN WARS
    C. William H. Prescott - SPANISH IN AMERICA
    D. Edmund C. Stedman - THE RISE OF AMERICAN CIVILIZATION

9. Of the following pairs of subjects of biographies and biographers, the one containing items INCORRECTLY paired is:

    A. Mark Twain - Van Wyck Brooks
    B. Benjamin Franklin - Mark Van Doren
    C. Edgar Allan Poe - Joseph W. Krutch
    D. Herman Melville - Henry S. Canby

10. Gandhi's tactic of *passive resistance* was derived, in part, from the thinking of

    A. Henry David Thoreau
    B. Walt Whitman
    C. John Dewey
    D. Bronson Alcott

11. The character, Queequeg, appears in

    A. THE LAST OF THE MOHICANS
    B. MOBY DICK
    C. DRUMS ALONG THE MOHAWK
    D. ARUNDEL

12. THE SCIENCE OF ENGLISH VERSE was written by the author of

    A. ANNABEL LEE
    B. SONG OF THE CHATTAHOOCHEE
    C. THANATOPSIS
    D. SNOWBOUND

13. The author of DEMOCRATIC VISTAS was also the author of

    A. SELF RELIANCE
    B. WALDEN
    C. DRUM TAPS
    D. THE EPIC OF AMERICA

14. All of the following wrote humor based on dialect EXCEPT

    A. Ed Howe
    B. Josh Billings
    C. Artemus Ward
    D. Finley Peter Dunne

15. THE ROMANTIC COMEDIANS was written by the author of

    A. VEIN OF IRON
    B. DEATH COMES TO THE ARCHBISHOP
    C. HOUSE OF MIRTH
    D. BLACK OXEN

16. James Joyce wrote all of the following EXCEPT

    A. PORTRAIT OF THE ARTIST AS A YOUNG MAN
    B. THE CICADAS
    C. CHAMBER MUSIC
    D. DUBLINERS

17. All of the following novels deal with the problem of racial antagonism EXCEPT

    A. INDIGO
    B. INTRUDER IN THE DUST
    C. ANGEL PAVEMENT
    D. A PASSAGE TO INDIA

18. T.S. Eliot wrote all of the following EXCEPT

    A. MURDER IN THE CATHEDRAL   B. PALM SUNDAY
    C. FOR LANCELOT ANDREWES   D. ASH WEDNESDAY

19. Of the following pairs, the one in which the items are INCORRECTLY paired is:

    A. THOREAU - Henry Seidel Canby
    B. AND GLADLY TEACH - Henry Van Dyke
    C. A GOODLY FELLOWSHIP - Mary Ellen Chase
    D. A PECULIAR TREASURE - Edna Ferber

20. All of the following are autobiographies EXCEPT

    A. UPSTREAM   B. EXILE'S RETURN
    C. PERSONAL HISTORY   D. TOMORROW AND TOMORROW

21. The American critic who wrote a study of Matthew Arnold is

    A. Alfred Kazin   B. Lionel Trilling
    C. Harry Levin   D. Philip Rahv

22. All of the following wrote poetry about their World War I experiences EXCEPT

    A. Louis MacNeice   B. Rupert Brooke
    C. Siegfried Sassoon   D. Wilfred Owen

23. All of the following are prominent as both poets and novelists EXCEPT

    A. D.H. Lawrence   B. W.H. Auden
    C. Thomas Hardy   D. Aldous Huxley

24. All of the following are connected with the existentialist movement EXCEPT

    A. Andre Malraux   B. Simone Beauvoir
    C. Albert Camus   D. Jean Paul Sartre

25. All of the following are Black poets EXCEPT

    A. Du Bose Heyward   B. Langston Hughes
    C. Countee Cullen   D. James Weldon Johnston

KEY (CORRECT ANSWERS)

1. C
2. A
3. D
4. A
5. B

6. C
7. C
8. D
9. D
10. A

11. B
12. B
13. C
14. A
15. A

16. B
17. C
18. B
19. B
20. D

21. B
22. A
23. B
24. A
25. A

EXAMINATION SECTION
TEST 1

DIRECTIONS: Each question or incomplete statement is followed by several suggested answers or completions. Select the one that BEST answers the question or completes the statement. *PRINT THE LETTER OF THE CORRECT ANSWER IN THE SPACE AT THE RIGHT.*

1. The following historical novels are based on the events noted EXCEPT:

    A. DRUMS ALONG THE MOHAWK - the American Revolution
    B. NORTHWEST PASSAGE - French and Indian Wars
    C. THE RED BADGE OF COURAGE - the Civil War
    D. THREE SOLDIERS - Spanish-American War

2. Thomas Wolfe's literary career was helped MOST by

    A. Maxwell Perkins
    B. Burton Rascoe
    C. Hiram Haydon
    D. Albert Jay Nock

3. THE PORTABLE FAULKNER was edited by

    A. Edmund Wilson
    B. Allen Tate
    C. Malcolm Cowley
    D. Bernard DeVoto

4. F. Scott Fitzgerald wrote all of the following EXCEPT

    A. TENDER IS THE NIGHT
    B. THE ENORMOUS ROOM
    C. THIS SIDE OF PARADISE
    D. THE LAST TYCOON

5. In the biography TERESA AND HER DEMON LOVER, the *demon lover* is

    A. Byron
    B. Keats
    C. Shelley
    D. Wordsworth

6. All of the following have written biographies of Byron EXCEPT

    A. Peter Quennell
    B. Robert Graves
    C. Andre Maurois
    D. Frances Winwar

7. All of the places listed below have been written about by the authors indicated EXCEPT

    A. Arabia - T.E. Lawrence
    B. South America - W.H. Hudson
    C. Iceland - Stephen Spender
    D. Yugoslavia - Rebecca West

8. AXEL'S CASTLE deals MAINLY with

    A. the symbolist movement
    B. Norse eddas
    C. Gothic architecture
    D. French historians

9. The *New Humanism* was a term associated with the writings of

    A. George Jean Nathan
    B. Paul Elmer More
    C. Van Wyck Brooks
    D. Bernard DeVoto

10. The term *genteel realism* was associated with the work of

    A. Betty MacDonald B. Edith Wharton
    C. Ellen Glasgow   D. Robert Nathan

11. THE AGE OF ANXIETY was written by

    A. W.H. Auden   B. C.D. Lewis
    C. Stephen Spender D. Eric Fromm

12. The American businessman is treated MOST sympathetically in the work entitled

    A. THE FINANCIER   B. USA
    C. DODSWORTH   D. THE PIT

13. The following literary sources of the musical plays indicated are correct EXCEPT:

    A. GREEN GROW THE LILACS - OKLAHOMA
    B. LILIOM - CAROUSEL
    C. THE TAMING OF THE SHREW - KISS ME, KATE
    D. BLACK HAMLET - LOST IN THE STARS

14. All of the following were written by John P. Marquand EXCEPT

    A. THE LAST ADAM   B. SO LITTLE TIME
    C. GOODBYE, MR. MOTO   D. WICKFORD POINT

15. A biographer of Chaucer and of Shakespeare is

    A. Marchette Chute B. Edith Rickert
    C. Howard Patch   D. Theodore Spencer

16. THE MUDLARK, by Theodore Bonnet, has among its characters all of the following EXCEPT

    A. Queen Victoria   B. Disraeli
    C. Prince Albert   D. Wheeler, a ragamuffin

17. The lines
    The world stands out on either side
    No wider than the heart is wide;
    Above the world is stretched the sky, -
    No higher than the soul is high.
    The heart can push the sea and land
    Farther away on either hand;
    The soul can split the sky in two,
    And let the face of God shine through
    were written by

    A. Millay   B. Dickinson   C. Wylie   D. Frost

18. THE AMERICAN SCHOLAR is an

    A. essay by Henry David Thoreau
    B. address by Ralph Waldo Emerson
    C. essay by Phillips Brooks
    D. essay by Oliver Wendell Holmes

19. All of the following were members of the *Imagist* school EXCEPT

   A. Amy Lowell
   B. John Gould Fletcher
   C. Vachel Lindsay
   D. Hilda Doolittle

20. In the poem EXCELSIOR by Longfellow, the young man

   A. failed to reach the highest glacier
   B. was encouraged to continue on his way
   C. died in his effort to achieve his purpose
   D. heeded the warning of the maiden

21. Arthur Dimmesdale appears in

   A. THE HOUSE OF THE SEVEN GABLES
   B. THE BLITHEDALE ROMANCE
   C. THE SCARLET LETTER
   D. THE MARBLE FAUN

22. THE VIRGINIAN was written by

   A. Thackeray   B. Wister   C. Roberts   D. Brand

23. Vachel Lindsay wrote all of the following EXCEPT

   A. DEATH OF THE HIRED MAN
   B. ABRAHAM LINCOLN WALKS AT MIDNIGHT
   C. THE SANTA FE TRAIL
   D. GENERAL BOOTH ENTERS HEAVEN

24. The one of the following which is NOT a work of Mark Twain is

   A. THE MYSTERIOUS STRANGER
   B. COLONEL SELLERS
   C. THE MAN THAT CORRUPTED HADLEYBURG
   D. THE GILDED AGE

25. ELSIE VENNER was written by

   A. James Russell Lowell
   B. Oliver Wendell Holmes
   C. Nathaniel Hawthorne
   D. Bayard Taylor

KEY (CORRECT ANSWERS)

1. D
2. A
3. C
4. B
5. A

6. B
7. C
8. A
9. B
10. B

11. A
12. C
13. D
14. A
15. A

16. C
17. A
18. B
19. C
20. C

21. C
22. B
23. A
24. B
25. B

TEST 2

DIRECTIONS: Each question or incomplete statement is followed by several suggested answers or completions. Select the one that BEST answers the question or completes the statement. *PRINT THE LETTER OF THE CORRECT ANSWER IN THE SPACE AT THE RIGHT.*

1. Of the following pairs of plays and playwrights, INCORRECTLY matched is: 1.____

    A. THE SILVER CORD - Sidney Howard
    B. CRAIG'S WIFE - George Kelly
    C. WINTERSET - Maxwell Anderson
    D. IDIOT'S DELIGHT - William Saroyan

2. The writer who was NOT a member of the Transcendentalist group was 2.____

    A. Ralph Waldo Emerson   B. Nathaniel Hawthorne
    C. Herman Melville   D. Bronson Alcott

3. The voyage described in TWO YEARS BEFORE THE MAST was undertaken because of 3.____

    A. illness   B. business venture
    C. war   D. scientific research

4. Mr. Philip Nolan, in Edward Kale's story, was a(n) 4.____

    A. American consul
    B. farmer
    C. journalist
    D. officer in the United States Army

5. In the story THE RANSOM OF RED CHIEF, the ransom was paid by the 5.____

    A. victim   B. parents   C. neighbors   D. kidnappers

6. The play THE INNOCENTS was based on 6.____

    A. THE TURN OF THE SCREW   B. DAISY MILLER
    C. WASHINGTON SQUARE   D. THE BOSTONIANS

7. Robert Jordan appears in the novel 7.____

    A. TO HAVE AND HAVE NOT   B. A FAREWELL TO ARMS
    C. THE SUN ALSO RISES   D. FOR WHOM THE BELL TOLLS

8. In the novel THE LATE GEORGE APLEY, the hero lived in 8.____

    A. New York   B. Boston
    C. Chicago   D. San Francisco

9. The following plays and playwrights are paired correctly EXCEPT 9.____

    A. THE SHOW OFF - George Kelly
    B. THE PHILADELPHIA STORY - Christopher Morley
    C. STREET SCENE - Elmer Rice
    D. THEY KNEW WHAT THEY WANTED - Sidney Howard

10. Edgar Allan Poe wrote all of the following EXCEPT

    A. THE FRINGED GENTIAN
    B. ISRAFEL
    C. THE CITY IN THE SEA
    D. THE CONQUEROR WORM

11. Hawthorne's ambitious guest, in the story by that name,

    A. won great fortune
    B. married his host's daughter
    C. met his death in an avalanche
    D. wore a black veil

12. In Amy Lowell's PATTERNS, the girl receives a message that

    A. her lover was killed in action
    B. her lover will be home soon
    C. a battle has been won
    D. she must prepare her home to receive wounded soldiers

13. It is GENERALLY believed that Emily Dickinson's life of seclusion was caused, in part, by

    A. chronic invalidism
    B. an unhappy love affair
    C. woman's social inferiority
    D. scholastic study

14. The term Salmagundi is associated with

    A. Addison   B. Irving   C. Dryden   D. Defoe

15. THE AMERICAN LANGUAGE was written by

    A. Noah Webster
    B. George Jean Nathan
    C. Frank Vizetelly
    D. Henry Mencken

16. All of the following statements are true EXCEPT that

    A. Kenneth Roberts was born in Maine
    B. he has written a series of novels about early America
    C. in his novel OLIVER WISWELL he depicted the plight of the rebels sympathetically
    D. he has documented his books carefully

17. Fruitlands, established in 1842 by Bronson Alcott, resembled

    A. Mount Vernon
    B. Brook Farm
    C. Johnson's Circle
    D. The Cockney School

18. Critical studies of recent American novelists have been written by

    A. Horace Gregory
    B. Maxwell Geisman
    C. George Jean Nathan
    D. Arthur Schlesinger, Jr.

19. PEDER VICTORIUS is a sequel to the novel entitled

    A. GIANTS IN THE EARTH
    B. MUTINY ON THE BOUNTY
    C. SONS
    D. THE RETURN OF PETER GRIMM

20. A *misanthropic* poet of the Far West was

    A. E.A. Robinson
    B. Robert W. Service
    C. Edwin Markham
    D. Robinson Jeffers

21. Of the following, the one NOT in SPOON RIVER ANTHOLOGY is

    A. Lucinda Matlock
    B. Miniver Cheevy
    C. Ann Rutledge
    D. Petit, the Poet

22. All of the following were written by Theodore Dreiser EXCEPT

    A. THE TITAN
    B. JENNIE GERHARDT
    C. THE GENIUS
    D. ELMER GANTRY

23. All of the following writers may be considered *naturalists* EXCEPT

    A. John Dos Passes
    B. Sinclair Lewis
    C. James T. Farrell
    D. Jack London

24. The Maule curse is referred to in a novel by

    A. Edith Wharton
    B. Willa Cather
    C. Nathaniel Hawthorne
    D. Herman Melville

25. Laurence Olivier was associated with

    A. The Abbey Theater
    B. The Old Vic
    C. The Mercury Theater
    D. The Group Theater

KEY (CORRECT ANSWERS)

1. D
2. C
3. A
4. D
5. D

6. A
7. D
8. B
9. B
10. A

11. C
12. A
13. B
14. B
15. D

16. C
17. B
18. B
19. A
20. D

21. B
22. D
23. B
24. C
25. B

TEST 3

DIRECTIONS: Each question or incomplete statement is followed by several suggested answers or completions. Select the one that BEST answers the question or completes the statement. *PRINT THE LETTER OF THE CORRECT ANSWER IN THE SPACE AT THE RIGHT.*

1. This American poet read his poetry, rich in vivid imagery and striking dramatic and auditory effects, from lecture platforms in an effort to cultivate a love of poetry among people generally. His work emphasized American subjects and heroes, patriotism, and a mystic love of nature and beauty. He was an unusual personality and led an adventurous, wandering life.
   The poet characterized is

   A. Frost B. Whitman C. Lindsay D. Sandburg

1.____

2. This American novelist and short story writer is best known for her stories of the lives of members of New York society in the 19th century. She employed psychological characterization, was interested in moral problems, followed approved artistic forms.
   The writer characterized is

   A. Willa Cather B. Edith Wharton
   C. Ellen Glasgow D. Zona Gale

2.____

3. This American novelist and short story writer is famous for his style: colloquial, short sentences, monosyllabic words, simple narrative technique. He has written stories and essays featuring danger and physical violence.
   The writer characterized is

   A. Steinbeck B. Hemingway
   C. Dos Passos D. Lewis

3.____

4. This American critic, poet, and short story writer of the 19th century is considered one of the most important of American writers. His short stories are considered important forerunners of the typical 20th century story. His criticism contains some of the first statements of literary principles in the art for art's sake area. His poetry is marked by metrical experiment, atmosphere, and striking imagery.
   The writer characterized is

   A. Poe B. Hawthorne C. Irving D. Whitman

4.____

5. All of the following statements are true EXCEPT that

   A. William Faulkner has created a fictitious county in Mississippi which he has peopled with various families
   B. these families appear and reappear in his novels
   C. in recounting the violent incidents in their lives, Faulkner has used a simple, straightforward style
   D. one of his recent books, KNIGHT'S GAMBIT, appeared, in parts, in the SATURDAY EVENING POST

5.____

6. The poet all of whose work was published posthumously was

   A. Elinor Wylie B. Emily Dickinson
   C. Amy Lowell D. Lizette Reese

6.____

7. The one of the following who did NOT write stories with a New England background is   7.____

   A. Sarah Orne Jewett   B. Edith Wharton
   C. Thomas Page   D. Mary E. Wilkins

8. GREEN PASTURES was written by   8.____

   A. DuBose Heyward   B. Marc Connelly
   C. Joel Chandler Harris D. Paul Green

9. All of the following statements are true EXCEPT: 9.____

   A. Mark Twain spent his boyhood in Hannibal, Missouri, on the banks of the Mississippi.
   B. He used many of his experiences as a master pilot in his book ROUGHING IT.
   C. His INNOCENTS ABROAD is filled with an irreverent attitude toward European culture.
   D. He ridiculed the caste system of the Middle Ages in A CONNECTICUT YANKEE IN KING ARTHUR'S COURT.

10. Of the following, the field in which Edgar Allan Poe did NOT excel is   10.____

    A. criticism   B. the short story
    C. poetry   D. the novel

11. THE HARTFORD WITS included all of the following EXCEPT   11.____

    A. John Trumbull   B. Charles Brockden Brown
    C. Timothy Dwight   D. Joel Barlow

12. American literature before 1776 may be characterized by each of the following adjectives EXCEPT   12.____

    A. descriptive   B. imaginative
    C. historical   D. theological

13. The Old Manse in Concord was the residence of   13.____

    A. Nathaniel Hawthorne B. James Russell Lowell
    C. Bronson Alcott   D. Margaret Fuller

14. IN THE MIDST OF LIFE was written by   14.____

    A. Ambrose Bierce   B. Richard Henry Dana
    C. Winston Churchill   D. Gamaliel Bradford

15. The one of the following items concerning Emerson which is INCORRECT is   15.____

    A. dependence on a logical and philosophical system as a means of arriving at truth
    B. sentences in the *aphoristic* style
    C. belief in the worth and dignity of the individual
    D. a stimulating ethical force in America

16. The novels of Cooper may be characterized by all of the following EXCEPT

    A. repetition of situation
    B. realistic portrayal of women
    C. limited geographical range
    D. heroes on a *grand* scale

17. The connoisseur in Poe's story was asked to taste

    A. Montrachet   B. Port
    C. Amontillado   D. Burgundy

18. Hosea Bigelow appears in the poetry of

    A. Whittier   B. Lowell   C. Frost   D. Masters

19. The Kentucky hills furnish the background for the novels and stories of

    A. Jesse Stuart   B. Harry Sylvester
    C. Frances Parkinson Keyes   D. Conrad Richter

20. The Gant family appears in the novels of

    A. Theodore Dreiser   B. Thomas Wolfe
    C. Sherwood Anderson   D. Sinclair Lewis

21. The chief character in T.S. Eliot's THE COCKTAIL PARTY is a(n)

    A. poet   B. psychiatrist
    C. artist   D. diplomat

22. The one of the following who is NOT a writer of radio plays is

    A. Norman Corwin   B. Lucille Fletcher
    C. Kathryn Forbes   D. Arch Oboler

23. A writer who has NOT written a novel dealing with the theme of racial or religious prejudice is

    A. Ernest Hemingway   B. Sinclair Lewis
    C. Arthur Miller   D. Laura Hobson

24. The *stream of consciousness* technique was used by all of the following EXCEPT

    A. Dorothy Richardson   B. Arnold Bennett
    C. Virginia Woolf   D. James Joyce

25. All of the following statements are true EXCEPT:

    A. E. A. Robinson spent his childhood in Gardiner, Maine, the *Tilbury* of his poems.
    B. President Theodore Roosevelt appointed him to a position in the New York Customs House.
    C. In later years, he was honored widely by universities and learned societies.
    D. His poetry is marked by an optimism and a buoyancy that are typically American.

KEY (CORRECT ANSWERS)

1.	C	11.	B
2.	B	12.	B
3.	B	13.	A
4.	A	14.	A
5.	C	15.	A
6.	B	16.	B
7.	C	17.	C
8.	B	18.	B
9.	B	19.	A
10.	D	20.	B

21. B
22. C
23. A
24. B
25. D

TEST 4

DIRECTIONS: Each question or incomplete statement is followed by several suggested answers or completions. Select the one that BEST answers the question or completes the statement. *PRINT THE LETTER OF THE CORRECT ANSWER IN THE SPACE AT THE RIGHT.*

1. Similar in theme to Chekhov's THE CHERRY ORCHARD is 1.___

   A. DETECTIVE STORY
   B. THE WISTERIA TREES
   C. DEATH OF A SALESMAN
   D. LOST IN THE STARS

2. The one of the following who was NOT associated with the *Theatre Guild* is 2.___

   A. Elia Kazan
   B. Lee Simonson
   C. Lawrence Langner
   D. Theresa Helburn

3. The author who has won the Pulitzer Prize for both the novel and the drama is 3.___

   A. Booth Tarkington
   B. Elmer Rice
   C. Thornton Wilder
   D. William Saroyan

4. The novel 1984 deals with 4.___

   A. a Utopian civilization
   B. a war among the animals in a barnyard
   C. totalitarian society
   D. war between the United States and China

5. All of the following were associated with the newspapers indicated EXCEPT 5.___

   A. Heywood Brown - THE NEW YORK WORLD
   B. H.L. Mencken - THE BALTIMORE SUN
   C. William Allen White - THE EMPORIA GAZETTE
   D. Simeon Strunsky - THE NEW YORK HERALD-TRIBUNE

6. The literary column of J. Donald Adams appeared regularly in the publication 6.___

   A. SATURDAY REVIEW OF LITERATURE
   B. NEW YORK TIMES BOOK REVIEW
   C. HERALD-TRIBUNE BOOK REVIEW
   D. THE NEW YORKER

7. Lunt and Fontanne appeared in 7.___

   A. ALL FOR LOVE
   B. I KNOW MY LOVE
   C. LOVE FOR LOVE
   D. LOVE'S LABOUR'S LOST

8. The name among the following which does NOT belong with the others is 8.___

   A. Norman Bel-Geddes
   B. Robert Edmund Jones
   C. Lee Simonson
   D. Lewis Mumford

9. All of the following statements are true EXCEPT: 9.___

   A. W.D. Howells became American consul in Venice as recompense for a campaign biography of Lincoln.

B. Howells sought to depict the average man in his ordinary life.
C. While Howells would not have approved of modern-day realism, he was a realist himself in his own day.
D. Silas Lapham, at the end of the novel, is a failure both financially and morally.

10. All of the following statements are true EXCEPT:

    A. Poe's PHILOSOPHY OF COMPOSITION is devoted mainly to an analysis of ANNABEL LEE as an example of his procedure in composing poetry.
    B. In the preface to the first edition of LEAVES OF GRASS, Whitman explained the function of the ideal poet.
    C. In the preface to the second edition of LYRICAL BALLADS, Wordsworth expounded his poetical principles.
    D. In his CRITICISM AND FICTION, Howells summed up his literary beliefs.

11. The biography BENJAMIN FRANKLIN was written by the author of

    A. THE AMERICAN NOVEL   B. JONATHAN GENTRY
    C. JOHN BROWN'S BODY   D. RIP TIDE

12. Each of the following was the first editor of his or her respective magazine EXCEPT

    A. Margaret Fuller - THE DIAL
    B. James Russell Lowell - THE ATLANTIC MONTHLY
    C. Oswald Garrison Villard - THE NATION
    D. Henry S. Canby - THE SATURDAY REVIEW OF LITERATURE

13. Of the following statements, the one NOT true is:

    A. It is the simple, honest, helpful Ernest himself who resembles THE GREAT STONE FACE.
    B. THE BLITHEDALE ROMANCE reflected Hawthorne's Brook Farm experience.
    C. Hester Prynne is the heroine of THE HOUSE OF SEVEN GABLES.
    D. THE MARBLE FAUN and THE SCARLET LETTER show the effect on character of hiding and revealing sin.

14. Each of the following was a best seller in its day EXCEPT

    A. UNCLE TOM'S CABIN   B. GONE WITH THE WIND
    C. LEAVES OF GRASS   D. DAY OF DOOM

15. The following ships are correctly matched with their respective books EXCEPT

    A. Pequod - MOBY DICK
    B. Hispaniola - TREASURE ISLAND
    C. Patua - LORD JIM
    D. Puritan - TWO YEARS BEFORE THE MAST

16. Of the following statements, the one NOT made by Emerson is:

    A. Things are in the saddle and ride mankind.
    B. Books are for the scholar's idle times.
    C. Hitch your wagon to a star.
    D. I quietly declare war with the state.

17. The Transcendentalists did each of the following EXCEPT

   A. emphasize the importance of sincere feeling and intuition
   B. establish a church
   C. try an experiment in community living at Brook Farm
   D. publish a magazine called THE DIAL

18. A novelist devoted to a portrayal of the back country of Florida is

   A. Marjorie Kinnan Rawlings
   B. Conrad Richter
   C. Erskine Caldwell
   D. Louis Bromfield

19. Lawrence Langner and Theresa Helburn were associated with

   A. INVITATION TO LEARNING
   B. THEATRE GUILD OF THE AIR
   C. AUTHOR MEETS THE CRITICS
   D. TOWN HALL OF THE AIR

20. Poe believed in each of the following EXCEPT:

   A. A great piece of writing must be short enough to be read at one sitting
   B. Literature to be great must be moral
   C. The writer should build up to a single effect
   D. The death of a beautiful woman is an excellent theme for literature

21. Of the following, the one NOT identified with the ONE HUNDRED GREAT BOOKS movement is

   A. Gardner Murphy   B. Stringfellow Barr
   C. Mortimer Adler   D. Robert M. Hutchins

22. Of the following, the one who has NOT written in the field of semantics is

   A. Curme   B. Korzybski
   C. Hayakawa   D. Stuart Chase

23. Of the following, the one whose action is NOT laid chiefly in Pennsylvania is

   A. I WENT TO PIT COLLEGE B. VALLEY OF DECISION
   C. OUR TOWN   D. HUGH WYNNE

24. Of the following, the one which does NOT deal with political corruption is

   A. BOTH YOUR HOUSES
   B. THE LAST PURITAN
   C. THE GENTLEMAN FROM INDIANA
   D. CONISTON

25. Of the following, the one NOT in the field of literary criticism or history is   25._____

    A. MAIN CURRENTS IN AMERICAN THOUGHT
    B. THE FLOWERING OF NEW ENGLAND
    C. THE SUMMING UP
    D. BEYOND LIFE

KEY (CORRECT ANSWERS)

1.	B	11.	A
2.	A	12.	C
3.	C	13.	C
4.	C	14.	C
5.	D	15.	D
6.	B	16.	C
7.	B	17.	B
8.	D	18.	A
9.	D	19.	B
10.	A	20.	B

21. C
22. A
23. C
24. B
25. D

TEST 5

DIRECTIONS: Each question or incomplete statement is followed by several suggested answers or completions. Select the one that BEST answers the question or completes the statement. *PRINT THE LETTER OF THE CORRECT ANSWER IN THE SPACE AT THE RIGHT.*

1. A biographical detail NOT to be associated with the author of THE WEB AND THE ROCK is that he   1.____

   A. was born in Asheville, North Carolina
   B. taught at New York University
   C. obtained a degree from Harvard
   D. was successful as a playwright

2. Douglas Southall Freeman's themes are similar to those of   2.____

   A. George Ticknor   B. Bruce Catton
   C. John Dos Passos   D. Saul Padover

3. She realizes that experience has brought to her some of the rewards as well as most of the disappointments of the corrupt culture into which she has been betrayed.   3.____
   This passage decribes

   A. The Princess Casamassima   B. Isabel Archer
   C. Daisy Miller   D. Mrs. Newsome

4. All of the following are quotations from the works of Ralph Waldo Emerson EXCEPT: 4.____

   A. The only gift is a portion of thyself
   B. Self-trust is the essence of heroism
   C. Hitch your wagon to a star
   D. All great truths begin as blasphemies

5. The author of THE MARSHES OF GLYNN also wrote   5.____

   A. THE SCIENCE OF ENGLISH VERSE and THE SONG OF THE CHATTA-HOOCHEE
   B. IN OLE VIRGINIA and UNCLE REMUS
   C. A NEW ENGLAND NUN and COUNTRY OF THE POINTED FIRS
   D. MY STUDY WINDOW and AMONG MY BOOKS

6. I. Emily Dickinson - Bronson Alcott   6.____
   II. Walt Whitman - Ralph Waldo Emerson
   III. Thomas Wolfe - Maxwell Perkins
   IV. Herman Melville - Nathaniel Hawthorne
   V. F. Scott Fitzgerald - James Joyce
   Of the above, writers are CORRECTLY matched with men who played important roles in their literary careers in

   A. I, III, IV   B. II, III, IV
   C. II, III, V   D. I, II, V

38

7. I. William Carlos Williams
    II. Hart Crane
    III. Wallace Stevens
    IV. Oliver Wendell Holmes
    Of the above, the two poets who practiced medicine were

    A. I, II   B. I, III   C. I, IV   D. III, IV

8. All of the following have written several novels about the South EXCEPT

    A. Ellen Glasgow
    B. Robert Penn Warren
    C. George Washington Cable
    D. Dorothy Canfield Fisher

9. A noted literary critic who has done considerable work in the area of semantics is

    A. Malcolm Cowley
    B. I.A. Richards
    C. Granville Hicks
    D. John Ciardi

10. All of the following were known both as philosophers and as men of letters EXCEPT

    A. Louis Sullivan
    B. George Santayana
    C. Josiah Royce
    D. William James

11. In Henry James' THE TURN OF THE SCREW, the actual existence of the two ghosts is

    A. never verified
    B. established in the boy's statement at the close
    C. established when the governess challenges the girl, Flora
    D. verified by the narrator in his postscript to the story

12. The lines
    The world stands out on either side
    No wider than the heart is wide
    are from the early poetry of

    A. A.E. Housman
    B. Edna St. Vincent Millay
    C. Rupert Brooke
    D. William Wordsworth

13. Of the following statements, the one which may NOT be applied to Walt Whitman is that

    A. in the late 1840's and early 1850's he abandoned rhyme
    B. he was a male nurse during the Civil War
    C. he was born in Camden, New Jersey
    D. he wrote for THE BROOKLYN EAGLE

14. All of the following American novels have their principal setting in Europe EXCEPT

    A. DODSWORTH
    B. THE GOLDEN BOWL
    C. THE MARBLE FAUN
    D. IN DUBIOUS BATTLE

15. GOD'S ANGRY MAN, by Leonard Ehrlich, is a fictionalized biography of

    A. Daniel Webster
    B. Paul Revere
    C. John Brown
    D. Martin Luther

16. All of the following were educated at Harvard EXCEPT

    A. T.S. Eliot
    B. George Santayana
    C. Ralph Waldo Emerson
    D. Herman Melville

17. *For genius, all over the world, stands hand in hands; and one shock of recognition runs the whole circle round.* The above line is quoted from the work of

    A. Herman Melville
    B. Ralph Waldo Emerson
    C. Edmund Wilson
    D. Matthew Arnold

18. I. D.H. Lawrence
    II. James Joyce
    III. Sherwood Anderson
    IV. Robert Penn Warren
    V. Frank Norris

    Of the above novelists, the three that have made notable contributions in poetry are

    A. I, III, V
    B. I, II, IV
    C. II, IV, V
    D. II, III, IV

19. I. THE WIND IN THE WILLOWS
    II. RING OF BRIGHT WATER
    III. BORN FREE
    IV. THE AGE OF OVERKILL

    Of the above works, the ones in which animals play a leading part are

    A. I, II, IV
    B. II, III
    C. I, II, III
    D. III, IV

20. All of the following authors wrote novels in the 1930's which were considered *revolutionary* in theme EXCEPT

    A. John Steinbeck
    B. Andre Malraux
    C. Ignazio Silone
    D. Hervey Allen

21. John Galbraith has USUALLY been identified with

    A. studies of contemporary society
    B. emancipation of the 20th Century Black
    C. the Birch Society
    D. criticism of works by England's *angry young men*

22. A teacher associated with the training of several prominent American playwrights was

    A. George Pierce Baker
    B. Joseph Warren Beach
    C. William Lyon Phelps
    D. Wallace Stegner

23. Jose Quintero's O'Neill enterprise off-Broadway was his direction of

    A. MOURNING BECOMES ELECTRA
    B. A TOUCH OF THE POET
    C. THE ICEMAN COMETH
    D. DESIRE UNDER THE ELMS

24. The author of THE PLAGUE wrote all of the following EXCEPT

    A. THE STRANGER
    B. CALIGULA
    C. THE MYTH OF SISYPHUS
    D. TIGER AT THE GATES

25. I. Jason Compson
    II. Gilbert Osmond
    III. Robert Jordan
    IV. Carol Kennicott

Of the above, the characters who represent decadence in the books in which they appear are

  A. I, II B. I, III C. III, IV D. II, IV

KEY (CORRECT ANSWERS)

1. D
2. B
3. B
4. D
5. A
6. B
7. C
8. D
9. B
10. A

11. A
12. B
13. C
14. D
15. C
16. D
17. A
18. B
19. C
20. D

21. A
22. A
23. D
24. D
25. A

EXAMINATION SECTION
TEST 1

DIRECTIONS: Each question or incomplete statement is followed by several suggested answers or completions. Select the one that BEST answers the question or completes the statement. *PRINT THE LETTER OF THE CORRECT ANSWER IN THE SPACE AT THE RIGHT.*

1. A play by Eugene O' Neill which has NOT been produced in this country but which has been produced in Sweden is

   A. MASKS OF ANGELS
   B. LEDA AND THE SWAN
   C. MORE STATELY MANSIONS
   D. CORRUPTION IN THE PALACE OF JUSTICE

   1.____

2. The author of the screenplay, LAWRENCE OF ARABIA, also wrote the play

   A. ROSS
   B. A MAN FOR ALL SEASONS
   C. THE AFFAIR
   D. BECKETT

   2.____

3. WHO'S AFRAID OF VIRGINIA WOOLF? is by the author of

   A. WAITING FOR GODOT
   B. THE SAND BOX
   C. THE CONNECTION
   D. THE MILK TRAIN DOESN'T STOP HERE ANYMORE

   3.____

4. I. PIGEON FEATHERS
   II. HONEY AND SALT
   III. THE DYER'S HAND
   IV. THE CAPE COD LIGHTER
   V. TALE FOR THE MIRROR

   Of the above works, those that are titles of short story collections are

   A. I, III, IV
   B. I, IV, V
   C. II, III
   D. II, IV, V

   4.____

5. "*I believe that man will not merely endure: he will prevail. He is immortal, not because he alone among creatures has an inexhaustible voice, but because he has a soul,*" is part of a quotation from

   A. Carl Sandburg
   B. John Steinbeck
   C. William Faulkner
   D. Woodrow Wilson

   5.____

6. An attempt to explain human history in terms of the laws of physics was made in the writings of

   A. Karl Marx
   B. William H. Prescott
   C. Charles Lyell
   D. Henry Adams

   6.____

7. All of the following one-act plays are correctly described EXCEPT

   A. THE VALIANT - A brother lies to his sister to put her mind at ease

   7.____

B. MY CLIENT CURLEY - An advertising man is disillusioned by his Madison Avenue experiences
C. SPREADING THE NEWS - A bit of gossip brings a humorous crisis to a village
D. SORRY, WRONG NUMBER - A woman overhears the plan for her own murder

8. Poems and their authors are correctly matched in all of the following EXCEPT   8.____

   A. THE RHODORA - Ralph Waldo Emerson
   B. CLAREL - Herman Melville
   C. PASSAGE TO INDIA - Walt Whitman
   D. MASQUE OF REASON - Edwin Arlington Robinson

9. The following characters are correctly paired according to the works in which they appear EXCEPT   9.____

   A. Frederick Henry - Catherine Barkley
   B. Fleur Forsyte - Michael Mont
   C. Milly Theale - Merton Densher
   D. Carl Linstrum - Antonio Shimerda

10. The novel NOT written by the author of the other three is   10.____

    A. HENDERSON THE RAIN KING
    B. THE ADVENTURES OF AUGIE MARCH
    C. THE VICTIM
    D. LIE DOWN IN DARKNESS

11. Thomas Mann's works include all of the following titles EXCEPT   11.____

    A. TONIO KROGER   B. BUDDENBROOKS
    C. THE WORLD'S ILLUSION D. DEATH IN VENICE

12. The experiences of Americans in Europe are delineated in all of the following novels EXCEPT   12.____

    A. TENDER IS THE NIGHT   B. TO HAVE AND HAVE NOT
    C. DAISY MILLER   D. REDBURN

13. I.   Maxwell Geismar   13.____
    II. Lionel Trilling
    III. Arnold Tate
    IV. Matthew Arnold
    Of the writers listed above, those who have achieved distinction for both their literary criticisms and their poetry are

    A. I, II   B. III, IV   C. I, III   D. II, IV

14. The author of THE RISE AND FALL OF THE THIRD REICH also wrote   14.____

    A. INTO THE VALLEY   B. BERLIN DIARY
    C. RUSSIA AND THE WEST   D. THE BERLIN WALL

15. All of the following were early works of their authors EXCEPT   15.____

    A. HISTORY OF NEW YORK - Washington Irving
    B. FANSHAWE - Nathaniel Hawthorne

C. BILLY BUDD - Herman Melville
D. SISTER CARRIE - Theodore Dreiser

16. All of the following had strong elements of transcendentalism in their thinking EXCEPT   16.____

    A. Walt Whitman   B. Henry David Thoreau
    C. James Russell Lowell   D. Theodore Parker

17. *"How dull it is to pause, to make an end,*   17.____
    To rust unburnish'd, not to shine in use."
    are lines written by the author of

    A. Saw the Vision of the world, and all the wonder that would be
    B. The year's at the spring
       And day's at the morn
    C. And we are here as on a darkling plain
    D. Lead, kindly Light, amid the encircling gloom

18. The author of the lines,   18.____
    "Bliss it was in that dawn to be alive,
    But to be young was very heaven,"
    also wrote

    A. Let not Ambition mock their useful toil
    B. And much it grieved my heart to think What Man has made of Man
    C. There is a pleasure in the pathless woods
    D. Forever wilt thou love, and she be fair

19. Gerard Manley Hopkins is an exemplar of the poetic technique known as   19.____

    A. antiphonal verse   B. sprung rhythm
    C. polyphonic prose   D. asymmetric verse

20. Of the following, the selection INCORRECTLY quoted is   20.____

    A. I must go down to the seas again, for the call of the running tide,
       Is a sweet call and a wild call I cannot turn aside
    B. Go down to Kew in lilac-time, in lilac-time, in
       lilac-time;
       Go down to Kew in lilac-time (it isn't far from London!)
       And you shall wander hand in hand with love in
       summer's wonderland
    C. Break, break, break
       On thy cold gray stones, O Sea!
       And I would that my tongue could utter
       The thoughts that arise in me
    D. Oh, to be in England
       Now that April's there,
       And whoever wakes in England
       Sees, some morning, unaware,
       That the lowest boughs and the brushwood sheaf
       Round the elm-tree bole are in tiny leaf

21. GODEY'S LADY'S BOOK was a   21.____

    A. periodical for women
    B. series of pamphlets remonstrating against denial of women's suffrage
    C. primer for governesses
    D. portfolio of paintings by women artists

22. ISRAFEL is an appellation associated with the author of the lines,   22.____

    A. In Heaven a spirit doth dwell
       Whose heartstrings are a lute
    B. Whither midst falling dew
       While glow the heavens with the last steps of day
    C. This is the Arsenal. From floor to ceiling,
       Like a huge organ, rise the burnished arms
    D. This is the ship of pearl, which, poets feign,
       Sails the unshadowed main

23. Author and book are correctly paired in all of the following EXCEPT   23.____

    A. William Gilmore Simms - NARRATIVE OF DAVY CROCKETT
    B. Charles Brockden Brown - WIELAND
    C. Washington Irving - LIFE OF GEORGE WASHINGTON
    D. Oliver Wendell Holmes - ELSIE VENNER

24. The author of THE INNOCENTS ABROAD wrote all of the following EXCEPT   24.____

    A. LETTERS FROM THE EARTH   B. WHAT IS MAN?
    C. THE MYSTERIOUS STRANGER   D. A CHANCE ACQUAINTANCE

25. *"He lives to learn, in life's hard school,*   25.____
    How few who pass above him
    Lament their triumph and his loss,
    Like her - because they love him"
    are lines from the works of

    A. Emerson   B. Whittier   C. Burns   D. Holmes

KEY (CORRECT ANSWERS)

1.	C	11.	C
2.	B	12.	B
3.	B	13.	B
4.	B	14.	B
5.	C	15.	C
6.	D	16.	C
7.	B	17.	A
8.	D	18.	B
9.	D	19.	B
10.	D	20.	A

21. A
22. A
23. A
24. D
25. B

TEST 2

DIRECTIONS: Each question or incomplete statement is followed by several suggested answers or completions. Select the one that BEST answers the question or completes the statement. *PRINT THE LETTER OF THE CORRECT ANSWER IN THE SPACE AT THE RIGHT.*

1. The one of the following men of letters whose final days and burial place are clouded in obscurity is

    A. Edgar Allan Poe
    B. William Sidney Porter
    C. Ambrose Bierce
    D. Hamlin Garland

2. All of the following writers and their native states are correctly paired EXCEPT

    A. John Steinbeck - California
    B. Elizabeth Madox Roberts - Kentucky
    C. Edward Eggleston - Indiana
    D. Eudora Welty - Florida

3. "'Warren?' she questioned.
   'Dead,' was all he answered"
   are the concluding lines of a poem written by the author of

    A. THE WHIPPOORWILL
    B. HARD TIMES
    C. THE CODE
    D. WESTERN STAR

4. All of the following fictional characters and descriptive phrases are appropriately paired EXCEPT

    A. Starbuck - prudent and pragmatic sailor
    B. Santiago - stoic and brave fisherman
    C. Jay Gatsby - pursuer of a delusory dream
    D. Eliza Gant - sensitive woman dedicated to esthetic values

5. The story DR. HEIDEGGER'S EXPERIMENT deals with a

    A. fatal landslide
    B. veil used as a mask
    C. search for the renewal of youth
    D. heart of stone

6. I. Dylan Thomas - *"Let us go then, you and I,
   When the evening is spread out against
   the sky
   Like a patient etherized upon a table"*

   II. Vachel Lindsay - *"A bronzed, lank man! His suit of
   ancient black
   A famous high top hat and plain worn
   shawl
   Make him the quaint great figure that
   men love"*

   III. T.S. Eliot - *"A poem should not mean
   But be"*

IV. W.B. Yeats - *"An aged man is but a paltry thing,*
         A tattered coat upon a stick, unless
         Soul clap its hands and sing"
V. Emily Dickinson - *"Dust thou art, to dust returnest*
         Was not spoken of the soul"

Of the above, authors and selections are CORRECTLY paired in

   A. I, III   B. III, IV, V   C. II, IV   D. I, II, V

7. Conrad Richter's THE LIGHT IN THE FOREST depicts

   A. the American pioneer in the West
   B. a white boy's life in Indian captivity
   C. beginnings of law and order in the western part of the United States
   D. the corrosion of loneliness endured by *mountain men*

8. I. Dwight Macdonald - AGAINST THE AMERICAN GRAIN
   II. Mary McCarthy - ON THE CONTRARY
   III. Randell Jarrell - CONTEMPORARIES
   IV. Elizabeth Hardwick - A VIEW OF MY OWN
   V. Gore Vidal - A SAD HEART AT THE SUPERMARKET

   Of the above, critics of the literary, social, or political scene are CORRECTLY paired with their works in

   A. I, II, V   B. I, II, IV   C. III, IV, V   D. II, III, V

9. I. LUST FOR LIFE - THE AGONY AND THE ECSTASY
   II. HENRY ESMOND - THE VIRGINIANS
   III. ADVISE AND CONSENT - A SHADE OF DIFFERENCE
   IV. THE BARBER OF SEVILLE - THE MARRIAGE OF FIGARO

   Of the above, the original and the sequel are NOT correctly matched in

   A. I only   B. I, II   C. II, III   D. IV only

10. The title of the novel LORD OF THE FLIES is derived from the name

    A. Belial   B. Satan   C. Lucifer   D. Beelzebub

11. I. TWO TRAMPS IN MUD TIME - Carl Sandburg
    II. ODE TO THE CONFEDERATE DEAD - Allen Tate
    III. THE SECOND COMING - William Butler Yeats
    IV. ARS POETICA - Archibald MacLeish

    Of the above, poem and author are CORRECTLY matched in

    A. I, IV   B. I, II, III
    C. II, III, IV   D. II, IV

12. *"It was my thirtieth year to heaven"* is the FIRST line of a poem by

    A. Richard Hovey   B. John Ciardi
    C. Karl Shapiro   D. Dylan Thomas

13. The one of the following which is a novel in the form of hearings before a Standing Committee on Education is

    A. EXCELLENCE
    B. THE BRAIN WATCHERS
    C. TEACHING MACHINES
    D. THE CHILD BUYER

14. THE STUDENTS' RIGHT TO READ was a publication of

    A. The Ford Foundation
    B. New York Association of Teachers of English
    C. National Association of Independent Schools
    D. National Council of Teachers of English

15. The central figure is an unpaid sexton of a run-down synagogue in the novel

    A. OF STREETS AND STARS
    B. THE ASSISTANT
    C. YOUNGBLOOD HAWKE
    D. COAT UPON A STICK

16. LEFT HAND, RIGHT HAND and THE SCARLET TREE are volumes in the autobiographical series by

    A. Robert Graves
    B. Osbert Sitwell
    C. Sacheverell Sitwell
    D. Virginia Woolf

17. Paul Pennyfeather, Peter Pastmaster, and Captain Grimes are characters in

    A. CROME YELLOW
    B. DECLINE AND FALL
    C. POINT COUNTERPOINT
    D. VILE BODIES

18. In the Barsetshire novels, Anthony Trollope created an English shire complete with place and family names.
    The modern novelist who has written books dealing with the same imaginary shire is

    A. Jon Godden
    B. Sheila Kaye-Smith
    C. Mazo de la Roche
    D. Angela Thirkell

19. Of the following pairs of authors and quotations, the one INCORRECTLY matched is

    A. Paine - "These are the times that try men's souls"
    B. Stevenson - "I loaf and invite my soul"
    C. Pope - "Whatever is is right"
    D. Emerson - "I greet you at the beginning of a great career"

20. All of the following are autobiographies EXCEPT

    A. Louis Untermeyer's FROM ANOTHER WORLD
    B. Edna Ferber's A PECULIAR TREASURE
    C. Hans Zinsser's AS I REMEMBER HIM
    D. Lewis Mumford's GREEN MEMORIES

21. Attempted suicide through sledding into a great elm is an important event in a work of fiction by

    A. Edith Wharton
    B. Willa Gather
    C. Elinor Wylie
    D. Ellen Glasgow

22. A STREETCAR NAMED DESIRE is by 22.____

    A. Lillian Hellman   B. Erskine Caldwell
    C. Caldwell Taylor   D. Tennessee Williams

23. The poet who said he would not exchange *"Manhattan crowds with their turbulent musical chorus"* for a *"rural domestic life"* was 23.____

    A. Masters   B. Whitman   C. Frost   D. Sandburg

24. Of the following, the poem with the LEAST onomatopoeia in it is 24.____

    A. THE CATARACT OF LODORE - Southey
    B. SONG OF THE CHATTAHOOCHEE - Lanier
    C. THE BELLS - Poe
    D. MIRACLES - Whitman

25. Of the following plays, the one NOT concerned with the theme of a son's avenging his father's murder is 25.____

    A. O'Neill's MOURNING BECOMES ELECTRA
    B. Sartre's THE FLIES
    C. Jeffers' MEDEA
    D. Sophocles' ELECTRA

KEY (CORRECT ANSWERS)

1.	C	11.	C
2.	D	12.	D
3.	C	13.	D
4.	D	14.	D
5.	C	15.	D
6.	C	16.	B
7.	B	17.	B
8.	B	18.	D
9.	A	19.	B
10.	D	20.	C

21.	A
22.	D
23.	B
24.	D
25.	D

TEST 3

DIRECTIONS: Each question or incomplete statement is followed by several suggested answers or completions. Select the one that BEST answers the question or completes the statement. *PRINT THE LETTER OF THE CORRECT ANSWER IN THE SPACE AT THE RIGHT.*

1. *"After the first powerful plain manifesto*
   The black statement of pistons, without more fuss
   But gliding like a queen, she leaves the station."
   These lines were written by

   A. W.H. Auden
   B. C. Day Lewis
   C. Louis MacNeice
   D. Stephen Spender

   1._____

2. Which one of the following is NOT a quotation from the poetry of T.S. Eliot?

   A. *"Here I am, an old man in a dry month,*
      Being read to by a boy, waiting for rain."
   B. *"The worlds revolve like ancient women*
      Gathering fuel in vacant lots."
   C. *"And what rough beast, its hour come round at last,*
      Slouches toward Bethlehem to be born?"
   D. *"I should have been a pair of ragged claws*
      Scuttling across the floors of silent seas."

   2._____

3. Which of the following adjectives is LEAST appropriate in characterizing 17th century American literature?

   A. Belletristic
   B. Imitative
   C. Religious
   D. Utilitarian

   3._____

4. *"The literal, detailed and inflexible elaboration of the idea of God as King and Judge"* is BEST exemplified in the writings of

   A. Charles Brockden Brown
   B. Philip Freneau
   C. Noah Webster
   D. Michael Wigglesworth

   4._____

5. THE TENTH MUSE LATELY SPRUNG UP IN AMERICA was written by

   A. Anne Bradstreet
   B. Emily Dickinson
   C. Sarah Kemble Knight
   D. Mary Rowlandson

   5._____

6. Which one of the following associations is NOT correct?

   A. James Fenimore Cooper - romanticism
   B. Nathaniel Hawthorne - neo-classicism
   C. Washington Irving - antiquarianism
   D. Alexis de Tocqueville - individualism

   6._____

7. Which one of the following poetic lines was NOT written by Ralph Waldo Emerson?

   A. *"Dust thou art, to dust returnest,*
      Was not spoken of the soul."
   B. *"Then Beauty is its own excuse for being."*
   C. *"When half-gods go,*

The Gods arrive. "
    D. *"The passive Master lent his hand
       To the vast soul that o'er him planned."*

8. Edgar Allan Poe's poetic principles did NOT include the idea that   8.____

    A. melancholy is a legitimate aspect of poetic beauty
    B. a poetic mood cannot be sustained in a long poem
    C. prosody is concerned with the regular alternation of long and short syllables
    D. a stanza should contain lines arranged in strict patterns

9. Which one of the following was NOT employed by Oliver Wendell Holmes as a chief conversationalist in his BREAKFAST-TABLE essays?   9.____

    A. THE AUTOCRAT   B. THE PHYSICIAN
    C. THE POET   D. THE PROFESSOR

10. The FIRST editor-in-chief of the ATLANTIC MONTHLY was   10.____

    A. Thomas Bailey Aldrich   B. Oliver Wendell Holmes
    C. William Dean Howells   D. James Russell Lowell

11. Which one of the following was the ONLY mid-nineteenth century American dramatist of consequence?   11.____

    A. George Henry Boker   B. John Esten Cooke
    C. Frances Anne Kemble   D. William Gilmore Simms

12. *"He seems to have taken the science of bumps (phrenology) as seriously as many recent writers have employed the theories of psychoanalysis."*
    This description applies MOST aptly to   12.____

    A. John Kendrick Bangs   B. Jack London
    C. Mark Twain   D. Walt Whitman

13. The hero, mesmerized in 1887, wakes up in the year 2000 to find Boston a paradise of cleanliness and material prosperity in a novel by   13.____

    A. Henry Brooks Adams   B. Edward Bellamy
    C. Christopher Morley   D. Lew Wallace

14. SHORT SIXES is a baker's dozen of clever and piquant tales by   14.____

    A. Henry Cuyler Bunner   B. Frances Marion Crawford
    C. Richard Harding Davis   D. Fitz-James O'Brien

15. Which one of the following definitions of poetry was written by Emily Dickinson?   15.____

    A. *"Poetry is ... the spontaneous overflow of powerful
       feelings recollected in tranquility."*
    B. *"...my homely definitions of prose and poetry; -
       that is, prose, - words in their best order; poetry; -
       the best words in their best order. "*
    C. *"If I feel physically as if the top of my head were
       taken off, I know that is poetry. "*

D. "That is to say, permanence in poetry as in love is
perceived instantly.
It hasn't to await the test of time."

16. THE OLD SWIMMIN' HOLE, LITTLE ORPHAN ANNIE, and WHEN THE FROST IS ON 16.____
THE PUNKIN are dialect poems by

   A. Paul Laurence Dunbar
   B. Eugene Field
   C. Bret Harte
   D. James W. Riley

17. THE RISE OF SILAS LAPHAM concludes with 17.____

   A. his suicide
   B. the loss of his fortune
   C. the marriage of his daughter to an aristocrat
   D. the settlement of the strike at his paint factory

18. The legendary Johnny Appleseed pursued his eccentric avocation in 18.____

   A. New England
   B. Ohio and Indiana
   C. the Mississippi Valley
   D. California

19. Which one of the following is an INCORRECT pairing of title and author? 19.____

   A. RED ROCK - John Fox, Jr.
   B. NIGHTS WITH UNCLE REMUS - Joel Chandler Harris
   C. PIKE COUNTY BALLADS - John Hay
   D. SONGS OF THE SIERRAS - Joaquin Miller

20. "He wrote many grim, vivid stories, reminiscent of Poe's tales of horror, and marked by 20.____
an ingenious use of the surprise ending, a sardonic humor, and a realistic study of tense
emotional states."
This quotation MOST aptly applies to

   A. Ambrose Bierce
   B. Stephen Crane
   C. O. Henry
   D. Henry James

21. Which one of the following influenced the literary theories of Henry James LEAST? 21.____

   A. Honoré de Balzac
   B. Thomas Hardy
   C. Nathaniel Hawthorne
   D. Ivan Turgenev

22. Millet's painting of a peasant was the inspiration for a a famous poem by 22.____

   A. Emma Lazarus
   B. Edwin Markham
   C. Carl Sandburg
   D. Louis Untermeyer

23. GLEANINGS IN BUDDHA-FIELDS and A JAPANESE MISCELLANY were written by 23.____

   A. Pearl S. Buck
   B. Louis Imogen Guiney
   C. Lafcadio Hearn
   D. George Santayana

24. An American literary critic whose work gave great emphasis to the defense of traditions 24.____
and standards, as against the disruptive forces of his time, was

   A. Irving Babbitt
   B. Van Wyck Brooks
   C. W.C. Brownell
   D. H.L. Mencken

25. An early leader of the group who called themselves the *New Humanists* was   25._____

    A. Gamaliel Bradford   B. Brander Matthews
    C. Paul Elmer More   D. Bliss Perry

KEY (CORRECT ANSWERS)

#	Ans	#	Ans
1.	D	11.	A
2.	C	12.	D
3.	A	13.	B
4.	D	14.	A
5.	A	15.	C
6.	B	16.	D
7.	A	17.	B
8.	C	18.	B
9.	B	19.	A
10.	D	20.	A

21. B
22. B
23. C
24. C
25. C

TEST 4

DIRECTIONS: Each question or incomplete statement is followed by several suggested answers or completions. Select the one that BEST answers the question or completes the statement. *PRINT THE LETTER OF THE CORRECT ANSWER IN THE SPACE AT THE RIGHT.*

1. Which one of the following groupings to titles and poets is INCORRECT?

    A. THE BRIDGE - Hart Crane
    B. CAN GRANDE'S CASTLE - Amy Lowell
    C. CANTOS - Ezra Pound
    D. TRIBUTE TO THE ANGELS - Elinor Wylie

2. Which pairing of title and author is INCORRECT?

    A. MAMBA'S DAUGHTERS - Hervey Allen
    B. IN THIS OUR LIFE - Ellen Glasgow
    C. THE GREAT MEADOW - Elizabeth Madox Roberts
    D. TEEFTALLOW - T.S. Stribling

3. The saga of an imaginary Yoknapatawpha County in Mississippi was developed by

    A. Sherwood Anderson   B. James Branch Cabell
    C. Erskine Caldwell   D. William Faulkner

4. Thea Kronberg's life is expressed and bound up in her career in the novel

    A. THE BRIMMING CUP   B. A LOST LADY
    C. ONE MORE SPRING   D. SONG OF THE LARK

5. Which one of the following names does NOT represent a fictional character?

    A. Martin Arrowsmith   B. Nancy Ashford
    C. Christopher Bean   D. Sarah Cleghorn

6. Which one of the following reference books is of MAJOR assistance in reading the works of Jack Kerouac and Allen Ginsberg?

    A. Bartlett's FAMILIAR QUOTATIONS
    B. Benet's THE READER'S ENCYCLOPEDIA
    C. DICTIONARY OF AMERICAN SLANG
    D. STANDARD DICTIONARY OF FOLKLORE

7. Which one of the following is INCORRECTLY paired with its author(s) or editor(s)?

    A. CYCLOPEDIA OF EDUCATION - Paul Monroe
    B. SECRETARY'S HANDBOOK - Sarah A. Taintor and Kate M. Monro
    C. TWENTIETH CENTURY AUTHORS - Fred B. Millet and Edith Rickert
    D. WRITER'S GUIDE AND INDEX TO ENGLISH - Porter G. Perrin

8. A TRUE RELATION is *primarily* concerned with

    A. denunciation of witchcraft in colonial New England
    B. opposition to theocratic education in Plymouth colony

C. settlement of Rhode Island
D. events in the Jamestown colony

9. The DEATH CHANT occurs in Whitman's poem

   A. O CAPTAIN! MY CAPTAIN!
   B. WHEN LILACS LAST IN THE DOORYARD BLOOM'D
   C. THE LAST INVOCATION
   D. BEAT! BEAT! DRUMS

10.
    I. THE GERM - Dante Gabriel Rossetti
    II. THE YELLOW BOOK - Max Beerbohm
    III. POETRY - Richard Hovey
    IV. SATURDAY REVIEW - Edward A. Weeks
    V. THE DIAL - Ralph Waldo Emerson

    Literary magazine and figure importantly associated with it are correctly paired in each of the above EXCEPT

    A. I, V   B. I, II, IV
    C. III, IV   D. II, III, V

11.
    I. THE MYSTERIES OF UDOLPHO
    II. SENSE AND SENSIBILITY
    III. JOSEPH ANDREWS
    IV. CASTLE OF OTRANTO
    V. VATHEK

    Of the above works, the description "gothic novel" MOST appropriately applies to

    A. I, III, IV   B. II, III, IV
    C. II, III, V   D. I, IV, V

12. Author and place with which his name is prominently associated are correctly paired in each of the following EXCEPT

    A. D.H. Lawrence - Taos
    B. Robert L. Stevenson - Samoa
    C. Ernest Hemingway - Cuba
    D. Ezra Pound - Leipsig

13. The one which is NOT a part of the Leatherstocking series is

    A. THE LAST OF THE MOHICANS   B. THE DEERSLAYER
    C. THE SPY   D. THE PATHFINDER

14.
    I. THE ROSE TATTOO
    II. COME BACK, LITTLE SHEBA
    III. SUMMER AND SMOKE
    IV. A VIEW FROM THE BRIDGE
    V. THE GLASS MENAGERIE
    VI. LOST IN THE STARS

    Of the works listed above, the author of A STREETCAR NAMED DESIRE and CAT ON A HOT TIN ROOF also wrote all the following

    A. I, II, III   B. IV, V, VI
    C. I, III, V   D. II, IV, VI

15. The author of THE SONG OF CHATTAHOOCHEE was also all of the following EXCEPT   15.____

    A. a soldier in the Confederate Army
    B. a flutist in a symphony orchestra
    C. author of THE YEMASSEE
    D. author of THE BOYS' KING ARTHUR

16. Poems and the persons to which they refer are correctly paired in all the following EXCEPT   16.____

    A. WHEN LILACS LAST IN THE DOORYARD BLOOM'D - Abraham Lincoln
    B. ICHABOD - Daniel Webster
    C. THE LOST LEADER - William Wordsworth
    D. DUNCIAD - Thomas Shadwell

17. I. William Faulkner - Georgia   17.____
    II. Robert Tristram Coffin - Vermont
    III. Robinson Jeffers - California
    IV. Marjorie Kinnan Rawlings - Florida

    Author and region with which the name is MOST appropriately associated are CORRECTLY paired above in

    A. I, II, III   B. II, IV
    C. III, IV   D. I, III, IV

18. Of the following, the one NOT noted as the author of important poems about World War I is   18.____

    A. Wilfred Owen   B. Siegfried Sassoon
    C. Stephen Spender   D. Robert Graves

19. I. General Robert E. Lee - Douglas Freeman   19.____
    II. Andrew Jackson - Marquis James
    III. Benjamin Franklin - Carl Van Doren
    IV. Mark Twain - Albert Bigelow Paine

    Of the above pairs of famous Americans and their biographers, all those CORRECTLY matched are

    A. I, III, IV   B. I, II, III, IV
    C. II, III   D. I, II, IV

20. I. LYSISTRATA   20.____
    II. TIGER AT THE GATES
    III. LOYALTIES
    IV. THE GREAT GATSBY
    V.   ALL QUIET ON THE WESTERN FRONT

    Of the above, those with pervading anti-war themes are

    A. I, II, III   B. I, II, V
    C. II, IV, V   D. III, IV, V

21. I. Phineas Fogg
    II. Job Trotter
    III. Becky Sharp
    IV. Captain Nemo
    V. Meg Merrilies
    VI. Scarlett O'Hara
    Of the above, the characters created by the same author are

    A. II, III, V   B. I, IV
    C. II, V, VI   D. III, V

22. I. GIANTS IN THE EARTH
    II. THE GOLDEN BOWL
    III. VANITY FAIR
    IV. THE SILVER CORD
    V. LOOK HOMEWARD ANGEL
    The titles of the famous works above which are NOT Biblical quotations are

    A. I, III   B. III, V   C. II, IV   D. I, V

23. I. OLYMPIO - Victor Hugo
    II. KING OF PARIS - Alexandre Dumas
    III. ARIEL - P. B. Shelley
    IV. ISRAFEL - Charles Baudelaire
    V. LELIA - George Eliot
    Of the above, the subjects CORRECTLY matched with the books about them are

    A. II, IV, V   B. I, II, III
    C. III, IV, V   D. I, IV, V

24. The borough of Brooklyn is treated in the well-known writings of all of the following EXCEPT

    A. Walt Whitman   B. Walter D. Edmonds
    C. Hart Crane   D. Thomas Wolfe

25. Work and author are correctly paired in all of the following EXCEPT

    A. AN ECONOMIC INTERPRETATION OF THE CONSTITUTION OF THE UNITED STATES - Beard
    B. HISTORY OF THE CONQUEST OF MEXICO - Parkman
    C. THE FRONTIER IN AMERICAN HISTORY - Turner
    D. THE AMERICAN COMMONWEALTH - Bryce

KEY (CORRECT ANSWERS)

1. D
2. A
3. D
4. D
5. D

6. C
7. C
8. A
9. B
10. C

11. D
12. D
13. C
14. C
15. C

16. D
17. C
18. C
19. B
20. B

21. B
22. B
23. B
24. B
25. B

TEST 5

DIRECTIONS: Each question or incomplete statement is followed by several suggested answers or completions. Select the one that BEST answers the question or completes the statement. *PRINT THE LETTER OF THE CORRECT ANSWER IN THE SPACE AT THE RIGHT.*

1. Of the following poems, the one MOST closely resembling Whittier's SNOW-BOUND is　　1.____

   A. Gray's ELEGY WRITTEN IN A COUNTRY CHURCHYARD
   B. Hood's SONG OF THE SHIRT
   C. Burn's COTTER'S SATURDAY NIGHT
   D. Keat's ODE TO AUTUMN

2. The statement about Henry James that is NOT true is:　　2.____

   A. He is often concerned with the interaction of American and European cultures.
   B. Although living in England for many years, he retained his American citizenship.
   C. Some of his stories have been successfully adapted to the stage.
   D. His prose tends to be involved, with many qualifying phrases and clauses.

3. Of the following novels, the one which does NOT deal in a large measure with the education of the young is　　3.____

   A. NICHOLAS NICKLEBY   B. RICHARD FEVEREL
   C. THE VARMINT   D. STRANGE FRUIT

4. All of the following statements about Ezra Pound are true EXCEPT:　　4.____

   A. In his earlier writing, he showed his affinity to the Imagist school.
   B. His later work is marked by the inclusion of many lines of poetry in foreign languages.
   C. The basic purpose of his longest work, CANTOS, is to reaffirm, in poetic form, the principles of twentieth century American democracy.
   D. Many prominent critics questioned the propriety of his receipt of the Bollingen prize for poetry in 1949.

5. Of the following poets, the one whose works give evidence of his spirit of affirmation and optimism is　　5.____

   A. Edwin Arlington Robinson   B. Robinson Jeffers
   C. Carl Sandburg   D. Edgar Lee Masters

6. Of the following characters, the one NOT created by Mark Twain is　　6.____

   A. Tom Canty   B. Becky Thatcher
   C. Colonel Sellers   D. Hester Prynne

7. Of the following authors, the one who does NOT write chiefly of the South is　　7.____

   A. Eudora Welty   B. Ellen Glasgow
   C. Louis Bromfield   D. DuBose Heyward

8. Of the following important Americans, the one who was NOT an immigrant to the country is

    A. Edward Bok
    B. Jacob Riis
    C. Arthur Schlesinger
    D. Mary Antin

9. Of the following pairs, the one containing two items INCORRECTLY paired is

    A. Sidney Porter - O. Henry
    B. Washington Irving - Knickerbocker
    C. Charles Dickens - Boz
    D. John Milton - Scriblerus

10. The author of DEMOCRACY AND EDUCATION is

    A. Horace Mann
    B. John Dewey
    C. John Erskine
    D. Edward Thorndike

11. Of the following characters from the Old Testament, the one paired with the WRONG city is

    A. Lot - Canaan
    B. Joshua - Jericho
    C. Moses - Egypt
    D. Esther - Moab

12. Henry Fleming is the hero of

    A. THE JUNGLE
    B. THE OCTOPUS
    C. THE RED BADGE OF COURAGE
    D. THE FINANCIER

13. The playwright and play NOT correctly paired are

    A. Clifford Odets - GOLDEN BOY
    B. Robert Sherwood - ABE LINCOLN IN ILLINOIS
    C. Maxwell Anderson - WINTERSET
    D. Elmer Rice - DEAD END

14. LIFE ON THE MISSISSIPPI is

    A. a sequel to HUCKLEBERRY FINN
    B. the story of the author's career as a pilot
    C. an account of the American tour of two European vagabonds
    D. a collection of fanciful legends of the Mississippi River Valley

15. All of the following are novels of the soil EXCEPT

    A. GIANTS IN THE EARTH
    B. NEW ENGLAND INDIAN SUMMER
    C. BARREN GROUND
    D. SO BIG

16. A writer often described as a recluse is

    A. Edna St. Vincent Millay
    B. Willa cather
    C. Edith Wharton
    D. Emily Dickinson

17. The poems PETIT, THE POET, LUCINDA MATLOCK, and ANNE RUTLEDGE appear in

    A. WAR IS KIND
    B. SPOON RIVER
    C. THE SINGLE HOUND
    D. MEN, WOMEN, AND GHOSTS

18. All of the following were associated with the newspaper or magazine with which they are paired EXCEPT 18.____

   A. William Cullen Bryant - NEW YORK EVENING POST
   B. Walt Whitman - Brooklyn DAILY EAGLE
   C. William Dean Howells - ATLANTIC MONTHLY
   D. Edward Eggleston - AMERICAN MERCURY

19. T.S. Eliot was born in 19.____

   A. the United States   B. England
   C. Ireland   D. Canada

20. An author and pseudonym NOT correctly associated are 20.____

   A. Mark Twain and Samuel Clemens
   B. George Eliot and Aurora Dupin
   C. Currer Bell and Charlotte Bronte
   D. O. Henry and William Sidney Porter

21. The author of THE PROFESSOR AT THE BREAKFAST TABLE also wrote 21.____

   A. THE VISION OF SIR LAUNFAL   B. THE CHAMBERED NAUTILUS
   C. DEMOCRATIC VISTAS   D. THE PSALM OF LIFE

22. The author of AN AMERICAN TRAGEDY also wrote 22.____

   A. THE PIT
   B. THE FINANCIER
   C. WINESBURG, OHIO
   D. MAGGIE: A GIRL OF THE STREETS

23. A person designated as a Babbitt is notably a 23.____

   A. conformer   B. rebel   C. creator   D. destroyer

24. The author of LOOK HOMEWARD, ANGEL also wrote 24.____

   A. YOU CAN'T GO HOME AGAIN
   B. HOME - THOUGHTS FROM ABROAD
   C. THE CLOISTER AND THE HEARTH
   D. THE HOME OF THE BRAVE

25. In all of the plays, THE SHRIKE, POINT OF NO RETURN, and DEATH OF A SALESMAN, the protagonist is 25.____

   A. indifferent to money
   B. concerned about material success
   C. successful in a material way
   D. engaged in a crusade against materialism

KEY (CORRECT ANSWERS)

1. B
2. D
3. C
4. D
5. C

6. C
7. A
8. C
9. D
10. B

11. D
12. B
13. C
14. D
15. B

16. A
17. C
18. C
19. A
20. C

21. D
22. B
23. C
24. D
25. C

EXAMINATION SECTION
TEST 1

DIRECTIONS: Each question or incomplete statement is followed by several suggested answers or completions. Select the one that BEST answers the question or completes the statement. *PRINT THE LETTER OF THE CORRECT ANSWER IN THE SPACE AT THE RIGHT.*

1. The one of the following NOT considered one of the Transcendentalists is   1.____

   A. Emerson
   B. Oliver Wendell Holmes, Sr.
   C. Hawthorne
   D. Thoreau

2. The writer of local color stories NOT correctly paired with a region is   2.____

   A. Mary E. Wilkins Freeman - New England
   B. Joel Chandler Harris - Georgia
   C. George Washington Cable - Louisiana
   D. Helen Hunt Jackson - the Middle West

3. BILLY BUDD, formerly dramatized on the New York stage, is based on a work by   3.____

   A. Hawthorne
   B. Cooper
   C. Melville
   D. Bret Harte

4. Emerson's philosophy is BEST expressed by the statement: 4.____

   A. It is the duty of each man to know foreign cultures well before he can appreciate his own.
   B. Each person must have a feeling of humility and must be prepared to accept that status decreed for him by the laws of society.
   C. Some persons have been endowed by nature with greater gifts than others. The less fortunate should be willing to accept the leadership of the more gifted.
   D. Each man must be true to his inner convictions and intuitions even though this may bring him into conflict with the established code of society.

5. The *Maule curse* is an element of the story in   5.____

   A. THE DEERSLAYER
   B. THE AMBASSADORS
   C. THE RISE OF SILAS LAPHAM
   D. THE HOUSE OF SEVEN GABLES

6. All of the following criticisms of James Fenimore Cooper's novels have validity EXCEPT: 6.____

   A. His heroines are unnatural, stiff, and artificial
   B. His plots lack novelty; his characters and situations are repeated with little variation
   C. He is in no sense an innovator, merely retelling stories that were created by others
   D. Although his narratives are spirited, his style is often excessively ponderous

7. Of the following, all are by the same author EXCEPT   7.____

   A. PAUL REVERE'S RIDE
   B. SNOW-BOUND
   C. BARBARA FRIETCHIE
   D. THE BAREFOOT BOY

8. Of the following statements concerning the novel MOBY DICK, the one that is NOT true is:

   A. The story is interrupted by digressions on the habits of the whale and the practices of whalers
   B. Moby Dick, the white whale, is a symbol of the force of evil that must be hunted down relentlessly
   C. Although Melville had written many other books before it, it was not until the publication of MOBY DICK that he gained fame and recognition
   D. Only the narrator, Ishmael, survives the wreck of the Pequot

9. The author and historical work NOT correctly paired are

   A. Hough - THE OREGON TRAIL
   B. Motley - THE RISE OF THE DUTCH REPUBLIC
   C. Prescott - THE CONQUEST OF MEXICO
   D. Irving - HISTORY OF THE LIFE AND VOYAGES OF CHRISTOPHER COLUMBUS

10. Of the following works of Edna St. Vincent Millay, the one that differs GREATLY in both mood and theme from the others listed is

    A. JUSTICE IN MASSACHUSETTS
    B. RENASCENCE
    C. CONVERSATION AT MIDNIGHT
    D. THE MURDER OF LIDICE

11. The poet who tried to bring his poetry to the public by selling it himself was

    A. Stephen Crane
    B. Edwin Markham
    C. Edgar Lee Masters
    D. Vachel Lindsay

12. Of the following works, the one that is LARGELY autobiographical is

    A. THE SONG OF THE LARK
    B. A SON OF THE MIDDLE BORDER
    C. THE CUSTOM OF THE COUNTRY
    D. THE AMERICAN

13. Sinclair Lewis did NOT write

    A. DODSWORTH
    B. IT CAN'T HAPPEN HERE
    C. THE GREAT GATSBY
    D. KINGSBLOOD ROYAL

14. An author who was also a physician was

    A. James Russell Lowell
    B. Thomas Bailey Aldrich
    C. Bret Harte
    D. Oliver Wendell Holmes, Sr.

15. Of the following authors, the one whose work MOST often deals with sin and pangs of guilt is

    A. William Gilmore Simms
    B. Nathaniel Hawthorne
    C. William Dean Howells
    D. Booth Tarkington

16. Life close to nature is described in   16.____
    A. WALDEN   B. SISTER CARRIE
    C. INNOCENTS ABROAD   D. THE MILL ON THE FLOSS

17. Mourning for the death of a beautiful and beloved woman is a repeated subject in the   17.____
    works of

    A. Bryant   B. Lanier   C. Poe   D. Whitman

18. A MODERN COMEDY continues the story begun in   18.____
    A. JOAN AND PETER   B. ESTHER WATERS
    C. THE FORSYTE SAGA   D. A PASSAGE TO INDIA

19. Ernest Hemingway did NOT create the character of   19.____
    A. John Ward Moorehouse   B. Frederic Henry
    C. Robert Jordan   D. Lady Brett Ashley

20. A poetical work NOT concerned with a political question is   20.____
    A. ICHABOD   B. THE BIGELOW PAPERS
    C. THE HARP-WEAVER   D. ODE IN TIME OF HESITATION

21. All of the following are by the same author EXCEPT   21.____

    A. THE BLITHEDALE ROMANCE
    B. THE MARBLE FAUN
    C. MOSSES FROM AN OLD MANSE
    D. BRACEBRIDGE HALL

22. An American poet, who was also a college professor, whose poetry has been popular   22.____
    with children, is

    A. Edwin Markham   B. Henry Wadsworth Longfellow
    C. Robert Louis Stevenson   D. Rudyard Kipling

23. Walt Whitman wrote all of the following lines EXCEPT   23.____

    A. "I sound my barbaric yawp over the roofs of the world"
    B. "O Captain! my Captain! our fearful trip is done!"
    C. "I never saw a moor"
    D. "I celebrate myself, and sing myself"

24. A book that was NOT on the best-seller lists within recent years is   24.____
    A. THE CRUEL SEA   B. THE SEA AROUND US
    C. UNDER THE SEA-WIND   D. THE SEA WOLF

25. Of the following writers, the one who frequently used New England, specifically Maine, as   25.____
    a setting is

    A. Margaret Mitchell   B. George Washington Cable
    C. Sarah Orne Jewett   D. Bret Harte

KEY (CORRECT ANSWERS)

1.	B	11.	D
2.	D	12.	B
3.	C	13.	C
4.	D	14.	D
5.	D	15.	B
6.	C	16.	A
7.	A	17.	C
8.	C	18.	C
9.	A	19.	A
10.	B	20.	C

21. D
22. B
23. C
24. D
25. C

TEST 2

DIRECTIONS: Each question or incomplete statement is followed by several suggested answers or completions. Select the one that BEST answers the question or completes the statement. *PRINT THE LETTER OF THE CORRECT ANSWER IN THE SPACE AT THE RIGHT.*

1. Of the following, the writer whose work is LEAST in the realistic tradition is 1.____

   A. Ernest Hemingway B. James Branch Cabell
   C. Sinclair Lewis D. Willa Cather

2. The author of SNOW-BOUND also wrote 2.____

   A. BARBARA FRITCHIE B. THE LAST LEAF
   C. THE VISION OF SIR LAUNFAL D. THANATOPSIS

3. Of the following stories, the one which is NOT largely concerned with an animal is 3.____

   A. BAMBI B. THE YEARLING
   C. THE CALL OF THE WILD D. THE OCTOPUS

4. A television program using a film and a discussion group, with subjects ranging from the United Nations to juvenile delinquency, was called 4.____

   A. MEET THE PRESS B. YOUTH ON THE MARCH
   C. IT'S WORTH KNOWING D. SEE IT NOW

5. THE LIVING BLACKBOARD was a television program produced by 5.____

   A. The New York City Board of Education
   B. Teachers College, Columbia University
   C. New York University
   D. Johns Hopkins

6. In the following groups, the one in which all three names are NOT properly classified together is 6.____

   A. Alton Cook, Otis L. Guernsey, Jr., Bosley Crowther
   B. Brooks Atkinson, George Jean Nathan, John Crosby
   C. Grantland Rice, Red Smith, Dan Parker
   D. Walter Lippman, Mark Sullivan, Joseph Alsop

7. Among the following reviewers, the one who can NOT properly be grouped with the others is 7.____

   A. Sterling North B. Ward Morehouse
   C. Lewis Gannett D. Charles Poore

8. Of the newspaper features and writers below, all are correctly paired EXCEPT 8.____

   A. MATTER OF FACT - Joseph and Stewart Alsop
   B. TODAY IN WASHINGTON - David Lawrence
   C. SEEING THINGS - John Mason Brown
   D. IN AND OUT OF BOOKS - J. Donald Adams

9. Of the following radio productions, the one for which Norman Corwin was NOT responsible is

   A. THE PLOT TO OVERTHROW CHRISTMAS
   B. SPOTLIGHT, NEW YORK
   C. THIS IS WAR
   D. ON A NOTE OF TRIUMPH

10. THIS I BELIEVE was a radio presentation associated with

    A. Edward R. Murrow
    B. George Sokolsky
    C. Drew Pearson
    D. Walter Winchell

11. Of the following groups, the one containing an item that does NOT belong with the others in the same group is

    A. Meet the Press, People's Platform, American Forum
    B. Best Plays, Family Theater, Broadway-TV Theater
    C. Larry Lesueur, Robert Trout, Elmer Davis
    D. Stan Lomax, Phil Rizzuto, Bill Stern

12. Of the following magazine features, the one that is NOT matched correctly is

    A. ACCENT ON LIVING - THE ATLANTIC MONTHLY
    B. THE EASY CHAIR - HARPER'S
    C. TALK OF THE TOWN - SEVENTEEN
    D. THE PERISCOPE - NEWSWEEK

13. Of the following pairs of magazines and editors, the pair INCORRECTLY matched is

    A. THE SATURDAY REVIEW - Edward A. Weeks
    B. HARPER'S - Frederick L. Allen
    C. POETRY - Karl Shapiro
    D. CURRENT HISTORY - D.G. Redmond

14. Of the following pairs of writers and magazines, the pair INCORRECTLY matched is

    A. Bernard de Voto - HARPER'S
    B. Stanley High - THE READER'S DIGEST
    C. James T. Shotwell - CURRENT HISTORY
    D. John Mason Brown - ATLANTIC MONTHLY

15. Of the following, the one who was editor-in-chief of more than one nationally circulated magazine was

    A. Henry R. Luce
    B. Ben Hibbs
    C. Malcolm Muir
    D. Norman Cousins

16. A magazine sponsored by the National Council of Teachers of English is

    A. THE ENGLISH REVIEW
    B. THE ENGLISH RECORD
    C. THE ENGLISH TEACHER
    D. THE ENGLISH JOURNAL

17. The author of HARVEY also wrote

    A. THE SEVEN YEAR ITCH
    B. THE SKIN OF OUR TEETH
    C. WISH YOU WERE HERE
    D. MRS. MCTHING

18. Of the following statements, the one that is INCORRECT is:

    A. PAINT YOUR WAGON was a musical comedy dealing with the forty-niners
    B. PAL JOEY grew out of the writings of John O' Hara
    C. THE MALE ANIMAL was about a college professor, his job, and his principles
    D. THE KING AND I was a thinly disguised biography of the British royal family

19. Katherine Hepburn made a hit in London in

    A. Shaw' s HEARTBREAK HOUSE
    B. Henry James' THE HEIRESS
    C. Shaw' s THE MILLIONAIRESS
    D. O'Neill' s MARCO MILLIONS

20. Of the following pairs of stage personalities, the one which was NOT a husband and a wife is

    A. Helen Hayes and Charles MacArthur
    B. Katherine Cornell and John Golden
    C. Lynn Fontanne and Alfred Lunt
    D. Lili Palmer and Rex Harrison

21. John Van Druten's play, I AM A CAMERA, was adapted from an autobiographical book by

    A. Christopher Isherwood   B. Christopher Fry
    C. T.S. Eliot   D. Erich Remarque

22. Of the following pairs of Broadway stage productions and their authors, the pair INCORRECTLY matched is

    A. THE CHILDREN'S HOUR - Lillian Hellman
    B. THE TRAITOR - Herman Wouk
    C. THE HAPPY TIME - Samuel Taylor
    D. JEZEBEL'S HUSBAND - Robert Sherwood

23. The winner of Academy Awards for his direction of HOW GREEN WAS MY VALLEY, THE GRAPES OF WRATH, and THE INFORMER was

    A. David Wark Griffith   B. Darryl Zanuck
    C. John Ford   D. John Huston

24. The dramatic program on television that based MOST of its productions on Pulitzer prize plays, or plays written by Pulitzer prize winners, was known as

    A. THE KRAFT THEATER   B. THE CELANESE THEATER
    C. LUX VIDEO   D. PHILCO PLAYHOUSE

25. Of the motion pictures below, the one that did NOT deal with wars of the twentieth century is

    A. RED BADGE OF COURAGE   B. RED BALL EXPRESS
    C. THE BIG PARADE   D. DESERT VICTORY

KEY (CORRECT ANSWERS)

1.	B	11.	B
2.	A	12.	C
3.	D	13.	A
4.	C	14.	D
5.	A	15.	A
6.	B	16.	D
7.	B	17.	D
8.	D	18.	D
9.	B	19.	C
10.	A	20.	B

21. A
22. D
23. C
24. B
25. A

TEST 3

DIRECTIONS: Each question or incomplete statement is followed by several suggested answers or completions. Select the one that BEST answers the question or completes the statement. *PRINT THE LETTER OF THE CORRECT ANSWER IN THE SPACE AT THE RIGHT.*

1. Of the following, the statement that is NOT correct is: 1._____

    A. THE ASPHALT JUNGLE is about jewel thieves in a midwestern city
    B. BITTER RICE describes the rice harvesters in the Po Valley
    C. MAN OF ARAN deals with Irish island life
    D. OPEN CITY describes operations of the French underground in Paris

2. Both John Huston and Walter Huston had much to do with the success of the motion picture 2._____

    A. THE HEIRESS
    B. ALL ABOUT EVE
    C. THE TREASURE OF SIERRA MADRE
    D. DODSWORTH

3. Of the following, the statement that is NOT correct is: 3._____

    A. In THE LAVENDER HILL MOB, a mousy little clerk steals a million dollars from the Bank of England
    B. OUTCAST OF THE ISLANDS is based on a Somerset Maugham story of Malaya
    C. MISS JULIE is a Swedish film
    D. THE INFORMER is a drama of Dublin in 1922 during the Sinn Fein rebellionz

4. Of the following statements, the one that is NOT correct is: 4._____

    A. THE AFRICAN QUEEN, based on a Conrad novel, was produced by William Wyler
    B. Both THE TEMPEST and THE WINTER'S TALE have been presented on the stage in summer theaters
    C. John Gielgud is cast as Cassius in a Hollywood filming of JULIUS CAESAR
    D. The writings of W. Somerset Maugham are the basis of QUARTET and ENCORE

5. A film dealing with the first experiences of young children with books is 5._____

    A. THE IMPRESSIONABLE YEARS
    B. NO RESTING PLACE
    C. THROUGH THE ENCHANTED GATE
    D. HAPPIEST DAYS OF YOUR LIFE

6. Of the following plays, the one INCORRECTLY matched with an author is 6._____

    A. BORN YESTERDAY - Garson Kanin
    B. THE IMPORTANCE OF BEING EARNEST - Oscar Wilde
    C. THE SHRIKE - Clare Booth Luce
    D. NIGHT MUST FALL - Emlyn Williams

7. Of the following statements, the one which is NOT true is:

    A. POINT OF NO RETURN deals with the iron of success
    B. The entire action of THE FOURPOSTER takes place in a bedroom
    C. Tennessee Williams won a Pulitzer prize for his play, A STREETCAR NAMED DESIRE
    D. UNDER THE RED SEA deals with an incident in World War II

8. The screen actor who starred in TWELVE O'CLOCK HIGH also played in

    A. KIND HEARTS AND CORONETS
    B. GENTLEMEN'S AGREEMENT
    C. THE BEST YEARS OF OUR LIVES
    D. LOST WEEKEND

9. Of the following motion pictures, the one which CANNOT be grouped with the others on the basis of setting is

    A. THE BIG SKY   B. THE SNOWS OF KILIMANJARO
    C. IVORY HUNTER   D. THE AFRICAN QUEEN

10. In the following pairs, the play or moving picture is paired with the name of the author upon whose work it is based EXCEPT in the case of

    A. SOUTH PACIFIC - James A. Michener
    B. FULL HOUSE - O. Henry
    C. GUYS AND DOLLS - Damon Runyon
    D. THE MAN IN THE WHITE SUIT - Maxwell Anderson

11. Of the following novelists, the one LEAST concerned with ethical problems is

    A. William Dean Howells   B. James Fenimore Cooper
    C. Nathaniel Hawthorne   D. Sinclair Lewis

12. The writer in this group who has NOT depicted life in the Middle West is

    A. Hamlin Garland   B. George W. Cable
    C. Edgar Eggleston   D. Booth Tarkington

13. The author among the following who did NOT use some phase of the Round Table theme is

    A. John Erskine   B. Mark Twain
    C. Edwin Arlington Robinson D. James Branch Cabell

14. All of the following newspaper men were drama critics EXCEPT

    A. Brooks Atkinson   B. Arthur Krock
    C. Ward Morehouse   D. Bowsley Brothers

15. When Emerson said, *"His heart was as great as the world, but there was no room in it to hold the memory of a wrong,"* he referred to

    A. George Washington   B. Thomas Jefferson
    C. Abraham Lincoln   D. Jesus Christ

16. The one writer in this group who did NOT write on religious subjects is

    A. William Ellery Channing
    B. Henry Ward Beecher
    C. Jonathan Edwards
    D. Vernon L. Parrington

17. Of the following characters, the one that does NOT belong in THE SCARLET LETTER is

    A. Arthur Dimmesdale
    B. Hester Prynne
    C. Judge Pyncheon
    D. Roger Chillingworth

18. Of the following, the writer NOT properly grouped with the others from the point of view of regional setting is

    A. Ellen Glasgow
    B. Margaret Mitchell
    C. Sarah Orne Jewett
    D. Marjorie Kinnan Rawlings

19. Of the following, the author whose literary style was LEAST affected by *stream of consciousness* psychology was

    A. Thomas Wolfe
    B. Gertrude Stein
    C. Sherwood Anderson
    D. Willa Cather

20. Moby Dick, as a symbol, represents

    A. the conflict between man and his fate
    B. a vengeance hunt for a white whale
    C. a study of fishermen under stress
    D. the effect of environment on man

21. Of the following novels, the one NOT written by Theodore Dreiser is

    A. THE FINANCIER
    B. THE TITAN
    C. THE PIT
    D. THE GENIUS

22. Of the following works, the ONLY one that employed the supernatural to a great extent is

    A. RAMONA
    B. ELSIE VENNER
    C. MARIA CHAPDELAINE
    D. MISS LULU BETT

23. Gaylord Ravenal is a character created by

    A. Edna Ferber
    B. Gertrude Atherton
    C. William Faulkner
    D. James Farrell

24. Of the following novels, the one which does NOT end tragically is

    A. GREEN MANSIONS
    B. MY ANTONIA
    C. A MODERN INSTANCE
    D. ETHAN FROME

25. A book by Jack London which is largely autobiographical is

    A. THE SEA WOLF
    B. BURNING DAYLIGHT
    C. WAR OF THE CLASSES
    D. MARTIN EDEN

KEY (CORRECT ANSWERS)

1. D
2. C
3. B
4. A
5. A

6. C
7. D
8. B
9. A
10. D

11. B
12. B
13. A
14. B
15. C

16. D
17. C
18. C
19. D
20. A

21. C
22. B
23. A
24. B
25. D

TEST 4

DIRECTIONS: Each question or incomplete statement is followed by several suggested answers or completions. Select the one that BEST answers the question or completes the statement. *PRINT THE LETTER OF THE CORRECT ANSWER IN THE SPACE AT THE RIGHT.*

1. Amory Blaine is the LEADING character in 1.____

    A. THE BRIMMING CUP   B. AH! WILDERNESS
    C. THIS SIDE OF PARADISE   D. SEVENTEEN

2. Carol Kennicott fights provincialism and narrowness in the novel 2.____

    A. ARROWSMITH   B. MAIN STREET
    C. BABBITT   D. IT CAN'T HAPPEN HERE

3. The setting of the following books is largely Europe, with the EXCEPTION of 3.____

    A. THE MARBLE FAUN   B. DODSWORTH
    C. THE JUNGLE   D. DAISY MILLER

4. All of the following were 19th century humorists EXCEPT 4.____

    A. Artemus Ward   B. David Crockett
    C. Bill Ney   D. Robert Ingersoll

5. Washington Irving wrote all of the following EXCEPT 5.____

    A. CONQUEST OF GRANADA
    B. THE RISE OF THE DUTCH REPUBLIC
    C. KNICKERBOCKER'S HISTORY OF NEW YORK
    D. THE LIFE OF GEORGE WASHINGTON

6. The one of the following writers who is known CHIEFLY as an essayist is 6.____

    A. Thomas Bailey Aldrich   B. Zona Gale
    C. William Saroyan   D. James Huneker

7. The one of the following who was NOT connected with the *muckraking* movement is 7.____

    A. Upton Sinclair   B. Lincoln Steffens
    C. Hamlin Garland   D. Ida M. Tarbell

8. The theme of WINTERSET was suggested by 8.____

    A. the Haymarket Riots
    B. the case of the Scottsboro Boys
    C. the Sacco-Vanzetti case
    D. John Brown's raid

9. All of the following plays by Eugene O'Neill use symbolic characters EXCEPT 9.____

    A. THE ICEMAN COMETH   B. LAZARUS LAUGHED
    C. THE GREAT GOD BROWN D. DESIRE UNDER THE ELMS

10. All of the following were written by the same author EXCEPT

   A. SO LITTLE TIME
   B. THE FLOWERING OF NEW ENGLAND
   C. THE LIFE OF EMERSON
   D. THE TIMES OF MELVILLE AND WHITMAN

11. All of the following were inhabitants of Spoon River EXCEPT

   A. Lucinda Matlock
   B. Anna Rutledge
   C. Fiddler Jones
   D. Richard Cory

12. Of the following poems, the one MOST clearly directed at exposing a social wrong was

   A. CHICAGO
   B. MINIVER CHEEVY
   C. FACTORIES
   D. BIRCHES

13. Of the following works, the one which is a poem describing the poet's contemporaries is

   A. THE POET AT THE BREAKFAST TABLE
   B. THE HEIGHT OF THE RIDICULOUS
   C. A FABLE FOR CRITICS
   D. BRUTE NEIGHBORS

14. The author of JOHN BROWN'S BODY also wrote

   A. THE WAR YEARS
   B. THE CONGO
   C. THE DUST WHICH IS GOD
   D. THE DEVIL AND DANIEL WEBSTER

15. Of the following poets, the one LEAST concerned with literary criticism is

   A. Adelaide Crapsey
   B. Harriet Monroe
   C. Amy Lowell
   D. Louis Untermeyer

16. The poem in this group NOT connected with some phase of the history of the United States is

   A. THE COURTSHIP OF MILES STANDISH
   B. ELDORADO
   C. THE CONCORD HYMN
   D. WHEN LILACS LAST IN THE DOORYARD BLOOM'D

17. A heated literary dispute raged around the award of the Bollingen prize for poetry in 1949 because it was awarded to

   A. Robert Frost
   B. Ezra Pound
   C. Peter Viereck
   D. W.H. Auden

18. All of the following won the Nobel Prize EXCEPT

   A. Upton Sinclair
   B. William Faulkner
   C. Sinclair Lewis
   D. Pearl Buck

19. Of the following lines, the one taken from THE RHODORA is: 19.____

    A. Into each life some rain must fall
    B. Then beauty is its own excuse for being
    C. It takes life to love life
    D. This is the compass-flower, that the finger of God has planted

20. "*She named the infant Pearl, as being of great price, - purchased with all she had*" is a quotation from the novel 20.____

    A. THE PEARL
    B. THE SCARLET LETTER
    C. THE SONG OF THE LARK
    D. AN AMERICAN TRAGEDY

21. The CORRECT words for the closing of the poem whose opening lines are, "*To him who in the love of nature holds Communion with her visible forms...*" are: 21.____

    A. Shall fold their tents, like the Arabs, And as silently steal away
    B. Like one who wraps the drapery of his couch About him, and lies down to pleasant dreams
    C. Till from the trumpet's mouth is pealed The blast of triumph o'er thy grave
    D. O, be my friend, and teach me to be thine!

22. The line, *"Truth, crushed to earth, shall rise again,"* is a quotation from a poem by 22.____

    A. William Cullen Bryant
    B. Edward Roland Sill
    C. Ralph Waldo Emerson
    D. James Russell Lowell

23. "*Build thee more stately mansions, O my soul,
    As the swift seasons roll!
    Leave thy low-vaulted past!*"
    is a quotation from 23.____

    A. THANATOPSIS
    B. THE CHAMBERED NAUTILUS
    C. FORBEARANCE
    D. THE VISION OF SIR LAUNFAL

24. *"Because I could not stop for Death
    He kindly stopped for me;
    The carriage held but just ourselves
    and Immortality..."*
    was written by 24.____

    A. Vachel Lindsay
    B. Eunice Tietjens
    C. Conrad Aiken
    D. Emily Dickinson

25. Of the following motion pictures, the one NOT based on a novel is 25.____

    A. RED BADGE OF COURAGE
    B. KIM
    C. HARVEY
    D. A PLACE IN THE SUN

KEY (CORRECT ANSWERS)

1. C
2. B
3. C
4. D
5. B

6. D
7. C
8. C
9. A
10. A

11. D
12. C
13. C
14. D
15. B

16. B
17. B
18. A
19. B
20. B

21. B
22. A
23. B
24. D
25. C

TEST 5

DIRECTIONS: Each question or incomplete statement is followed by several suggested answers or completions. Select the one that BEST answers the question or completes the statement. *PRINT THE LETTER OF THE CORRECT ANSWER IN THE SPACE AT THE RIGHT.*

1. Alex Guinness appeared in all of the following motion pictures EXCEPT   1._____
   - A. THE LAVENDER HILL MOB
   - B. MUDLARK
   - C. A CHRISTMAS CAROL
   - D. OLIVER TWIST

2. The motion picture, MIRACLE IN MILAN, was concerned with   2._____
   - A. miraculous cures of the sick
   - B. escape from war-time bombing
   - C. timely relief from floods
   - D. the need for goodness in the world

3. Of the following pairs, the one in which the items are INCORRECTLY matched is   3._____
   - A. VIVA ZAPATA - Marlon Brando
   - B. SHOWBOAT - Dorothy Kirsten
   - C. HARVEY - Josephine Hull
   - D. THE LIGHT TOUCH - Pier Angeli

4. A motion picture that presented heroism of a high order in World War II was   4._____
   - A. DECISION BEFORE DAWN
   - B. RED BADGE OF COURAGE
   - C. WHEN WORLDS COLLIDE
   - D. DISTANT DRUMS

5. Of the following motion pictures, the one which Cecil B. DeMille did NOT direct is   5._____
   - A. QUO VADIS
   - B. HE GREATEST SHOW ON EARTH
   - C. DAVID AND BATHSHEBA
   - D. THE TEN COMMANDMENTS

6. A motion picture that presented a tragedy based on racial differences in a country other than the United States of America was   6._____
   - A. INTRUDER IN THE DUST
   - B. CRY THE BELOVED COUNTRY
   - C. NO WAY OUT
   - D. PINKY

7. A motion picture that was filmed in Japan was   7._____
   - A. RASHOMON
   - B. EAST IS EAST
   - C. JAPANESE WAR BRIDE
   - D. GO FOR BROKE

8. Of the following motion pictures, the one NOT originally a play was   8._____
   - A. A STREETCAR NAMED DESIRE
   - B. DEATH OF A SALESMAN
   - C. DETECTIVE STORY
   - D. AN AMERICAN IN PARIS

9. Julie Harris, the principal in I AM A CAMERA, attracted wide attention as a *teenager* in   9._____
   - A. REMAINS TO BE SEEN
   - B. THE HAPPY TIME
   - C. SOUTH PACIFIC
   - D. MEMBER OF THE WEDDING

10. Shaw's Cleopatra and Shakespeare's differ in that the former is more   10._____

    A. scheming and devious
    B. strikingly beautiful
    C. child-like and dependent
    D. dominant and imperious

11. Of the following theatrical productions, the one in which Celeste Holm did NOT appear was   11._____

    A. JANE   B. ANNA CHRISTIE
    C. OKLAHOMA   D. AFFAIRS OF STATE

12. Of the following plays, the one which is NOT a musical comedy is   12._____

    A. THE KING AND I   B. THE MOON IS BLUE
    C. PAINT YOUR WAGON   D. CALL ME MADAM

13. Of the following plays and names connected with them, the ones that do NOT belong together are   13._____

    A. THE GRASS HARP - Audrey Hepburn
    B. GOLDEN BOY - John Garfield
    C. POINT OF NO RETURN - Henry Fonda
    D. MRS. McTHING - Brandon DeWilde

14. Because of his ventures in verse drama, Christopher Fry has been linked with the author of   14._____

    A. A NIGHT AT AN INN   B. MURDER IN THE CATHEDRAL
    C. THE BROWNING VERSION   D. THE BALLAD OF READING GAOL

15. A play that concerned the reactions of a sane man confined to a mental hospital was   15._____

    A. REMAINS TO BE SEEN   B. POINT OF NO RETURN
    C. THE SHRIKE   D. PAL JOEY

16. Of the following plays, the one with which Jose Ferrer was NOT associated as producer, director, or performer was   16._____

    A. THE FOURPOSTER   B. TWENTIETH CENTURY
    C. DARKNESS AT NOON   D. STALAG 17

17. Laurence Olivier was a *graduate* of   17._____

    A. GRUB STREET   B. OLD VIC
    C. COMMEDIA DEL'ARTE   D. THEATER IN THE ROUND

18. An actor who did NOT get his dramatic start in England was   18._____

    A. Michael Redgrave   B. Edmund Gwenn
    C. Alfred Lunt   D. George Arliss

19. Emlyn Williams scored a Broadway success in his readings from   19._____

    A. Charles Dickens   B. William Thackeray
    C. George B. Shaw   D. Hugh Walpole

20. All of the following Broadway shows were based on short stories or sketches which appeared originally in magazines EXCEPT 20.____

    A. SOUTH PACIFIC B. PAL JOEY
    C. THE KING AND I D. GUYS AND DOLLS

21. An artist famous for his magazine covers was 21.____

    A. Norman Rockwell B. Salvador Dali
    C. Pablo Picasso D. Rube Goldberg

22. The reviewer who conducted in a New York newspaper a department devoted to books for boys and girls was 22.____

    A. Babette Deutsch B. Louise S. Bechtel
    C. Sterling North D. Amy Loveman

23. The *lead* of a news story is 23.____

    A. a banner headline across the front page
    B. a sub-head breaking up a lengthy story
    C. the first sentence or two answering the questions: Who? What? When? Where?
    D. the name of the town and the date preceding a news story sent in by an out-of-town reporter or by a news agency

24. The term *Associated Press* refers to 24.____

    A. the union to which reporters belong
    B. a world-wide news service supplying news to member papers
    C. a nation-wide organization of publishers
    D. an association of men who operate the newspaper presses

25. Excellence in the field of journalism is recognized by the awarding of 25.____

    A. Nobel Prizes B. Pulitzer Prizes
    C. Critics Awards D. Newspaper Guild Trophies

KEY (CORRECT ANSWERS)

1. B
2. D
3. B
4. A
5. A

6. B
7. A
8. D
9. D
10. C

11. A
12. B
13. A
14. B
15. C

16. C
17. B
18. C
19. A
20. D

21. A
22. B
23. C
24. B
25. B

EXAMINATION SECTION
TEST 1

DIRECTIONS: Each question or incomplete statement is followed by several suggested answers or completions. Select the one that BEST answers the question or completes the statement. *PRINT THE LETTER OF THE CORRECT ANSWER IN THE SPACE AT THE RIGHT.*

1. *The woods are lovely, dark and deep*
   But I have promises to keep
   And miles to go before I sleep
   is a quotation from a poem by

   A. Edward A. Robinson B. Emily Dickinson
   C. William Rose Benet D. Robert Frost

   1.____

2. *Born in Amherst, lived in Amherst, died in Amherst* has been given as an enigmatic description of the life of

   A. Sara Teasdale B. Nathaniel Hawthorne
   C. Henry Thoreau D. Emily Dickinson

   2.____

3. A story whose climax depends on a remarkable coincidence is

   A. THE GOLD BUG B. GIFT OF THE MAGI
   C. THE NECKLACE D. QUALITY

   3.____

4. Of the following, the work MOST influenced by Freudian psychology is

   A. AN AMERICAN TRAGEDY B. MY ANTONIA
   C. GRAPES OF WRATH D. WINESBURG, OHIO

   4.____

5. A character in a poem, who died at the age of 96 after a rich and fruitful life, is

   A. Lucinda Matlock B. Aaron Stark
   C. Silas, the hired man D. Captain Craig

   5.____

6. ROUGHING IT is based upon Mark Twain's experiences

   A. in the Far West B. on the Mississippi
   C. in the Confederate Army D. in the Holy Land

   6.____

7. A writer who often dealt with the theme of the conflict of American and European culture was

   A. William Dean Howells B. Henry James
   C. Edith Wharton D. Herman Melville

   7.____

8. Oliver LaFarge's autobiography is entitled

   A. LAUGHING BOY B. RAW MATERIAL
   C. ALL THE YOUNG MEN D. LONG PENNANT

   8.____

9. *People who habitually drive their own cars at fifty miles*
   an hour turn vermillion and magenta
   If you go over fifteen or twenta...
   is typical of the style of

   A. Phyllis McGinley B. Charles Addams
   C. James Thurber D. Ogden Nash

   9.____

10. In his novel, ACROSS THE RIVER AND INTO THE TREES, Ernest Hemingway returns to the country of his earlier

    A. THE SUN ALSO RISES
    B. A FAREWELL TO ARMS
    C. FOR WHOM THE BELL TOLLS
    D. TO HAVE AND HAVE NOT

11. Of the following, the one whose career is associated with the practice of medecine as well as with the writing of poetry is

    A. Robert Frost
    B. Wallace Stevens
    C. Conrad Aiken
    D. William C. Williams

12. A famous poet who participated in the television feature WHAT'S MY LINE? is

    A. W.H. Auden
    B. Louis Untermeyer
    C. Carl Sandburg
    D. Norman Corwin

13. Henry Morgan Robertson's THE CARDINAL pictures Stephen Fermoyle as a parish priest in the environs of

    A. Chicago
    B. Boston
    C. New York
    D. San Francisco

14. JANE MECOM: FRANKLIN'S FAVORITE SISTER was written by

    A. Mark Van Doren
    B. Henry Steel Cominger
    C. Carl Van Doren
    D. Carl Carmer

15. All of the following are correctly matched EXCEPT

    A. Jesse Stuart - THE THREAD THAT RUNS SO TRUE
    B. Bliss Perry - AND GLADLY TEACH
    C. Mary Ellen Chase - ONE SMALL HEAD
    D. Sean O'Casey - I KNOCK AT THE DOOR

16. Of the following authors, the one NOT noted for satire is

    A. Anatole France
    B. Jonathan Swift
    C. Theodore Dreiser
    D. Aldous Huxley

17. Of the following, all were written by Sinclair Lewis EXCEPT

    A. BABBITT
    B. A MODERN COMEDY
    C. WORK OF ART
    D. IT CAN'T HAPPEN HERE

18. Of the following, the one NOT properly grouped with the others is

    A. Edwin Markham
    B. James Boswell
    C. Lytton Strachey
    D. Carl Sandburg

19. The relationship of parent and child is an important element in all of these works EXCEPT

    A. THE ORDEAL OF RICHARD FEVEREL
    B. SILAS MARNER
    C. THE SCARLET LETTER
    D. MAIN STREET

20. All of the following are historical novelists EXCEPT 20.____

    A. Samuel Shellabarger   B. Winston Churchill
    C. Katherine Mansfield   D. Rafael Sabatini

21. The drama critic often referred to as *The American Shaw* was 21.____

    A. George Jean Nathan   B. Robert Chapman
    C. Brooks Atkinson   D. John Mason Brown

22. Washington Irving did NOT write 22.____

    A. TALES OF A TRAVELLER   B. BRACEBRIDGE HALL
    C. TWICE-TOLD TALES   D. THE ALHAMBRA

23. *A foolish inconsistency is the hobgoblin of little minds* is a quotation from an essay by 23.____

    A. Thoreau   B. Emerson   C. Irving   D. Webster

24. All of the following are correctly matched EXCEPT 24.____

    A. Charlotte Bronte - Currer Bell
    B. Washington Irving - Geoffrey Crayon
    C. Mary Ann Evans - George Eliot
    D. Evelyn Waugh - George Orwell

25. The following books were written by Robert Penn Warren with the EXCEPTION of 25.____

    A. ALL THE KING'S MEN   B. THE BIG SKY
    C. WORLD ENOUGH AND TIME   D. NIGHT RIDER

KEY (CORRECT ANSWERS)

1. D
2. D
3. B
4. D
5. A

6. A
7. B
8. B
9. D
10. B

11. D
12. B
13. B
14. C
15. C

16. C
17. B
18. A
19. D
20. C

21. A
22. C
23. B
24. D
25. B

TEST 2

DIRECTIONS: Each question or incomplete statement is followed by several suggested answers or completions. Select the one that BEST answers the question or completes the statement. *PRINT THE LETTER OF THE CORRECT ANSWER IN THE SPACE AT THE RIGHT.*

1. In the essay, MARY WHITE, William Allen White pays tribute to his   1.____
   A. mother   B. aunt   C. wife   D. daughter

2. SEEDS OF TREASON is a study of the trial of   2.____
   A. Earl Browder   B. Ben Davis
   C. Harry Bridges   D. Alger Hiss

3. ISRAFEL by Hervey Allen is a biography of   3.____
   A. Nathaniel Hawthorne   B. Edgar Allan Poe
   C. Stephen Crane   D. Henry James

4. Of the following writers, the one whose short stories are naturalistic interpretations of American life in small towns is   4.____
   A. Fannie Hurst   B. Sherwood Anderson
   C. George Washington Cable   D. Frank Stockton

5. The characters in the musical comedy GUYS AND DOLLS are taken from the short stories of   5.____
   A. Damon Runyon   B. Jack Tait
   C. Ben Hecht   D. Earl Wilson

6. The author of THE COCKTAIL PARTY did NOT write   6.____
   A. ASH WEDNESDAY   B. GERONTION
   C. PATTERNS   D. FOUR QUARTETS

7. TALES OF THE SOUTH PACIFIC won the Pulitzer Prize for its author   7.____
   A. Merle Miller   B. James A. Michener
   C. Thomas B. Costain   D. John Hersey

8. Eugene Gant is the central figure in novels by   8.____
   A. Sherwood Anderson   B. James Branch Cabell
   C. Theodore Dreiser   D. Thomas Wolfe

9. THE WALL is an account of life in   9.____
   A. medieval China   B. the Warsaw Ghetto
   C. Puritan New England   D. fascist Italy

10. A series of novels in which Lanny Budd is the central character was written by   10.____
    A. Sinclair Lewis   B. Upton Sinclair
    C. Alex Waugh   D. Irwin Shaw

11. In Stephen Crane's THE RED BADGE OF COURAGE, there is a description of a battle that was fought in the

    A. War of 1812
    B. Crimean War
    C. Civil War
    D. Spanish-American War

12. Ellen Glasgow's novels are USUALLY concerned with life in

    A. the South
    B. New York City
    C. the Middle West
    D. New England

13. In his novels, John P. Marquand frequently satirizes

    A. New Englanders
    B. Westerners
    C. Southerners
    D. Canadians

14. The retreat of the Italians from Caporetto is described by Hemingway in

    A. THE SUN ALSO RISES
    B. A FAREWELL TO ARMS
    C. DEATH IN THE AFTERNOON
    D. MEN WITHOUT WOMEN

15. World War II did NOT influence the lives of the people depicted in

    A. THE NAKED AND THE DEAD
    B. THE YOUNG LIONS
    C. BRAVE NEW WORLD
    D. INTO THE VALLEY

16. The story of Joseph and his brothers is the subject of several novels by

    A. Reinhold Niebuhr
    B. Thomas Mann
    C. Albert Schweitzer
    D. Fulton Oursler

17. Of the following works, the one NOT written by Carl Sandburg is

    A. THE PEOPLE, YES
    B. ROOTABAGA STORIES
    C. ABRAHAM LINCOLN, THE WAR YEARS
    D. JOHN BROWN'S BODY

18. NINETEEN EIGHTY FOUR was written by the author of

    A. THE ANIMAL FARM
    B. HATTER'S CASTLE
    C. DUSTY ANSWER
    D. SCOOP

19. Of the following poems, the one which is an elegy on the death of Lincoln is

    A. WHEN LILACS LAST IN THE DOORYARD BLOOM'D
    B. THRENODY
    C. THANATOPSIS
    D. THE MAN AGAINST THE SKY

20. An American poet actively interested in the abolitionist movement was

    A. Poe
    B. Dickinson
    C. Whittier
    D. Lanier

21. A poet who has consistently shown his concern about our national, social, and cultural heritage is

    A. Wallace Stevens
    B. Alfred Kreymborg
    C. Mark Van Doren
    D. Archibald MacLeish

22. The FIRST important published poem of Edna St. Vincent Millay was 22.____
    A. SECOND APRIL
    B. RENASCENCE
    C. FATAL INTERVIEW
    D. EUCLID ALONE HAS LOOKED ON BEAUTY BARE

23. Unusual typographical devices are to be found in some of the poems of 23.____
    A. Louis Untermeyer   B. E.E. Cummings
    C. John Gould Fletcher   D. Robert Bridges

24. The author of THE ROAD NOT TAKEN did NOT write 24.____
    A. AN OLD MAN'S WINTER NIGHT
    B. FIRE AND ICE
    C. MENDING WALL
    D. CHILDREN OF THE NIGHT

25. *The fog comes on little oat feet* is from a poem by 25.____
    A. Vachel Lindsay   B. Robert Frost
    C. Amy Lowell   D. Carl Sandburg

KEY (CORRECT ANSWERS)

1. D	11. C
2. D	12. A
3. B	13. A
4. B	14. B
5. A	15. C
6. C	16. B
7. B	17. D
8. D	18. A
9. B	19. A
10. B	20. C

21. D
22. B
23. B
24. D
25. D

TEST 3

DIRECTIONS: Each question or incomplete statement is followed by several suggested answers or completions. Select the one that BEST answers the question or completes the statement. *PRINT THE LETTER OF THE CORRECT ANSWER IN THE SPACE AT THE RIGHT.*

1. The motion picture, THE MAGNIFICENT YANKEE, gives a vivid picture of

    A. Franklin D. Roosevelt
    B. General Eisenhower
    C. Henry Cabot Lodge
    D. Justice Oliver Wendell Holmes

2. A young woman who joined a nursing order and went to Minkanja to help the natives was a character in

    A. LOST IN THE STARS
    B. THE COCKTAIL PARTY
    C. THE GREEN BAY TREE
    D. THE HAPPY TIME

3. Of the following, the play which centers around a Welsh miner is

    A. GREEN GROW THE LILACS
    B. GREEN PASTURES
    C. THE GREEN HAT
    D. THE CORN IS GREEN

4. Of the following plays, the one which was NOT written by Lillian Hellman is

    A. THE LITTLE FOXES
    B. TOMORROW THE WORLD
    C. THE AUTUMN GARDEN
    D. SEASON IN THE SUN

5. SECOND THRESHOLD, Philip Barry's unfinished play, was revised and completed by

    A. Robert Sherwood
    B. Maxwell Anderson
    C. Charles MacArthur
    D. Moss Hart

6. Of the following, the play which was NOT written by Augustus Thomas is

    A. THE HARVEST MOON
    B. RIO GRANDE
    C. THE SCARECROW
    D. THE WITCHING HOUR

7. Of the following plays, the one that does NOT attack the stupidities of war or the greed of munitions makers is

    A. THE TROJAN WOMEN
    B. IDIOT'S DELIGHT
    C. LYSISTRATA
    D. VALLEY FORGE

8. The theme of a race of masterless men allowing their city to fall before the advent of an empty symbol of tyranny was used by

    A. Norman Corwin
    B. Archibald Oboler
    C. Archibald MacLeish
    D. Christopher Isherwood

9. The use of blank verse as the medium for a realistic contemporary drama is found in Anderson's

    A. WINTERSET
    B. GODS OF THE LIGHTNING
    C. KNICKERBOCKER HOLIDAY
    D. SATURDAY'S CHILDREN

10. The story of an overpowering woman whose life has been fulfilled by completeness of   10._____
    her submission to her husband is told in
        A. THE GREEN BAY TREE   B. NOT FOR CHILDREN
        C. THE ROSE TATTOO   D. THE AUTUMN GARDEN

11. A revival of a play which was directed by Robert Lewis is   11._____
        A. TWENTIETH CENTURY   B. AN ENEMY OF THE PEOPLE
        C. KING LEAR   D. THE RELAPSE

12. Paul Green's THE LOST COLONY played for several summers at the   12._____
        A. University of Iowa
        B. University of North Carolina
        C. Washington University
        D. Little Theatre of Dallas, Texas

13. The element of the supernatural is NOT found in   13._____
        A. THE INNOCENTS   B. BELL, BOOK, AND CANDLE
        C. SUMMER AND SMOKE   D. DARK OF THE MOON

14. The unities of time and place are NOT observed in   14._____
        A. IPHIGENIA IN TAURIS   B. IDIOT'S DELIGHT
        C. THE TIME OF YOUR LIFE D. THE PETRIFIED FOREST

15. Hallie Flanagan is noted for her work in the   15._____
        A. Theatre in the Round   B. Federal Theatre
        C. Group Theatre   D. Theatre Guild

16. Eugene O'Neill's sole departure from his norm of harrowing soul searching was the   16._____
    delightful comedy,
        A. DAYS WITHOUT END   B. THE ICEMAN COMETH
        C. LAZARUS LAUGHED   D. AH, WILDERNESS!

17. Christopher Fry was NOT connected with the writing of   17._____
        A. A PHOENIX TOO FREQUENT B. THE LADY'S NOT FOR BURNING
        C. BLACK CHIFFON   D. RING ROUND THE MOON

18. Alec Guiness has NOT played on Broadway in   18._____
        A. THE COCKTAIL PARTY
        B. KIND HEARTS AND CORONETS
        C. THE MUDLARK
        D. AN ENEMY OF THE PEOPLE

19. The role of Elizabeth in THE BARRETTS OF WIMPOLE STREET was played on televi-   19._____
    sion by
        A. Mary Sinclair   B. Ruth Hussey
        C. Katherine Cornell   D. Helen Hayes

20. The one of the following who does NOT belong in the same category as the others is   20.____

   A. Herman Shumlin B. Lee Simonson
   C. George Abbott   D. Joshua Logan

21. Arch Oboler was BEST known as a   21.____

   A. radio actor   B. radio script writer
   C. television director D. stage actor

22. Of the following pairs, the one in which the items are NOT correctly matched is   22.____

   A. THE AMERICAN LANGUAGE - H.L. Mencken
   B. THE MODERN TEMPER - Joseph Wood Krutch
   C. MONT ST. MICHEL AND CHARTRES - Henry Adams
   D. AN ALMANAC FOR MODERNS - Van Wyck Brooks

23. THE JUST SO STORIES do NOT tell how the   23.____

   A. moose got his antlers
   B. elephant got his trunk
   C. rhinoceros got his wrinkled skin
   D. camel got his hump

24. The work among the following which is NOT autobiographical is   24.____

   A. MARTIN EDEN
   B. A SON OF THE MIDDLE BORDER
   C. ETHAN FROME
   D. A STORY TELLER'S STORY

25. A novel in which NONE of the action takes place in the southern part of the United States is   25.____

   A. SHADOWS ON THE ROCK   B. SANCTUARY
   C. LOOK HOMEWARD, ANGEL D. TOBACCO ROAD

KEY (CORRECT ANSWERS)

1. D
2. B
3. D
4. D
5. A

6. C
7. D
8. C
9. A
10. C

11. B
12. B
13. C
14. A
15. B

16. D
17. C
18. D
19. D
20. B

21. B
22. D
23. A
24. C
25. A

TEST 4

DIRECTIONS: Each question or incomplete statement is followed by several suggested answers or completions. Select the one that BEST answers the question or completes the statement. *PRINT THE LETTER OF THE CORRECT ANSWER IN THE SPACE AT THE RIGHT.*

1. YANKEE FROM OLYMPUS is a biography of

    A. President Wilson
    B. William Cullen Bryant
    C. Henry Wadsworth Longfellow
    D. Justice Holmes

2. *Farewell to barn and stack and tree,*
   Farewell to Severn shore,
   was written by

    A. Walter DeLaMare B. Rupert Brooke
    C. Wilfred Owen   D. A.E. Housman

3. *A foolish consistency is the hobgoblin of little minds* was written by

    A. Thoreau   B. Emerson   C. Lincoln   D. Melville

4. *One could do worse than be a swinger of birches* is a quotation from a poem by

    A. Edgar Lee Masters B. Elinor Wylie
    C. Robert Frost   D. Emily Dickinson

5. Difficulty in adjusting to a society in which they find themselves is the MAIN theme of THE

    A. DEERSLAYER   B. SACRED FONT
    C. RISE OF SILAS LAPHAM   D. FALL OF THE HOUSE OF USHER

6. Of the following, the one NOT an American historian is

    A. William Hickling Prescott
    B. George Bancroft
    C. Jared Sparks
    D. Charles Brockden Brown

7. The one of the following which is the name of the sailing vessel used in MOBY DICK is

    A. Hispaniola   B. Pequod
    C. Nevesink   D. Lucy Ann

8. The lines of Whittier,
   Let not the land once proud of him
   Insult him now,
   Nor brand with deeper shame his dim
   Dishonored brow,
   refer to

    A. Nathan Hale   B. Aaron Burr
    C. Benedict Arnold D. Daniel Webster

9. DRED, A TALE OF THE GREAT DISMAL SWAMP was written by the author of

   A. UNCLE TOM'S CABIN
   B. OMOO
   C. A SON OF THE MIDDLE BORDER
   D. THE LADY OF THE AROOSTOCK

10. Mabel L. Todd, T.W. Higginson, and Helen Hunt Jackson are names often associated with the name of

    A. Sara Teasdale
    B. Edna St. Vincent Millay
    C. Amy Lowell
    D. Emily Dickinson

11. Mark Twain did NOT write

    A. THE GILDED AGE
    B. THE SILVERADO SQUATTERS
    C. ROUGHING IT
    D. THE MAN THAT CORRUPTED HADLEYBURG

12. Of the following pairs of women writers, the pair which wrote about life below the Mason and Dixon line is

    A. Ellen Glasgow and Marjorie Kinnan Rawlings
    B. Edna Ferber and Agnes Repplier
    C. Mary Ellen Chase and Elizabeth Bowen
    D. Willa Cather and Edna St. Vincent Millay

13. The one of the following characters NOT created by Hawthorne is

    A. Billy Budd
    B. Robert Chillingworth
    C. Matthew Maule
    D. Donatello

14. Of the following, the one that is a pseudonym is

    A. Don Marquis
    B. Artemus Ward
    C. Sidney Porter
    D. Peter Finlay Dunn

15. The one of the following NOT a creation of Washington Irving is

    A. Diedrich Knickerbocker
    B. Tom Coffin
    C. King Boabdil of Granada
    D. Rip Van Winkle

16. Harvey Birch is a character in a novel by

    A. James Fenimore Cooper
    B. Herman Melville
    C. Nathaniel Hawthorne
    D. Mark Twain

17. In TO A WATERFOWL, Bryant

    A. saw nature's confirmation of the existence of omnipotent goodness
    B. expressed disapproval of bird shooting
    C. deplored the migration of birds to the South
    D. longed for the instinctive knowledge of a bird

18. The words *sink or swim, live or die, survive or perish, I give my hand and my heart to this vote* occurred in a speech by

    A. Lincoln B. Webster C. Calhoun D. Decatur

19. Martin Eden died

    A. in a train wreck
    B. of starvation
    C. of a bullet wound
    D. by drowning

20. THE BLITHEDALE ROMANCE dealt with life

    A. on Brook Farm
    B. in a New England seacoast village
    C. in a happy family
    D. in lower Fifth Avenue at the turn of the century

21. Of the following books, the one written by a male author was

    A. FRANKENSTEIN
    B. SCENES FROM CLERICAL LIFE
    C. OROONOKO
    D. CALEB WILLIAMS

22. Man's struggle against hostile forces of nature is the theme of all of the following EXCEPT

    A. GIANTS IN THE EARTH
    B. ARROWSMITH
    C. MOBY DICK
    D. WHITE TOWER

23. The one of the following plays NOT suggested by an earlier version of the same story is

    A. PYGMALION
    B. THE COCKTAIL PARTY
    C. CAROUSEL
    D. KISS ME, KATE

24. Of the following plays, the one which exemplifies a desirable father-son relationship is

    A. THE GREAT GOD BROWN
    B. STRANGE INTERLUDE
    C. AH! WILDERNESS
    D. THE EMPEROR JONES

25. *Powerful, western fallen star* is a reference to Lincoln appearing in

    A. O CAPTAIN! MY CAPTAIN
    B. LINCOLN, A MAN OF THE PEOPLE
    C. REMEMBRANCE ROCK
    D. WHEN LILACS LAST ON THE DOOR YARD BLOOM'D

KEY (CORRECT ANSWERS)

1. D
2. D
3. B
4. C
5. C

6. D
7. B
8. C
9. A
10. D

11. B
12. A
13. A
14. B
15. B

16. A
17. A
18. B
19. D
20. A

21. D
22. B
23. B
24. C
25. D

TEST 5

DIRECTIONS: Each question or incomplete statement is followed by several suggested answers or completions. Select the one that BEST answers the question or completes the statement. *PRINT THE LETTER OF THE CORRECT ANSWER IN THE SPACE AT THE RIGHT.*

1. The hero of MCTEAGUE, by Frank Norris, was a

   A. drayman
   B. longshoreman
   C. merchant
   D. dentist

2. There are important characters who are invisible to the audience in all of the following plays EXCEPT

   A. THE HAIRY APE
   B. PETER PAN
   C. MADWOMAN OF CHAILLOT
   D. EDWARD, MY SON

3. *A man can be God's mouthpiece* was an enunciated belief of

   A. A, Walt Whitman
   B. Charles Dickens
   C. Lincoln Steffens
   D. Oscar Wilde

4. The hero served a term in prison in

   A. THE FINANCIER
   B. SISTER CARRIE
   C. THE BULWARK
   D. JENNIE GERHARDT

5. THE ORDEAL OF MARK TWAIN, which provoked an honest reevaluation of the American cultural inheritance, was written by

   A. Randolph Bourne
   B. Van Wyck Brooks
   C. James Huneker
   D. Bernard de Voto

6. The one of the following who is a 19th century American dramatist is

   A. F. Marion Crawford
   B. Augustin Daly
   C. Paul Leicester Ford
   D. Meredith Nicholson

7. MAIN CURRENTS IN AMERICAN THOUGHT is a(n)

   A. history of American literature
   B. political compendium emphasizing the work of political writers
   C. survey of prose writers who shaped national thinking
   D. interpretation of the economic determinants of American literature

8. The quotation, *I went to the woods because I wished to live deliberately to front only the essential facts of life...* is from

   A. Walt Whitman
   B. Vachel Lindsay
   C. Henry David Thoreau
   D. James Fenimore Cooper

9. The lines,
   Lay me on an anvil, O God,
   Beat me and hammer me into a crowbar...
   are by

   A. Louis Untermeyer
   B. Robert Frost
   C. Edwin Markham
   D. Carl Sandburg

10. A milestone in the progress of naturalism in America was reached with the publication of   10.____

    A. DERE MABLE
    B. CONQUISTADOR
    C. THE RED BADGE OF COURAGE
    D. TO HAVE AND TO HOLD

11. Robert Jordan, in FOR WHOM THE BELL TOLLS, held on to life long enough to   11.____

    A. kill a lieutenant of the enemy forces
    B. marry Maria
    C. see his first-born son
    D. raise the flag of the Republic in Madrid

12. An IMPORTANT scene laid in the vaults of a New York bank occurs in Marquand's   12.____

    A. THE LATE GEORGE APLEY   B. B.F. 'S DAUGHTER
    C. SO LITTLE TIME   D. POINT OF NO RETURN

13. M' FINGAL is a(n)   13.____

    A. novel about an Irish pioneer in the Midwest
    B. account of the author's college days at Yale
    C. poem burlesquing American Tories
    D. tract advocating armed rebellion in the South

14. Babbitt accepted his son's marriage philosophically because he   14.____

    A. needed capital which Eunice's father could provide
    B. was relieved to have gossip so silenced
    C. admired the boy's courage in defying the wishes of the two families
    D. had secretly engineered the romance

15. LEAD, KINDLY, LIGHT is a(n)   15.____

    A. interpretation of Mahatma Gandhi's philosophy
    B. novel based on the life of Christ
    C. poem about a blind soldier
    D. biography of Cardinal Newman

16. In HOMEWARD BOUND, James Fenimore Cooper, after his return from Europe,   16.____

    A. expressed pleasure at the liberal influences at work in the United States
    B. recounted adventures which he had had abroad
    C. painted a romantic picture of life at sea
    D. criticized the extension of suffrage to classes unprepared for it

17. Vernon Louis Parrington's interpretation of literary history is based on a theory of   17.____

    A. economic determinism   B. aesthetic awareness
    C. social evolution   D. cultural cycles

18. Of the following statements, the one which does NOT apply to Clyde Griffiths, in Dreiser's AN AMERICAN TRAGEDY, is that he was

    A. the son of a street preacher
    B. the father of a baby boy
    C. tried for murder
    D. condemned to die in the electric chair

19. Of the following pairs of local colorists, the pair noted for portraying the same general region is

    A. Sarah Orne Jewett and Robert P. Tristram Coffin
    B. Charles Egbert Craddock and Joseph C. Lincoln
    C. Willa Cather and Mary E. Wilkins Freeman
    D. Sherwood Anderson and Thomas Nelson Page

20. The main characters in THE YOUNG LIONS are a(n)

    A. Jew, a Broadway producer, a Nazi
    B. Black, a Jew, a Nazi
    C. chaplain, a southern girl, a Black
    D. actress, an English general, a Nazi

21. Of the following novelists, the one whose stories are laid in pioneer days in Kentucky is

    A. Bess Streeter Aldrich
    B. Dorothy Canfield Fisher
    C. Ruth Suckow
    D. Elizabeth Madox Roberts

22. In THE GOLDEN DAY, Lewis Mumford interprets American culture through its

    A. imaginative literature
    B. art
    C. pioneer movements
    D. economic changes

23. Of the following statements, the one which can be associated MOST appropriately with *Brahminism* is:

    A. Literature should be the expression of the natural man
    B. True divinity dwells in the soul of each individual
    C. Literature belongs in the drawing room and the library, and it must observe the drawing room amenities
    D. Government should be the enactment of God's justice into human laws

24. The titles, authors, and characters are correctly matched for each of the following EXCEPT

    A. THE JUNGLE - Upton Sinclair - Jurgis Rudkus
    B. SISTER CARRIE - Theodore Dreiser - George Hurstwood
    C. THE PIT - Frank Norris - Curtis Jadwin
    D. MAIN STREET - Sinclair Lewis - Gustaf Sondelius

25. WINESBURG, OHIO is

    A. a collection of short stories about twisted village personalities
    B. a novel about a girl's escape from a small mill town
    C. the autobiography of Sherwood Anderson
    D. the story of the growth of a typical American tow

KEY (CORRECT ANSWERS)

1. D
2. A
3. A
4. A
5. B

6. B
7. A
8. C
9. D
10. C

11. A
12. D
13. C
14. C
15. A

16. D
17. A
18. B
19. A
20. A

21. D
22. A
23. C
24. D
25. A

EXAMINATION SECTION
TEST 1

DIRECTIONS: Each question or incomplete statement is followed by several suggested answers or completions. Select the one that BEST answers the question or completes the statement. *PRINT THE LETTER OF THE CORRECT ANSWER IN THE SPACE AT THE RIGHT.*

Questions 1-3.

DIRECTIONS: Questions 1 through 3 are to be answered on the basis of the following passage.

The young lady inspected her flounces and smoothed her ribbons again; and Winterbourne presently risked an observation upon the beauty of the view. He was ceasing to be embarrassed, for he had begun to perceive that she was not in the least embarrassed herself...He had a great relish for feminine beauty; he was addicted to observing and analysing it; and as regards this young lady's face he made several observations. It was not all insipid, but it was not exactly expressive; and though it was eminently delicate Winterbourne mentally accused it – very forgivingly – of a want of finish.

1. This passage is taken from

    A. THE HOUSE OF MIRTH
    B. THE TURN OF THE SCREW
    C. DAISY MILLER
    D. THE BEAST IN THE JUNGLE

2. The description, *It was not all insipid, but it was not exactly expressive,* mainly implies that

    A. although not ignorant, neither was her face particularly open or revealing
    B. her face revealed a great deal of emotional reservation
    C. her face revealed a degree of ignorance
    D. although not honest, her face was not ignorant

3. In the final phrase of the passage, the word *want* most nearly means

    A. need for
    B. overabundance
    C. desiring of
    D. lack

4. Which of the following writers wrote TO BE YOUNG, GIFTED AND BLACK and A RAISIN IN THE SUN?

    A. Gwendolyn Brooks
    B. Alice Walker
    C. Maya Angelou
    D. Lorraine Hansberry

5. In the short story A JURY OF HER PEERS, by Susan Glaspell, the canary symbolizes Mrs. Wright's

    A. lost youth
    B. death
    C. rage
    D. sorrow

6. Edith Wharton's HOUSE OF MIRTH focuses primarily on the

    A. class constraints presented to underclass women in turn-of-the-century Manhattan
    B. triumph of an underclass woman who rises to the heights of Manhattan society

- C. demise of a young woman who fails to adjust to the emotional constraints of upper-class society
- D. demise of a young woman who married for love rather than security

7. Toni Morrison wrote which of the following?

   A. THE COLOR PURPLE
   B. BELOVED
   C. THEIR EYES WERE WATCHING GOD
   D. All of the above

8. Sherwood Anderson, Gertrude Stein, and F. Scott Fitzgerald are commonly described by literary historians as

   A. colonialists
   B. realists
   C. romantics
   D. modernists

9. This poet gained national fame for his dialect poetry which depicted the idealized plantation life of slaves.

   A. James Baldwin
   B. Paul Laurence Dunbar
   C. Joel Chandler Harris
   D. George Washington Cable

10. NOTICE

    Persons attempting to find a motive in this narrative will be prosecuted; persons attempting to find a moral in it will be banished; persons attempting to find a plot in it will be shot.

    The above forward is found in which American masterpiece?

    A. THE ADVENTURES OF HUCKLEBERRY FINN
    B. THE ADVENTURES OF TOM SAWYER
    C. WALDEN
    D. BENITO CERENO

11. THE CRYING OF LOT 49 was written by

    A. Donald Bartheleme
    B. Norman Mailer
    C. Don Delillo
    D. Thomas Pynchon

Questions 12-15.

DIRECTIONS: Questions 12 through 15 are to be answered on the basis of the following passage.

Those Winter Sundays, Robert Hayden

*Sundays too my father got up early
and put his clothes on in the blueblack cold,
then with cracked hands that ached
from labor in the weekday weather made
banked fires blazed. No one ever thanked him.*

*I'd wake and hear the cold splintering, breaking.
When the rooms were warm, he 'd call,*

and slowly I would rise and dress,,
fearing the chronic angers of that house,

Speaking indifferently to him,
who had driven out the cold
and polished my good shoes as well.
What did I know, what did I know
of love's austere and lonely offices?

12. Lines 2 and 3 rely primarily on

    A. assonance
    B. alliteration
    C. iambic pentameter
    D. end rhyme

13. What is the meaning of *austere* as it is used in the last line of the poem?

    A. Stern
    B. Forbidding
    C. Disciplined
    D. Poor

14. What is the meaning of *offices* as it is used in the last line of the poem?

    A. Places of work
    B. Prestigious positions
    C. Titles
    D. Responsibilities

15. The theme of THOSE WINTER SUNDAYS is best stated that as a(n)

    A. adult, the narrator now fears his father
    B. adult, the narrator now understands his father's expressions of love
    C. child, the narrator was abused by his father
    D. child, the boy understood his father's expression of love

16. Whom of the following is the Sioux Medicine Man whose great vision of the end of the world was translated by John Niehardt?

    A. Black Elk
    B. Standing Bear
    C. Charles Alexander Eastman
    D. Mourning Dove

17. In A FAREWELL TO ARMS, Frederic Henry works as a(n)

    A. newspaper reporter
    B. mercenary soldier
    C. ambulance driver
    D. spy

Questions 18-20.

DIRECTIONS: Questions 18 through 20 are to be answered on the basis of the following passage.

Some years ago -- never mind how long precisely -- having little or no money in my purse, and nothing particular to interest me on shore, I thought I would sail about a little and see the watery part of the world.
Whenever I find myself growing grim about the mouth; whenever it is a damp, drizzly November in my soul; whenever I find myself involuntarily pausing before coffin warehouses,

and bringing up the rear of every funeral I meet; and especially whenever my hypos get such an upper hand of me, that it requires a strong moral principle to prevent me from deliberately stepping into the street, and methodically knocking people's hats off -- then, I account it high time to get to sea as soon as I can.

18. The sentences above are taken from the opening pages of 18.____

   A. THE SCARLET LETTER B. MOBY DICK
   C. WALDEN D. NATURE

19. The *watery part of the world* refers to 19.____

   A. the tropical islands
   B. weeping
   C. the sea
   D. England, where it rains all winter

20. The phrase *growing grim about the mouth* is best paraphrased by which of the following? 20.____

   A. Tired of the city B. Physically ill
   C. Overcome with rage D. Overcome with depression

21. Which of the following poets wrote THE BEAN EATERS, A BLACK WEDDING SONG, THE RITES FOR COUSIN VIT, and WE REAL COOL? 21.____

   A. Langston Hughes B. Gwendolyn Brooks
   C. Zora Neale Hurston D. Audre Lorde

22. The generation of writers which includes Hemingway, Dos Passes, and T.S. Eliot is referred to as the 22.____

   A. Lost Generation B. Romantics
   C. Minimalists D. Post-modernists

23. Which of the following writers is NOT among those writing and publishing at the end of the 19th century and beginning of the 20th? 23.____

   A. Kate Chopin B. Willa Cather
   C. Edith Wharton D. Zora Neale Hurston

24. Which of the following stories written by Washington Irving is based on a German folktale Irving discovered while living in England? 24.____

   A. RIP VAN WINKLE
   B. THE LEGEND OF SLEEPY HOLLOW
   C. THE SKETCH BOOK
   D. TALES OF A TRAVELER

Questions 25-28.

DIRECTIONS: Questions 25 through 28 are to be answered on the basis of the following passage.

I Saw in Louisiana A Live Oak Growing, Walt Whitman

I saw in Louisiana a live-oak growing,

All alone stood it and the moss hung down from the branches,
Without any companion it grew there uttering joyous leaves of dark green,
And its look, rude, unbending, lusty, made me think of myself,
But I wonder'd how it could utter joyous leaves standing alone there without its friend near, for I knew I could not,
And I broke off a twig with a certain number of leaves upon it, and twined around it a little moss,
And brought it away, and I have placed it in sight in my room,
It is not needed to remind me as of my own dear friends,
(For I believe lately I think of little else than of them,)
Yet it remains to me a curious token, it makes me think of manly love;
For all that, and though the live-oak glistens there in Louisiana solitary in a wide flat space,
Uttering joyous leaves all its life without a friend a lover near,
I know very well I could not.

25. In the poem above, the live-oak tree represents

    A. a loneliness the narrator could not endure
    B. the narrator's sense of loneliness
    C. the loneliness of mankind isolated from nature
    D. death

26. The line, *uttering joyous leaves of dark green,* depends mainly on

    A. end rhyme
    B. iambic pentameter
    C. assonance
    D. alliteration

27. The poem above is written in

    A. iambic pentameter
    B. free verse
    C. Shakespearean sonnet form
    D. villanelle form

28. Which of the following images advances the theme of loneliness throughout the poem?

    A. The plain upon which the tree grows
    B. Branches
    C. Moss
    D. Leaves

29. Who is the poet whose poems include THE RAVEN, DREAMLAND, and THE VALLEY OF UNREST?

    A. John Greenleaf Whittier
    B. Edgar Allan Poe
    C. Henry Wadsworth Longfellow
    D. T.S. Eliot

30. Who is the poet whose poems include DADD, METAPHORS, and THE MAGIC MOUNTAINS?

    A. Adrienne Rich
    B. Muriel Rukeyser
    C. Sylvia Plath
    D. Anne Sexton

31. Which of the following stories written by Nathaniel Hawthorne is an allegorical tale about artistic endeavor and struggle?

    A. YOUNG GOODMAN BROWN
    B. THE ARTIST OF THE BEAUTIFUL
    C. RAPPACCINI'S DAUGHTER
    D. THE MAYPOLE OF MERRY MOUNT

32. *During the whole of a dull, dark, and soundless day in the autumn of the year, when the clouds hung oppressively low in the heavens, I had been passing alone, on horseback, through a singularly dreary tract of country; and at length found myself, as the shades of the evening drew on, within view of the melancholy house.*
    The lines above open the short story entitled THE

    A. TELL-TALE HEART
    B. CASK OF AMONTILLADO
    C. PURLOINED LETTER
    D. FALL OF THE HOUSE OF USHER

33. Who is the poet whose poems include TO MY DEAR CHILDREN, CONTEMPLATIONS, and THE FLESH AND THE SPIRIT?

    A. Phillis Wheatley
    B. Anne Bradstreet
    C. Elizabeth Barret Browning
    D. Emily Dickinson

34. *Dear Son,*
    I have ever had a Pleasure in obtaining any little Anecdotes of my Ancestors. You may remember the Enquiries I made among the Remains of my Relations when you were with me in England; and the Journey I took for that purpose. Now imagining it may be equally agreeable to you to know the Circumstances of my Life, many of which you are yet unacquainted with; and expecting a Week's uninterrupted leisure in my present Country Retirement, I sit down to write them for you.
    The above lines open which of the following books?

    A. CIVIL DISOBEDIENCE
    B. WALDEN POND
    C. RULES BY WHICH A GREAT EMPIRE MAY BE REDUCED TO A SMALL ONE
    D. THE AUTOBIOGRAPHY OF BENJAMIN FRANKLIN

35. Which of the following poets' work is characterized by the use of degraded cities to explore themes of death, rebirth, and love?

    A. T.S. Eliot
    B. W.H. Auden
    C. William Carlos Williams
    D. Wallace Stevens

36. Which American writer had an ancestor who served as a judge during the Salem witchcraft trials?

    A. Ralph Waldo Emerson
    B. Herman Melville
    C. Walt Whitman
    D. Nathaniel Hawthorne

37. Which of the following men wrote THE WONDERS OF THE INVISIBLE WORLD and A PEOPLE OF GOD IN THE DEVIL'S TERRITORIES?

    A. Edward Taylor
    B. Cotton Mather
    C. Jonathon Edwards
    D. Roger Williams

38. Originally published in New York newspapers, this work was written to convince citizens of New York state to adopt the new Constitution.

    A. THE FEDERALIST
    B. COMMON SENSE
    C. THE DECLARATION OF INDEPENDENCE
    D. THE HASTY PUDDING

39. Who wrote the short story, AN OCCURRENCE AT OWL-CREEK BRIDGE?

    A. Paul Bowles
    B. Ernest Hemingway
    C. Stephen Crane
    D. Ambrose Bierce

40. *The thousand injuries of Fortunato I had borne as I best could, but when he ventured upon insult I vowed revenge. You, who so well know the nature of my soul, will not suppose, however, that I gave utterance to a threat.*
    At length I would be avenged; this was a point definitively settled -- but the very definitiveness with which it was resolved precluded the idea or risk. I must not only punish but punish with impunity.
    The lines above open the short story entitled THE

    A. TELL-TALE HEART
    B. CASK OF AMONTILLADO
    C. FALL OF THE HOUSE OF USHER
    D. PURLOINED LETTER

41. Which of the following writers wrote THE BEAST IN THE JUNGLE, THE GREAT GOOD PLACE, and THE TURN OF THE SCREW?

    A. Edith Wharton
    B. H. Lawrence
    C. William James
    D. Henry James

42. The narrative written by Mrs. Mary Rowlandson recounts her

    A. struggle to gain rights for women
    B. marriage to her famous husband
    C. captivity among Native Americans
    D. daily life as an English colonist

43. Louise Erdrich wrote which of the following?

    A. THE WAY TO RAINY MOUNTAIN
    B. LOVE MEDICINE

C. BELOVED
D. CEREMONY

44. Which of the following poets wrote BOAT! BOAT! DRUMS!, CAVALRY CROSSING A FORD, and O CAPTAIN! MY CAPTAIN!?

    A. Walt Whitman
    B. Emily Dickinson
    C. Henry Wadsworth Longfellow
    D. Zora Neale Hurston

45. Which of the following best describes THE SOUND AND THE FURY? A(n)

    A. exploration of a woman's spiritual awakening within the confines of a small Southern town
    B. exploration of the rise and fall of a mythic plantation family in a small Southern town
    C. dramatization of a family's efforts to return the mother's body home for burial
    D. exploration of the decline of a family and culture told in three successive narratives

46. Which of the following writers had the greatest influence on Walt Whitman?

    A. Ralph Waldo Emerson
    B. Henry David Thoreau
    C. Nathaniel Hawthorne
    D. Edgar Allan Poe

47. What is the title of the first pamphlet published in this country urging immediate and complete independence from England?

    A. THE DECLARATION OF INDEPENDENCE
    B. COMMON SENSE
    C. THE HASTY PUDDING
    D. THE CRISIS

48. Who was the African-American leader whose life and work came to embody the American dream of a poor child who achieves success through hard work and dedication?

    A. Langston Hughes
    B. Paul Laurence Dunbar
    C. Booker T. Washington
    D. W.E.B. DeBois

49. Which of the following writers wrote the poem THE DAY OF DOOM, considered the most popular poem ever written in America?

    A. Michael Wigglesworth
    B. Henry Wadsworth Longfellow
    C. Walt Whitman
    D. Edgar Allan Poe

50. Which of the following novels has as its primary focus the life of a young black woman in the American South?

    A. MY MORTAL ENEMY
    B. NIGHTWOOD
    C. THEIR EYES WERE WATCHING GOD
    D. THE AWAKENING

KEY (CORRECT ANSWERS)

1. C	11. D	21. B	31. B	41. D
2. A	12. B	22. A	32. D	42. C
3. D	13. C	23. D	33. B	43. B
4. D	14. D	24. A	34. D	44. A
5. A	15. B	25. A	35. A	45. D
6. C	16. A	26. C	36. D	46. A
7. B	17. C	27. B	37. B	47. B
8. D	18. B	28. D	38. A	48. C
9. B	19. C	29. B	39. D	49. A
10. A	20. D	30. C	40. B	50. C

TEST 2

DIRECTIONS: Each question or incomplete statement is followed by several suggested answers or completions. Select the one that BEST answers the question or completes the statement. *PRINT THE LETTER OF THE CORRECT ANSWER IN THE SPACE AT THE RIGHT.*

Questions 1-5.

DIRECTIONS: Questions 1 through 5 are to be answered on the basis of the following passage.

Stopping By the Woods on a Snowy Evening

Whose woods these are I think I know.
His house is in the village though;
He will not see me stopping here
To watch his woods fill up with snow.

My little horse must think it queer
To stop without a farmhouse near
Between the woods and frozen lake
The darkest evening of the year

He gives his harness bells a shake
To ask if there is some mistake.
The only other sound's the sweep
Of easy wind and downy flake.

The woods are lovely, dark and deep,
But I have promises to keep,
And miles to go before I sleep,
And miles to go before I sleep.

1. The author of this poem is

   A. William Auden　　　　B. Robert Frost
   C. Robert Penn Warren　　D. Robert Hayden

2. In the first line of the second stanza, the word *queer* is used to mean

   A. unusual　　B. usual
   C. exciting　　D. frightening

3. The repetition of the final lines in this poem suggests what on the part of the narrator?

   A. Boredom　　　B. Fear
   C. Enthusiasm　　D. Weariness

4. The last stanza of the poem relies primarily on

   A. iambic pentameter　　B. alliteration
   C. end rhyme　　　　　　D. internal rhyme

5. The woods in this poem primarily symbolize 5.____

   A. death   B. life   C. despair   D. hope

6. John Dos Passos is famous for writing which of the following? 6.____

   A. BABBITT
   B. TENDER IS THE NIGHT
   C. THE OPEN BOAT
   D. THE U.S. TRILOGY

7. Which of the following poets wrote THE CAPTURED GODDESS; VENUS TRANSIENS, MEETING-HOUSE HILL, and NEW HEAVENS FOR OLD? 7.____

   A. Emily Dickinson
   B. Denise Levertov
   C. Amy Lowell
   D. Sylvia Plath

8. Which of the following early American writers was the first to demonstrate that memorable and sophisticated fiction could be set in the United States? 8.____

   A. Washington Irving
   B. Booker T. Washington
   C. Oliver Wendell Holmes
   D. Henry Wadsworth Longfellow

9. Which of the following writers wrote a famous review of Nathaniel Hawthorne's TWICE-TOLD TALES, which influenced the shape of the American short story? 9.____

   A. Edgar Allan Poe
   B. Herman Melville
   C. Walt Whitman
   D. Ralph Waldo Emerson

10. In this novel, a young boy grows to respect the humanity of a runaway slave, although this acceptance goes against everything the boy has been taught about slaves and human nature in general. 10.____

    A. THE ADVENTURES OF TOM SAWYER
    B. THE ADVENTURE OF HUCKLEBERRY FINN
    C. LITTLE MEN
    D. UNCLE TOM'S CABIN

11. THE GREAT GATSBY is mainly an indictment of 11.____

    A. societal constraints
    B. class consciousness
    C. materialism
    D. the American dream of success

12. The novel BELOVED has as its main focus the 12.____

    A. life of an African-American woman who overcomes abuse at the hands of her stepfather and husband
    B. life of a runaway slave woman who decides to kill her child rather than let it be returned to slavery
    C. experiences of a slave on a Southern plantation before the Civil War
    D. experiences of an ex-slave searching for the woman he loves after the Civil War

13. Which of the following stories written by Nathaniel Hawthorne focuses on the arrogance of a young man who seeks adventure beyond the boundaries of his daily experience and foolishly underestimates the obstacles before him?

    A. THE ARTIST OF THE BEAUTIFUL
    B. RAPPACCINI'S DAUGHTER
    C. MY KINSMAN, MAJOR MOLINEUX
    D. YOUNG GOODMAN BROWN

14. Which of the following poets wrote THE YELLOW, THANATOPSIS, THE PRAIRIES, and VIOLET?

    A. Walt Whitman
    B. William Cullen Bryant
    C. Hart Crane
    D. T.S. Eliot

Questions 15-17.

DIRECTIONS: Questions 15 through 17 are to be answered on the basis of the following passage.

The Day of Doom

Still was the night, serene and bright,
  when all men sleeping lay;
Calm was the season, and carnal reason
  thought so 'twould last for aye.

Soul, take thine ease, let sorrow cease,
  much good thou has in store;
This was their song, their cups among,
  the evening before.

15. The lines above are written in

    A. free verse
    B. Finnish folk meter
    C. common hymn meter
    D. iambic pentameter

16. In line 3, the phrase *carnal reason* refers to

    A. physical desire
    B. spiritual desire
    C. spiritual reason
    D. physical debilitation

17. In line 4 of the poem, the word *aye* is used to mean

    A. often   B. sometimes   C. never   D. ever

18. Considered the first successful American novelist, this writer's works included PRECAUTION, LAST OF THE MOHICANS, and THE PILOT.

    A. James Fennimore Cooper
    B. Henry Wadsworth Longfellow
    C. Ralph Waldo Emerson
    D. Herman Melville

19. The feminist writer who is best known for portraying the lives and voices of working-class men and women in New York City.   19.____

    A. Grace Paley
    B. Toni Morrison
    C. Joyce Carol Oates
    D. Flannery O'Connor

20. Which of the following novels has as its main focus the efforts of a poor family to bury their mother forty miles from home?   20.____

    A. THE GRAPES OF WRATH
    B. THE SUN ALSO RISES
    C. AS I LAY DYING
    D. A LIGHT IN AUGUST

21. Which of the following poets is best known for the originality of her poetry and its unconventional system of punctuation?   21.____

    A. Elizabeth Barrett Browning
    B. Sylvia Plath
    C. Emily Dickinson
    D. Anne Sexton

22. THE NAKED AND THE DEAD has as its main focus the experiences of a young man during   22.____

    A. the Civil War
    B. World War I
    C. World War II
    D. the Vietnam War

23. Which of the following essays focuses on the variety of religious experiences open to man?   23.____

    A. THE POET
    B. SELF-RELIANCE
    C. NATURE
    D. THE OVER-SOUL

Questions 24-25.

DIRECTIONS: Questions 24 and 25 are to be answered on the basis of the following passage.

Thoughts on the Works of Providence

Arise, my soul, on wings enraptured, rise
To praise the monarch of the earth and skies,
Whose goodness and beneficence appear
As round its center moves the rolling year,
Or when the mourning glows with rosy charms,
Or the sun slumbers in the ocean's arms:
Of light divine by a rich portion lent
To guide my soul, and favor my intent.
Celestial muse, my arduous flight sustain,
And raise my mind to a seraphic strain!

24. The stanza above depends mainly upon the metaphor of   24.____

    A. flight   B. angels   C. clouds   D. wind

25. The *monarch of the earth and skies* in line 2 refers to   25.____

   A. angels   B. the stars   C. God   D. the sun

26. The novel THE RED BADGE OF COURAGE was written by   26.____

   A. Stephen Crane   B. William Dean Howells
   C. Ernest Hemingway   D. Jack London

Questions 27-30.

DIRECTIONS: Questions 27 through 30 are to be answered on the basis of the following passage.
From, *The White Heron*

Now look down again, Sylvia where the green marsh is set among the shining birches and dark hemlocks; there where you saw the white heron once you will see him again; look, look! a white spot of him like a single floating feather comes up from the dead hemlock and grows larger, and rises, and comes close at last, and goes by the landmark pine with steady sweep of wing and outstretched slender neck and crested head. (1) And wait! wait! do not move a foot or a finger, little girl, do not send an arrow of light and consciousness from your two eager eyes, for the heron has perched on a pine bough not far beyond yours and cries back to his mate on the nest and plumes his feathers for the new day!(2)

The child gives a long sigh a minute later when a company of shouting cat-birds comes also to the tree, and vexed by their flutterings and lawlessness the solemn heron goes away.(3)

27. In sentence 2, the phrase, *do not send an arrow of light and consciousness from your two eager eyes,* mainly implies that   27.____

   A. the intensity of Sylvia's excitement can be felt or sensed even if she remains still
   B. Sylvia is dreaming this image
   C. Sylvia has to close her eyes in order to hide her presence from the heron
   D. Sylvia intends to kill the heron

28. In sentence 3, *lawlessness* most nearly means   28.____

   A. unprecedented in the natural world
   B. beyond the boundaries of natural behavior
   C. loud, chaotic behavior
   D. violent attacks

29. In this passage, the heron mainly symbolizes   29.____

   A. joy   B. defeat   C. death   D. purity

30. The author of this story is   30.____

   A. Willa Cather   B. Sarah Orne Jewett
   C. Mary Wilkins Freeman D. Charlotte Perkins Gilman

31. Which of the following works was NOT written by Louisa May Alcott?   31.____

   A. MOODS
   B. THE FOREIGNER

C. WORK: A STORY OF EXPERIENCE
D. HOSPITAL SKETCHES

32. The Harlem Renaissance took place during the

    A. 1860's and 1870's
    B. 1890's and early 1900's
    C. 1920's and 1930's
    D. 1960's and 1970's

33. Which of the following novellas has as its primary focus the destruction of a young American woman traveling in Europe?

    A. DAISY MILLER
    B. MY MORTAL ENEMY
    C. THE TURN OF THE SCREW
    D. THE AGE OF GRIEF

34. For which of his contemporaries did Ralph Waldo Emerson compose a now-famous and widely-read eulogy?

    A. Herman Melville
    B. Walt Whitman
    C. Henry David Thoreau
    D. Emily Dickinson

35. In which of the following did Edgar Allan Poe outline his philosophy for short stories, calling for writers to decide upon a *desired effect* before inventing incidents to narrate?

    A. THE IMP OF THE PERVERSE
    B. THE POETIC PRINCIPLE
    C. THE PHILOSOPHY OF COMPOSITION
    D. A review of TWICE-TOLD TALES

36. Which Henry James novel explores themes of masculine aloofness by examining the lives of two young men living in London?

    A. THE BEAST IN THE JUNGLE
    B. DAISY MILLER
    C. THE TURN OF THE SCREW
    D. WASHINGTON SQUARE

37. The Ghost Dance vision which swept the Indian tribes on the Plains during the late 19th century led to which of the following events?
    The

    A. defeat of Custer
    B. massacre at Wounded Knee
    C. defeat of Crazy Horse
    D. beginning of reservation relocation

38. Which of the following is a short story which details a man's life in the moments just before his execution?

    A. AN OCCURRENCE AT OWL CREEK BRIDGE
    B. THE OPEN BOAT
    C. HILLS LIKE WHITE ELEPHANTS
    D. THE FLOWERING JUDAS

39. Which of the following authors wrote PALE HORSE, PALE RIDER, SHIP OF FOOLS, and OLD MORTALITY?

    A. Kate Chopin
    B. Katherine Anne Porter
    C. F. Scott Fitzgerald
    D. Stephen Crane

40. The era of literature defined by its stylistic innovations, disregard for traditional syntax and mixture of different genres is known as the _____ period.

   A. realistic
   B. contemporary
   C. romantic
   D. modern

41. This poet coined the phrase "make it new" to summarize the ideals of modern writers.

   A. Langston Hughes
   B. Gertrude Stein
   C. Ezra Pound
   D. T.S. Eliot

42. In the short story YOUNG GOODMAN BROWN, by Nathaniel Hawthorne, the main character's wife is named

   A. Faith
   B. Hope
   C. Charity
   D. Justice

Questions 43-46.

DIRECTIONS: Questions 43 through 46 are to be answered on the basis of the following passage.

From, *Old Woman Magoun*

The hamlet of Barry's Ford is situated in a sort of high valley among the mountains. (1) Below it the hills lie in moveless curves like a petrified ocean; above it they rise in green-cresting Waves which never break. (2) It is Barry's Ford because at one time the Barry family was the most important in the place; and Ford because just at the beginning of the hamlet the little turbulent Barry River is fordable. (3) There is, however, now a rude bridge across the river. (4)

Old Woman Magoun was largely instrumental in bringing the bridge to pass. (5) She haunted the miserable little grocery, wherein whiskey and hands of tobacco were the most salient features of the stock in trade, and she talked much. (6) She would elbow herself into the midst of a knot of idlers and talk. (7)

43. The author of this short story is

   A. Kate Chopin
   B. Sarah Orne Jewett
   C. Mary Wilkins Freeman
   D. Alice Dunbar-Nelson

44. Sentences 1 and 2 in the passage above depend mainly on

   A. irony
   B. allegory
   C. metaphor
   D. simile

45. In sentence 4, the word *rude* is used to mean

   A. rough
   B. dangerous
   C. large
   D. temporary

46. In sentence 6, the phrase *most salient features* mainly implies

   A. illegal purchases
   B. the most common commodities
   C. stolen goods
   D. the most expensive commodities

47. James Baldwin wrote all of the following EXCEPT
    A. SONNY'S BLUES
    B. INVISIBLE MAN
    C. THE FIRE NEXT TIME
    D. WHAT IT MEANS TO BE AN AMERICAN

48. Who is the Cherokee writer credited with finding a national audience, for the first time, for details about life in the Indian Territory. His works include OLD HARJO and WHEN THE GRASS GREW LONG.
    A. Mourning Dove
    B. John Niehardt
    C. John Milton Oskison
    D. Black Elk

49. *I was born a slave on a plantation in Franklin County, Virginia. I am not quite sure of the exact place or exact date of my birth, but at any rate I suspect I must have been born somewhere and at some time. As nearly as I have been able to learn, I was born near a crossroads post office called Hale's Ford, and the year was 1858 or 1859. I do not know the month or the day. The earliest impressions I can now recall are of the plantation and the slave quarters -- the latter being the part of the plantation where the slaves had their cabins.*
    These lines open

    A. UNCLE REMUS: HIS SONGS AND SAYINGS
    B. LIFT EVERY VOICE AND SING
    C. THE SOULS OF BLACK FOLK
    D. UP FROM SLAVERY

50. Who wrote COMMON SENSE and THE CRISIS?
    A. Thomas Jefferson
    B. Thomas Paine
    C. Benjamin Franklin
    D. John Adams

KEY (CORRECT ANSWERS)

1. B	11. D	21. C	31. B	41. C
2. A	12. B	22. C	32. C	42. A
3. D	13. C	23. D	33. A	43. C
4. C	14. B	24. A	34. C	44. D
5. A	15. C	25. C	35. D	45. A
6. D	16. A	26. A	36. A	46. B
7. C	17. D	27. A	37. B	47. B
8. A	18. A	28. C	38. A	48. C
9. A	19. A	29. D	39. B	49. D
10. B	20. C	30. B	40. D	50. B

TEST 3

DIRECTIONS: Each question or incomplete statement is followed by several suggested answers or completions. Select the one that BEST answers the question or completes the statement. *PRINT THE LETTER OF THE CORRECT ANSWER IN THE SPACE AT THE RIGHT.*

1. In MOBY DICK, which of the following characters is obsessed by his search for the great white whale?   1.____

    A. Ahab
    B. Ishmael
    C. Quuqueg
    D. All of the characters are equally obsessed by the search

2. Who wrote the following poems: THEME FOR ENGLISH B, DREAM DEFERRED, HOMECOMING, DREAM BOOGIE?   2.____

    A. Audre Lorde
    B. Cummings
    C. Gwendolyn Brooks
    D. Langston Hughes

Questions 3-5.

DIRECTIONS: Questions 3 through 5 are to be answered on the basis of the following passage.

From, A ROSE FOR EMILY

When Miss Emily Grierson died, our whole town went to her funeral: the men through a sort of respectful affection for a fallen monument, the women mostly out of curiosity to see the inside of her house, which no one save an old manservant -- a combined gardener and cook -- had seen in at least ten years. (1)

It was a big, squarish frame house that had once been white, decorated with cupolas and spires and scrolled balconies in the heavily lightsome style of the seventies, set on what had once been our most select street. (2) But garages and cotton gins had encroached and obliterated even the august names of that neighborhood; only Miss Emily's house was left, lifting its stubborn and coquettish decay above the cotton wagons and the gasoline pumps -- an eyesore among eyesores. (3) And now Miss Emily had gone to join the representatives of those august names where they lay in the cedar-bemused cemetery among the ranked and anonymous graves of Union and Confederate soldiers who fell at the battle of Jefferson.(4)

3. In this story, Miss Emily represents   3.____

    A. the old South
    B. the new South
    C. outdated Christian values
    D. the industrial North

4. In sentence 3, *coquettish* most nearly means   4.____

    A. decadent
    B. innocent
    C. childish
    D. flirtatious

5. Which of the following best describes the speaker's attitude toward Miss Emily? 5.____

   A. Pity B. Disgust C. Curiosity D. Anger

6. N. Scott Momaday wrote which of the following? 6.____

   A. CEREMONY
   B. BLESS ME, ULTIMA
   C. THE WAY TO RAINY MOUNTAIN
   D. LOVE MEDICINE

7. Which of the following novels focuses on the tribulations of a family of migrants as they make their way to California? 7.____

   A. TENDER IS THE NIGHT B. A LIGHT IN AUGUST
   C. THE SUN ALSO RISES D. THE GRAPES OF WRATH

8. In THE SCARLET LETTER, the heroine, Hester Prynne, is forced to wear which of the following identifying symbols? 8.____

   A. S, for Seductress B. A, for Adultery
   C. B, for Betrayer D. W, for Witch

9. This playwright's realistic portrayal of the lives of downtrodden characters caused him to be censored, but also paved the way for later playwrights like Arthur Miller and Tennessee Williams. 9.____

   A. Eugene O'Neill B. Theodore Dreiser
   C. Hart Crane D. Cummings

10. In the novel THE AWAKENING, the sea symbolizes 10.____

    A. the constraints of society
    B. an element of nature that encourages deep reflection
    C. an element of nature that is violent and oppressive
    D. the constraints of marriage

11. The style of writing in ON THE ROAD is best described as 11.____

    A. fantasy B. realism
    C. magic realism D. stream of consciousness

Questions 12-15.

DIRECTIONS: Questions 12 through 15 are to be answered on the basis of the following passage.

Fairyland, Edgar Allan Poe

Dim vales-and shadowy floods -
And cloudy-looking woods,
Whose forms we can't discover
For the tears that drip all over.
5 *Huge moons there wax and wane -*
Again—again—again
Ev 'ry moment of the night

*For ever changing places
And they put out the star-light*
10 *With the breath from their pale faces;
About twelve by the moon-dial
One, more filmy than the rest
(A sort which, upon trial,
They have found to be the best)*
15 *Comes down-still down-and down
With its centre on the crown
Of a mountain's circumference
In easy drapery falls
Over hamlets, and rich halls,*
20 *Wherever they may be -
O'er the strange woods-o'er the sea -
Over spirits on the wing
Over every drowsy thing -
And buries them up quite*
25 *In a labyrinth of light -
And then, how deep! O! deep!
Is the passion of their sleep!
In the morning they arise,
And their moony covering*
30 *Is soaring in the skies,
With the tempests as they toss,
Like-almost anything -
Or a yellow Albatross
They use that moon no more*
35 *For the same end as before -
Videlicet a tent -
Which I think extravagant:
It atomies, however,
Into a shower dissever,*
40 *Of which those butterflies,
Of Earth, who seek the skies,
And so come down again,
(The unbelieving things!)
Have brought a specimen*
45 *Upon their quivering wings.*

12. Which of the following serves as the primary image in this poem?   12._____

    A. Butterflies   B. Tents
    C. Moonlight   D. Dew

13. In lines 5 and 6, the rhyme scheme relies on which of the following?   13._____

    A. Latin meter   B. Iambic pentameter
    C. Alliteration   D. Assonance

14. In line 39, the word *dissever* most nearly means   14._____

    A. glimmer   B. explode   C. glitter   D. fall

15. Which of the following serves as the final image in this poem? 15.____

    A. Moonlight on butterfly wings
    B. The moon hovering above a mountain
    C. Moonlight on water
    D. The moon as it shines upon a tent

16. Of the following writers, whose work is mainly known for examining the corrupting influences of society by introducing naive Americans to highly sophisticated social circles, often in Europe? 16.____

    A. Nathaniel Hawthorne   B. H. Lawrence
    C. Edith Wharton   D. Henry James

Questions 17-19.

DIRECTIONS: Questions 17 through 19 are to be answered on the basis of the following passage.

The dark uniforms of the men were so coated with dust from the incessant wrestling of the two armies that the regiment almost seemed a part of the clay bank which shielded them from the shells. (1) On the top of the hill a battery was arguing in tremendous roars with some other guns and to the eye of the infantry, the artillerymen, the guns, the caissons, the horses, were distinctly outlined upon the blue sky. (2) When a piece was fired a red streak as round as a log flashed low in the heavens, like a monstrous bolt of lightning. (3) The men of the battery wore white duck trousers, which somehow emphasized their legs, and when they ran and crowded in little groups at the bidding of the shouting officers, it was more impressive than usual to the infantry. (4)

17. The imagery in sentence 1 mainly suggests 17.____

    A. timeless struggle   B. death
    C. peace   D. timeless hatred

18. Sentence 2 in the passage above depends mainly on 18.____

    A. irony   B. allegory   C. metaphor   D. simile

19. In sentence 3, the phrase *as round as a log* is an example of 19.____

    A. allegory   B. alliteration
    C. metaphor   D. simile

Questions 20-21.

DIRECTIONS: Questions 20 and 21 are to be answered on the basis of the following passage.

We wear the mask that grins and lies,
It hides our cheeks and shades our eyes,
This debt we pay to human guile;
With torn and bleeding hearts we smile,
And mouth with myriad subtleties.

20. In the last line, *myriad* means

    A. singular   B. dishonest   C. various   D. painful

21. The use of *subtleties* in the last line is an example of

    A. off-rime
    C. iambic rime
    B. exact rime
    D. alliteration

22. Stephen Crane, Mark Twain, and Jack London are all considered by literary historians to be

    A. colonialists
    C. realists
    B. romantics
    D. modernists

23. Which of the following writers once explained his literary philosophy by saying, *The dignity of the movement of an iceberg is due to only one-eighth of it being above water?*

    A. Norman Mailer
    C. William Faulkner
    B. John Steinbeck
    D. Ernest Hemingway

24. Which of the following writers wrote the poems URIEL, MERLIN, and ODE INSCRIBED TO W.H. CHANNING?

    A. Ralph Waldo Emerson
    C. William Cullen Bryant
    B. Walt Whitman
    D. Herman Melville

Questions 25-28.

DIRECTIONS: Questions 25 through 28 are to be answered on the basis of the following passage.

What determined the speech that startled him in the course of their encounter scaTcely matters, being probably but some words spoken by himself quite without intention -- spoken as they lingered and slowly moved together after their renewal of acquaintance. (1) He had been conveyed by friends an hour or two before to the house at which she was staying; the party of visitors at the other house, of whom he was one, and thanks to whom it was his theory, as always, that he was lost in the crowd, had been invited over to luncheon. (2) There had been after luncheon much dispersal, all in the interest of the original motive, a view of Wetherend itself and the fine things, intrinsic features, picture, heirlooms, treasures of all the arts, that made the place almost famous; and the great rooms were so numerous that guests could wander at their will, hang back from the principal group and in cases where they took such matters with the last seriousness give themselves up to mysterious appreciations and measurements. (3)

25. The passage above opens

    A. WASHINGTON SQUARE
    C. THE TURN OF THE SCREW
    B. DAISY MILLER
    D. THE BEAST IN THE JUNGLE

26. The passage above is mainly concerned with the

    A. meeting of a man and a woman
    B. meeting of two men

C. details of a social gathering
D. main character's alienation

27. In line 1, the phrase *renewal of acquaintance* mainly implies that

    A. the two will soon meet for the first time
    B. the two have met before
    C. the two have just met
    D. he can't stop thinking about her

28. In line 3, the opening clause, *There had been after luncheon much dispersal,* mainly implies that

    A. there was a great deal of noise
    B. there was a great deal of talking
    C. many people left at the same time
    D. people said their goodbye's at the same time

29. Which of the following writers was famous for retelling stories he had heard from slaves, and for creating the character of Uncle Remus?

    A. Joel Chandler Harris   B. Paul Laurence Dunbar
    C. Jean-ah Poquelin   D. Charles Waddell Chesnutt

30. Which of the following best states the theme of Willa Cather's short story masterpiece PAUL'S CASE?

    A. It is impossible for the artist to survive in a narrow-minded society.
    B. The individual's struggle against alienation is often overwhelming.
    C. It is impossible for the artist to survive in a materialistic society.
    D. The individual's struggle against alienation is often successful.

31. *There is a difference between one and another hour of life, in their authority and subsequent effect. Our faith comes in moments; our vice is habitual. Yet is there a depth in those brief moments, which constrains us to ascribe more reality to them than to all other experiences.*
    The lines above open the essay entitled

    A. THE OVER-SOUL   B. NATURE
    C. EXPERIENCE   D. THE POET

32. Who is the African-American leader who urged African-Americans to become self-sufficient and seize their civil rights through political and civil protest?

    A. Booker T. Washington   B. W. DuBois
    C. Paul Laurence Dunbar   D. Frederick Douglas

33. Which of the following writers was able to publish five novels, two volumes of poetry, and approximately 300 sketches and short stories before he died at the age of 24?

    A. Stephen Crane   B. Wilfred Owen
    C. Jack London   D. Walt Whitman

34. In which of the following autobiographies does Charles Eastman chronicle his childhood before he was sent away from his family to attend school with white children? 34._____
    A. LOVE MEDICINE
    B. INDIAN BOYHOOD
    C. BLACK ELK SPEAKS
    D. A VOICE PROM THE SOUTH

35. Isaac Babel wrote all of the following EXCEPT 35._____
    A. THE DEATH OF DOLGUSHOV
    B. SANDY THE CHRIST
    C. ENEMIES, A LOVE STORY
    D. MY FIRST GOOSE

36. Which of the following writers gained critical acclaim for the NICK ADAMS stories? 36._____
    A. Raymond Carver
    B. John Steinbeck
    C. William Faulkner
    D. Ernest Hemingway

Questions 37-39.

DIRECTIONS: Questions 37 through 39 are to be answered on the basis of the following passage.

Their foot shall slide in due time. (Deuteronomy 32.35)

In this verse is threatened the vengeance of God on the wicked unbelieving Israelites, who were God's visible people, and who lived under the means of grace, but who, notwithstanding all God's wonderful works towards them, remained (as in verse 28), void of counsel, having no understanding in them. (1) Under all the cultivations of heaven, they brought forth bitter and poisonous fruit, as in the two verses next preceding the text.(2)

37. These lines open which of the following? 37._____
    A. THE WONDERS OF THE INVISIBLE WORLD
    B. SINNERS IN THE HANDS OF AN ANGRY GOD
    C. A PEOPLE OF GOD IN THE DEVIL'S TERRITORIES
    D. THE DAY OF DOOM

38. In sentence 1, the phrase *void of counsel* mainly implies 38._____
    A. an unwillingness to follow God's advice
    B. an inability to follow God's advice
    C. that, having followed God's advice, the people are now waiting for the rewards
    D. that, having disobeyed God, the people are aware that they will be punished

39. In sentence 2, the phrase *under all the cultivations of heaven* mainly implies 39._____
    A. that, having followed God's instructions, they are waiting for their reward
    B. an inability to understand God's intentions
    C. strong religious instruction and training
    D. a lack of religious instruction and training

40. Which of the following writers wrote O, PIONEERS!, THE SONG OF THE LARK, and MY ANTONIA?

    A. Willa Cather
    B. Edith Wharton
    C. John Dos Passos
    D. Kate Chopin

41. In which of the following essays does Emerson provide his aesthetic philosophy on poetry and literary criticism?

    A. SELF-RELIANCE
    B. THE POET
    C. THE OVER-SOUL
    D. NATURE

42. For which of the following writers was the portrayal of the fallen South a major theme?

    A. F. Scott Fitzgerald
    B. Mark Twain
    C. John Steinbeck
    D. William Faulkner

43. *After the kings of Great Britain had assumed the right of appointing the colonial governors, the measures of the latter seldom met with the ready and general approbation, which had been paid to those of their predecessors, under the original charters. The people looked with most jealous scrutiny to the exercise of power, which did not emanate from themselves, and they usually rewarded the rulers with slender gratitude, for the compliances, by which, in softening their instructions from beyond the sea, they had incurred the reprehension of those who gave them.*
    The lines above open the short story entitled

    A. RAPPACCINI'S DAUGHTER
    B. MY KINSMAN, MAJOR MOLINEUX
    C. THE ARTIST OF THE BEAUTIFUL
    D. BARTELBY THE SCRIVENER

44. The novel THE RED BADGE OF COURAGE depicts which of the following wars?

    A. World War I
    B. Spanish-American War
    C. Civil War
    D. Revolutionary War

45. Which of the following has as its primary focus the experiences of a platoon of men during and after the Vietnam War?

    A. HENDERSON THE RAIN KING
    B. THE THINGS THEY CARRIED
    C. ARMIES OF THE NIGHT
    D. CATCH-22

46. Which of the following writers wrote CALL OF THE WILD, MARTIN EDEN, and IRON HEEL?

    A. John Dos Passos
    B. Ernest Hemingway
    C. Stephen Crane
    D. Jack London

47. The Ghost Dance Vision refers to the

    A. apocalyptic vision of a slave which led to the Nat Turner uprising
    B. apocalyptic vision of a Sioux Indian which predicted the restoration of Indian lands and buffalo herds
    C. dream which inspired THE HEADLESS HORSEMAN
    D. feminist vision of a Utopian society based on sexual equality

48. Which of the following short stories has as its main focus the troubled relationship between two brothers who grew up in Harlem and are finally reconciled by one brother's music?

   A. THE SKY IS GRAY
   B. A SOLO SONG: FOR DOC
   C. BATTLE ROYAL
   D. SONNY'S BLUES

49. In the short story by Joyce Carol Oates, WHERE ARE YOU GOING, WHERE HAVE YOU BEEN?, the character of Arnold Friend symbolizes

   A. a fairytale prince
   B. a terrifying version of a fairytale prince
   C. adult sexuality
   D. childhood innocence

50. Which of the following poets is generally regarded as the leading experimentalist in modern literature?

   A. Ezra Pound
   B. T.S. Eliot
   C. Allen Ginsburg
   D. William Carlos Williams

KEY (CORRECT ANSWERS)

1. A	11. D	21. A	31. A	41. B
2. D	12. C	22. C	32. B	42. D
3. A	13. D	23. D	33. A	43. B
4. D	14. B	24. A	34. B	44. C
5. C	15. A	25. D	35. C	45. B
6. C	16. D	26. A	36. D	46. D
7. D	17. A	27. B	37. B	47. B
8. B	18. C	28. C	38. A	48. D
9. A	19. D	29. A	39. C	49. B
10. B	20. C	30. B	40. A	50. A

EXAMINATION SECTION
TEST 1

DIRECTIONS: Each question or incomplete statement is followed by several suggested answers or completions. Select the one that BEST answers the question or completes the statement. *PRINT THE LETTER OF THE CORRECT ANSWER IN THE SPACE AT THE RIGHT.*

1. At the time of her death, only seven of this poet's poems had been published, all of them anonymously.   1.____

    A. Anne Sexton
    B. Sylvia Plath
    C. Elizabeth Barrett Browning
    D. Emily Dickinson

2. In the short story by Tillie Olsen, I STAND HERE IRONING, the final image of the iron mainly suggests   2.____

    A. oppression and defeat
    B. love and triumph
    C. death
    D. the endurance of maternal love

3. Which of the following poets wrote ILLUSTRIOUS ANCESTORS, A SOLITUDE, and A WOMAN ALONE?   3.____

    A. Sylvia Plath   B. Denise Levertov
    C. Adrienne Rich   D. Muriel Rukeyser

4. The novel HUCKLEBERRY FINN was written by   4.____

    A. Stephen Crane   B. Nathaniel Hawthorne
    C. Mark Twain   D. Henry David Thoreau

5. Before his death, who was the man who said he wished to be remembered first and foremost for writing THE DECLARATION OF INDEPENDENCE?   5.____

    A. Thomas Paine   B. Thomas Jefferson
    C. Alexander Hamilton   D. Benjamin Franklin

6. Which of the following writers exposed the Chicago meatpacking industry in his first novel, and then went on to run for Governor of California?   6.____

    A. Stephen Crane   B. Jack London
    C. Upton Sinclair   D. John Dos Passos

Questions 7-8.

DIRECTIONS: Questions 7 and 8 are to be answered on the basis of the following passage.

Until the Great Exposition of 1900 closed its doors in November, Adams haunted it, aching to absorb knowledge, and helpless to find it. He would have liked to know how much of it could have been grasped by the best-informed man in the world. While he Was thus meditating chaos, Langley came by, and showed it to him.

7. The passage above, taken from a chapter entitled *The Dynamo and the Virgin,* is found in which of the following books by Henry Adams?   7.____

    A. DEMOCRACY: AN AMERICAN NOVEL
    B. MOUNT-SAINT-MICHEL AND CHARTRES
    C. ESTHER: A NOVEL
    D. THE EDUCATION OF HENRY ADAMS

8. What is so unusual about the book which is quoted above?   8.____

    A. It's a biographical account written in the first person.
    B. It's an autobiographical account written in the third person.
    C. It exposed the dangerous working conditions of many Americans.
    D. The author put himself at risk in order to conduct research for the book, one of the first American journalists to do so.

9. WOMAN WARRIOR has as its primary focus the experiences of a   9.____

    A. Chinese-American woman and her immigrant family
    B. Chinese-American boy in turn-of-the-century San Francisco
    C. multi-racial woman struggling with her identity
    D. Chinese-American immigrant's journey back to China

Questions 10-11.

DIRECTIONS: Questions 10 and 11 are to be answered on the basis of the following passage.

I like to see it lap the Miles -
And lick the Valleys up -
And stop to feed itself at Tanks -
And then - prodigious step

Around a Pile of Mountains -
And supercilious peer
In Shanties - by the sides of Roads -
And then a Quarry pare

To fit its Ribs
And crawl between
Complaining all the while
In horrid - hooting stanza -
Then chase itself down Hill -

And neigh like Boanerges -
Then - punctual as a Star -
Stop - docile and omnipotent
At its own stable door -

10. This poem relies mainly on   10.____

    A. personification   B. metaphor
    C. a paradox   D. irony

11. The train is being compared to a

    A. bird   B. dog   C. storm   D. horse

12. Which of the following best states the theme of the short story masterpiece, THE YELLOW WALLPAPER?

    A. The stability of marriage can soothe a troubled mind.
    B. The artistic temperament is not suited to marriage.
    C. The bondage of conventional marriage parallels the bondage experienced by patients in a mental institution.
    D. There is no satisfactory cure for nervous prostration.

13. Saul Bellow, Toni Morrison, and N. Scott Momaday are considered by literary historians to be _____ writers.

    A. contemporary   B. modern
    C. romantic   D. minority

14. On the advice of Sherwood Anderson, this Southern writer began to focus on his *little postage stamp of soil,* Yoknapatawpha County, where all of his subsequent novels were set.

    A. Hart Crane   B. John Steinbeck
    C. William Faulkner   D. Ernest Hemingway

15. THE AWAKENING was written by

    A. Kate Chopin   B. Edith Wharton
    C. Willa Cather   D. Charlotte Perkins Gilman

Questions 16-19.

DIRECTIONS: Questions 16 through 19 are to be answered on the basis of the following passage.

Women

Women have no wilderness in them,
They are provident instead,
Content in the tight hot cell of their hearts
To eat dusty bread.

They do not see cattle cropping red winter grass,
They do not hear
Snow water going down under culverts
Shallow and clear

They wait, when they should turn to journeys,
They stiffen, when they should bend.
They use against themselves that benevolence
To which no man is friend.

They cannot think of so many crops to a field
Or of clean wood cleft by an axe.

Their love is an eager meaninglessness
Too tense, or too lax.

They hear in every whisper that speaks to them
A shout and a cry
As like as not, when they take life over their door-sills
They should let it go by.

16. The author of this poem is

    A. Louise Bogan
    C. Anne Sexton
    B. Sylvia Plath
    D. Emily Dickinson

17. The tone of this poem is best described as

    A. despairing
    C. accusing
    B. forgiving
    D. appeasing

18. In line 2, the word *provident* most nearly means

    A. ignorant B. lazy C. afraid D. practical

19. Which of the following best states the theme of this poem?

    A. Women should stop reducing their imaginations in order to gain security.
    B. Women will always reduce their imaginations in order to gain security.
    C. Women must imagine better lives for themselves if they want to achieve them.
    D. Men and women have different views of the world.

20. Which of the following best states the theme of the Eugene O'Neill play, THE ICEMAN COMETH?
    A

    A. self-deluding derelict works to deprive other derelicts of their life-sustaining lies
    B. self-deluding salesman works to deprive derelicts of their life-sustaining lies
    C. bitter salesman waits to die
    D. hopeful derelict unsuccessfully tries to gain entry into the world of commerce and productivity

21. Edith Wharton is commonly described by literary historians as a

    A. colonialist
    C. romantic
    B. realist
    D. modernist

22. Which of the following was written by Tennessee Williams?

    A. ENEMIES, A LOVE STORY
    C. THE CRUCIBLE
    B. A STREETCAR NAMED DESIRED
    D. DEATH OF A SALESMAN

23. Marge Piercy, Gwendolyn Brooks, and Amiri Baraka are all considered _____ writers.

    A. realistic
    C. modern
    B. romantic
    D. contemporary

24. The work of John Barth and Donald Bartheleme often makes a comment on the act of writing itself. This is referred to as 24.____

    A. metafiction B. magic realism
    C. fantasy D. shifting point of view

25. Characters struggling with the pioneering and immigrant experiences of life on the High Plains figure prominently in the fiction of 25.____

    A. Edith Wharton B. Willa Cather
    C. Kate Chopin D. Charlotte Perkins Gilma

26. *Where do we find ourselves? In a series of which we do not know the extremes, and believe that it has none. We wake and find ourselves on a stair; there are stairs below us, which we seem to have ascended; there are stairs above us, many a one, which go upward and out of sight. But the Genius which, according to the old belief, stands at the door by which we enter, and gives us the lethe to drink, that we may tell no tales, mixed the cup too strongly, and we cannot shake off the lethargy now at noonday.*
    The lines above begin which Emerson essay? 26.____

    A. SELF-RELIANCE B. THE POET
    C. NATURE D. EXPERIENCE

27. The poem HIAWATHA was written by 27.____

    A. Walt Whitman
    B. Henry Wadsworth Longfellow
    C. Washington Irving
    D. Robert Louis Stevenson

28. Which of the following rhythmic patterns does the poem HIAWATHA employ? 28.____

    A. Classic European meters B. Free verse
    C. Finnish folk meters D. Latin meters

Questions 29-31.

DIRECTIONS: Questions 29 through 31 are to be answered on the basis of the following passage.

A throng of bearded men, in sad-colored garments and gray, steeple-crowned hats, intermixed with women, some wearing hoods, and others bareheaded, was assembled in front of a wooden edifice, the door of which was heavily timbered with oak, and studded with iron spikes.

The founders of a new colony, whatever Utopia of human virtue and happiness they might originally project, have invariably recognized it among their earliest practical necessities to allot a portion of the virgin soil as a cemetery, and another portion as the site of a prison.

29. The passage above is taken from the opening pages of 29.____

    A. NATURE, by Ralph Waldo Emerson
    B. MOBY DICK, by Herman Melville
    C. THE SCARLET LETTER, by Nathaniel Hawthorne
    D. WALDEN, by Henry David Thoreau

30. In the second paragraph, the word *allot* is used to mean

    A. discuss   B. designate   C. reject   D. sell

31. The main implication of the second paragraph is best expressed by which of the following?

    A. In a truly Utopian society, there is no need for prisons or cemeteries.
    B. Utopians resist assigning valuable land to cemeteries and prisons, preferring to handle these problems in less conventional ways instead.
    C. Assigning valuable land for use as cemeteries and prisons is in line with Utopian ideals about the perfectibility of human nature.
    D. Despite their best intentions, idealists must acknowledge the presence of death and crime in their communities.

32. In Flannery O'Connor's short story, A GOOD MAN IS HARD TO FIND, the character of the Grandmother experiences which of the following just before she dies?

    A. Hatred   B. Rage   C. Grace   D. A seizure

Questions 33-34.

DIRECTIONS: Questions 33 and 34 are to be answered on the basis of the following passage.

From *THE CHRYSANTHEMUMS*

The high gray-flannel fog of winter closed off the Salinas Valley from the sky and from all the rest of the world. On every side it sat like a lid on the mountains and made of the great valley a closed pot. On the broad, level land floor the gang plows bit deep and left the black earth shining like metal where the shares had cut. On the foothill ranches across the Salinas River, the yellow stubble fields seemed to be bathed in pale cold sunshine, but there was no sunshine in the valley now in December. The thick willow scrub along the river flamed with sharp and positive yellow leaves.

33. The tone of this excerpt is best described as

    A. melancholy   B. despairing
    C. hopeful   D. expectant

34. In this excerpt, the writer depends primarily upon

    A. allegory   B. metaphor   C. irony   D. parody

Questions 35-36.

DIRECTIONS: Questions 35 and 36 are to be answered on the basis of the following passage.

*Man is his own star, and the soul that can
Render an honest and a perfect man,
Command all light, all influence, all fate,
Nothing to him falls early or too late.
Our acts our angels are, or good or ill,
Our fatal shadows that walk by us still.*

35. The verse above serves as the opening to

    A. SELF-RELIANCE
    B. WALDEN POND
    C. SONG OF MYSELF
    D. THE POET

36. The refrain, *I would prefer not to,* is uttered by the main character in the short story

    A. RAPPACCINI'S DAUGHTER
    B. THE ARTIST OF THE BEAUTIFUL
    C. BENITO CERENO
    D. BARTLEBY THE SCRIVENER

37. Which of the following novels exposed the dangerous and filthy conditions of the Chicago meat-packing industry in the early part of the 20th century?

    A. THE BEAST IN THE JUNGLE
    B. THE JUNGLE
    C. BABBITT
    D. THE RISE OF SILAS LAPHAM

38. Which of the following writers wrote ESTHER: A NOVEL, MOUNT-SAINT MICHEL AND CHARTRES, and DEMOCRACY: AN AMERICAN NOVEL?

    A. William James
    B. William Dean Howells
    C. Henry Adams
    D. Henry James

39. Which of the following women wrote an autobiography in the form of a religious conversion, or *accounting;* which provided a frank look at the cruelty and powerlessness many women faced in early America?

    A. Anne Bradstreet
    B. Elizabeth Ashbridge
    C. Abigail Adams
    D. Sarah Kemble Knight

40. This short story dramatizes the rebellion of an old mother who defies her husband by moving their family into the new barn her husband has built, so that they might live at least as well as her husband's livestock.

    A. THE FOREIGNER
    B. A CHURCH MOUSE
    C. THE REVOLT OF MOTHER
    D. CIRCUMSTANCE

41. Which of the following served as a parable for the McCarthy hearings of the 1950's?

    A. THE CRUCIBLE
    B. DEATH OF A SALESMAN
    C. JURY OF HER PEERS
    D. ENEMIES, A LOVE STORY

42. Which of the following poets wrote MY LOST YOUTH, A PSALM OF LIFE, and THE BUILDING OF THE SHIP?

    A. Robert Frost
    B. Herman Melville
    C. Walt Whitman
    D. Henry Wadsworth Longfellow

Questions 43-44.

DIRECTIONS: Questions 43 and 44 are to be answered on the basis of the following passage.

From, OUR AMERICA, by Jose Marti

The conceited villager believes the entire world to be his village. Provided that he can be mayor, or humiliate the rival Who stole his sweetheart, or add to the savings in his strongbox, he considers the universal order good, unaware of those giants with seven-league boots who can crush him underfoot, or of the strife in the heavens between comets that streak through the drowsy air-devouring worlds. (1) What remains of the village in America must rouse itself. (2) These are not the times for sleeping in a nightcap, but With weapons for a pillow, like the warriors of Juan de Castellanos – weapons of the mind, which conquer all others. (3) Barricades of ideas are worth more than barricades of stone. (4)

43. The main implication of this passage is that

    A. Americans must awaken their minds and spirits
    B. Americans must take up arms
    C. citizens must defend themselves by any means necessary
    D. the country is ripe for invasion

44. The main implication of the first sentence is that

    A. government is of no use with so much danger in the world
    B. politicians are greedy and inept
    C. because citizens are ignorant, they are happy with limited power
    D. most citizens don't know how to govern themselves

45. In the novel THE AWAKENING, Edna Pontellier awakens to

    A. a deeper sense of her maternal instincts
    B. a deeper, more sensual sense of herself
    C. the joys of independence
    D. the sorrows of being a woman

46. In the short story THE MAYPOLE OF MERRY MOUNT, by Nathaniel Hawthorne, the Maypole represents

    A. youth   B. female sexuality
    C. pagan beliefs   D. Christian beliefs

47. Which of the following women writers was also a humorist and enjoyed a popularity in her lifetime that rivaled that of her contemporary, Mark Twain?

    A. Marietta Holley   B. Louisa May Alcott
    C. Charlotte Perkins Gilman D. Anna Julia Cooper

48. Which of the following poetic forms originated among the Mexican-Americans of the southwest?

    A. Danza   B. Corrido   C. Copla   D. Villanelle

49. Of the following writers, whose work focuses primarily on social observations of the aristocracy of turn-of-the-century Manhattan and Europe?   49.____

    A. Gertrude Stein
    B. Kate Chopin
    C. Willa Catha
    D. Edith Wharton

50. This poet's use of open forms and unconventional subject matter had such a profound effect on American poetry that s/he has been called America's first poet.   50.____

    A. T.S. Eliot
    B. Emily Dickinson
    C. Walt Whitman
    D. Langston Hughes

KEY (CORRECT ANSWERS)

1. D	11. D	21. D	31. D	41. A
2. A	12. C	22. B	32. C	42. D
3. B	13. A	23. D	33. A	43. A
4. C	14. C	24. A	34. B	44. C
5. B	15. A	25. B	35. A	45. B
6. C	16. A	26. D	36. D	46. C
7. D	17. C	27. B	37. B	47. A
8. B	18. D	28. C	38. C	48. B
9. A	19. A	29. C	39. B	49. D
10. A	20. B	30. B	40. C	50. C

TEST 2

DIRECTIONS: Each question or incomplete statement is followed by several suggested answers or completions. Select the one that BEST answers the question or completes the statement. *PRINT THE LETTER OF THE CORRECT ANSWER IN THE SPACE AT THE RIGHT.*

1. THE CRYING OF LOT 49 has as its main concern the 1.___

    A. loss of individuality in a materialistic society
    B. loss of individuality in a technological society
    C. loss of individual privacy
    D. threat of nuclear war

Questions 2-3.

DIRECTIONS: Questions 2 and 3 are to be answered on the basis of the following passage.

We have yet had no genius in America, with tyrannous eye, which knew the value of our incomparable materials, and saw, in the barbarism and materialism of the times, another carnival of the same gods whose picture he so much admires in Homer; then in the middle age; then in Calvinism. . . . Our logrolling, our stumps and their politics, our fisheries, our Negroes, and Indians, our boasts, and our repudiations, the wrath of rogues, and the pusillanimity of honest men, the northern trade, the southern planting, the western clearing, Oregon, and Texas, are yet unsung. Yet America is a poem in our eyes; its ample geography dazzles the imagination, and it will not Wait long for metres.

2. The lines above are taken from which of the following essays by Ralph Waldo Emerson? 2.___

    A. NATURE   B. SELF-RELIANCE
    C. THE POET   D. EXPERIENCE

3. The last line from the passage above mainly implies that 3.___

    A. America is waiting for a formal poetry to evolve
    B. European poetry has more material to work with than does American poetry
    C. American poetry will not be as accomplished as European poetry
    D. American poetry will not be based on European meters and material

4. Which of the following poets wrote ICABOD, AMONG THE HILLS, and SNOW-BOUND: A WINTER IDYL? 4.___

    A. John Greenleaf Whittier
    B. Robert Frost
    C. Walt Whitman
    D. Henry Wadsworth Longfellow

5. Which of the following novellas has as its primary focus the tragic choice of a heroine who marries for love instead of security? 5.___

    A. DAISY MILLER   B. MY MORTAL ENEMY
    C. THE TURN OF THE SCREW   D. THE AGE OF GRIEF

6. Saul Bellow wrote which of the following? 6.___

    A. THE WAY TO RAINY MOUNTAIN   B. THE OLD MAN AND THE SEA
    C. ENEMIES, A LOVE STORY   D. HENDERSON THE RAIN KING

7. In the ADVENTURES OF HUCKLEBERRY FINN, the river that Huck and Jim travel represents

    A. freedom from the negative influences of human society
    B. human society
    C. slavery
    D. the American South

8. Which of the following poets became a major figure in the Harlem Renaissance in part because of his ability to incorporate jazz forms and rhythms into his work?

    A. T.S. Eliot
    B. Langston Hughes
    C. Jean Toomer
    D. George Samuel Schuyler

Questions 9-13.

DIRECTIONS: Questions 9 through 13 are to be answered on the basis of the following passage.

From *THE LOVE SONG OF J. ALFRED PRUFROCK*

Let us go then, you and I
When the evening is spread out against the sky
Like a patient etherized upon a table;
Let us go, through certain half-deserted streets,
The muttering retreats
Of restless nights in one-night cheap hotels
And sawdust restaurants with oyster-shells:
Streets that follow like a tedious argument
Of insidious intent
To lead you to an overwhelming question...
Oh, do not ask, "What is it?"
Let us go and make our visit.

9. The author of this poem is

    A. W.H. Auden   B. T.S. Eliot
    C. William Carlos Williams   D. Wallace Stevens

10. Lines 2 and 3 rely on

    A. simile   B. metaphor   C. allegory   D. irony

11. In line 9, the word *insidious* most nearly means

    A. expected   B. surprising
    C. stealthy   D. deceptive

12. These lines are written in which point of view?

    A. First person   B. Second person
    C. Third person limited   D. Third person omniscient

13. The tone of this excerpt is best described as

    A. maniacal
    B. melancholy
    C. hopeful
    D. joyful

14. Which of the following best describes ABSALOM, ABSALOM! The

    A. journey of a woman from a small southern town who goes to the city to find the father of her child
    B. struggle of a family to return the mother's body home for burial
    C. rise and fall of mythic plantation family in a small Southern town
    D. decline of a Southern family told in three successive narratives

15. A FAREWELL TO ARMS is mainly an indictment of

    A. the American dream
    B. idealized youth
    C. romantic love
    D. war

16. Which of the following American writers was the first to gain an international literary reputation for his work?

    A. Stephen Crane
    B. Washington Irving
    C. Walt Whitman
    D. Edgar Allen Poe

17. Who is the African-American poet whose poems include THOUGHTS ON THE WORKS OF PROVIDENCE and ON BEING BROUGHT FROM AFRICA TO AMERICA?

    A. Alice Dunbar Nelson
    B. Anne Bradstreet
    C. Paul Lawrence Dunbar
    D. Phillis Wheatley

18. Which of the following writers, whose works include THE WAY TO WEALTH, RULES BY WHICH A GREAT EMPIRE MAY BE REDUCED TO A SMALL ONE, and THE EPHEMERA?

    A. Ralph Waldo Emerson
    B. John Adams
    C. Benjamin Franklin
    D. Thomas Jefferson

19. Which of the following novelists gained a national reputation for his mastery of Creole life, and set most of his historical fiction in New Orleans?

    A. Alexander Lawrence Posey
    B. Charles Waddell Chestnutt
    C. Joel Chandler Harris
    D. George Washington Cable

20. In THE GREAT GATSBY, the billboard mainly symbolizes

    A. an absent god
    B. an amoral society
    C. an immoral society
    D. materialism

21. Which of the following essays written by Emerson is said to have set the stage for the work of Walt Whitman, America's first major poet?

    A. THE OVER-SOUL
    B. NATURE
    C. SELF-RELIANCE
    D. THE POET

22. Which of the following poets wrote BECAUSE I COULD NOT STOP FOR DEATH, IT DROPPED SO LOW IN MY REGARD, and VICTORY COMES LATE? 22.____

    A. Henry Wadsworth Longfellow
    B. Emily Dickinson
    C. Walt Whitman
    D. Elizabeth Barrett Browning

23. Of which of the following men did Walt Whitman once say, *I remained simmering, simmering, until (he) brought me to a boil?* 23.____

    A. Abraham Lincoln
    B. Stephen Crane
    C. Nathaniel Hawthorne
    D. Ralph Waldo Emerson

Questions 24-28.

DIRECTIONS: Questions 24 through 28 are to be answered on the basis of the following passage.

Because I could not stop for Death -
He kindly stopped for me -
The Carriage held but just Ourselves -
And Immortality.

We slowly drove - He knew no haste
And I had put away
My labor and my leisure too,
For His Civility -

We passed the School, where Children strove
At Recess - in the Ring -
We passed the Fields of Gazing Grain -
We passed the Setting Sun -

Or rather - He passed Us -
The Dews drew quivering and chill -
For only Gossamer, my Gown -
My Tippet - only Tulle -

We paused before a House that seemed
A Swelling of the Ground -
The Roof was scarcely visible -
The Cornice - in the Ground -

Since then - 'tis Centuries - and yet
Feels shorter than the Day
I first surmised the Horses' Heads
Were toward Eternity -

24. The author of this poem is

    A. Emily Dickinson
    B. Elizabeth Barrett Browning
    C. Walt Whitman
    D. Robert Frost

25. The first stanza relies primarily on

    A. irony   B. allegory   C. simile   D. metaphor

26. The last two lines of the first stanza mainly imply that

    A. death is a gentle experience
    B. death and immortality are intrinsically connected
    C. immortality is earned through hard work
    D. death and immortality are not necessarily connected

27. In stanza 3, the phrase *Fields of Gazing Grain* mainly implies that the

    A. natural world is indifferent to the narrator's death
    B. natural world is a witness to the narrator's death
    C. narrator lives near a farm
    D. narrator was in the midst of harvesting his/her grain

28. From what point in time is the narrator narrating this poem?

    A. Eternity
    B. After having returned home
    C. The past
    D. Moments before death

29. The book LIFE IN THE IRON MILLS was written by

    A. Louisa May Alcott   B. Rebecca Harding Davis
    C. Helen Keller   D. Charlotte Perkins Gilman

30. In the short story, A JURY OF HER PEERS, two housewives must decide whether

    A. the murderer is fit to stand trial
    B. the victim murdered his wife's canary
    C. another housewife was justified in murdering her husband
    D. another housewife is guilty of murdering her husband

31. Which of the following writers focused much of his fiction on the lives of farmers and workers in California?

    A. Ernest Hemingway   B. Ralph Ellison
    C. William Faulkner   D. John Steinbeck

32. Which of the following books has as its main theme an examination of the dueling claims of individuality and authority?

    A. BILLY BUDD, SAILOR   B. THE AWAKENING
    C. BENITO CERENO   D. UNCLE TOM'S CABIN

33. *(Found among the Papers of the Late Diedrich Knickerbocker)*
 A pleasing land of drowsy heat it was,
 Of dreams that wave before the half-shut eye;
 And of gay castles in the clouds that pass,
 Forever flushing round a summer sky
 The above lines open

   A. YOUNG GOODMAN BROWN
   B. MOBY DICK
   C. THE LEGEND OF SLEEPY HOLLOW
   D. RIP VAN WINKLE

34. Who wrote THE HASTY PUDDING, a poem which celebrated the simplicity of American manners?

   A. Thomas Paine B. Joel Barlow
   C. Royall Tyler D. Philip Freneau

35. Which of the following poets wrote 13 WAYS OF LOOKING AT A BLACKBIRD, THE DEATH OF A SOLDIER, and ASIDES ON THE OBOE?

   A. Wallace Stevens B. W.H. Auden
   C. T.S. Eliot D. William Carlos Williams

Questions 36-41.

DIRECTIONS: Questions 36 through 41 are to be answered on the basis of the following passage.

From, *BATTLE ROYAL*

 About eighty-five years ago they were told that they were free, united with others of our country in everything pertaining to the common good, and, in everything social, separate like the fingers of the hand. (1) And they believed it. (2) They exulted in it. (3) They stayed in their place, worked hard, and brought up my father to do the same. (4) But my grandfather is the one.(5) He was an odd guy, my grandfather, and I am told I take after him. (6) It was he who caused the trouble. (7) On his deathbed he called my father to him and said, "Son, after I'm gone I want you to keep up the good fight. (8) I never told you, but our life is a war and I have been a traitor all my born days, a spy in the enemy's country ever since I give up my gun back in the Reconstruction. (9) Live with your head in the lion's mouth. (10) I want you to overcome 'em with yeses, undermine 'em with grins, agree 'em to death and destruction, let 'em swoller you till they vomit or bust wide open." (11) They thought the old man had gone out of his mind. (12) He had been the meekest of men. (13) The younger children were rushed from the room, the shades drawn, and the flame of the lamp turned so low that it sputtered on the wick like the old man's breathing. (13)

36. The phrase, *separate like the fingers of the hand*, taken from sentence 1, refers to

   A. integration B. segregation
   C. freedom D. slavery

37. In sentence 3, *exulted* most nearly means

   A. resisted
   B. overcame
   C. endured
   D. celebrated

38. In sentence 9, who is the enemy the grandfather refers to?

   A. People outside the immediate family
   B. Society in general
   C. White people
   D. Other African-Americans

39. Sentence 11, which states, *I want you to overcome 'em with yeses, undermine 'em with grins, agree 'em to death and destruction, let 'em swoller you till they vomit or bust wide open,* mainly implies that

   A. the best way to overcome the enemy is to help him destroy himself
   B. people won't tolerate passive agreement
   C. the best way to remain safe is to never disagree with the enemy
   D. too much passive agreement can be dangerous

40. The parents' reaction to the grandfather's speech suggests that they find it

   A. humorous   B. senseless   C. harmless   D. dangerous

41. In sentence 13, the clause *sputtered on the wick like the old man's breathing* is an example of a(n)

   A. allegory   B. simile   C. metaphor   D. parody

42. *Our age is retrospective. It builds the sepulchres of the fathers. It writes biographies, histories, and criticism. The foregoing generations beheld God and nature fact to face; we, through their eyes. Why should not we also enjoy an original relation to the universe? Why should not we have a poetry and philosophy of insight and not of tradition, and a religion by revelation to us, and not the history of theirs?*
   The lines above are taken from the opening pages of

   A. SONG OF MYSELF, by Walt Whitman
   B. WALDEN POND, by Henry Thoreau
   C. NATURE, by Ralph Waldo Emerson
   D. THE POET, by Ralph Waldo Emerson

43. Which of the following women wrote THE MORGESON'S, a masterpiece renowned for its psychological portrait of obsessive characters living out their lives in restrictive social circumstances?

   A. Elizabeth Drew Stafford
   B. Harriet Beecher Stowe
   C. Kate Chopin
   D. Louisa May Alcott

44. Which of the following African-American authors wrote A BRAND PLUCKED FROM THE FIRE, an autobiography expressing early feminist ideals which attacked racism and sexism and called for equal treatment within the Church?

   A. Sojourner Truth
   B. Alice Dunbar Nelson
   C. Julia Foote
   D. Zora Neale Hurston

Questions 45-46.

DIRECTIONS: Questions 45 and 46 are to be answered on the basis of the following passage.

It is very seldom that mere ordinary people like John and myself secure ancestral halls for the summer.
A colonial mansion, a hereditary estate, I would say a haunted house, and reach the height of romantic felicity — but that would be asking too much of fate!
Still, I will proudly declare that there is something queer about it.
Else, why should it be let so cheaply? And why have stood so long untenanted?
John laughs at me, of course, but one expects that in marriage.

45. The passage above serves as the opening to THE

   A. AWAKENING
   B. YELLOW WALLPAPER
   C. REVOLT OF MOTHER
   D. TURN OF THE SCREW

46. The final line of the passage contributes to the tone of

   A. dissatisfaction
   B. whimsy
   C. confusion
   D. despair

47. Mark Twain wrote all of the following EXCEPT

   A. SOCIABLE JIMMY
   B. PUDD'NHEAD WILSON
   C. A CONNECTICUT YANKEE IN KING ARTHUR'S COURT
   D. PO' SANDY

48. Which of the following men wrote the sermons entitled, SINNERS IN THE HANDS OF AN ANGRY GOD and IMAGES OR SHADOWS OF DIVINE THINGS?

   A. William Bartram
   B. William Bird
   C. Jonathon Edwards
   D. Cotton Mather

49. What is the title of the short story, written by Harriet Spofford, which focuses on a woman who must call upon the hymns, prayers, and songs from her everyday life in order to survive when she is trapped by a wild animal?

   A. CIRCUMSTANCE
   B. THE WHITE HERON
   C. A CHURCH MOUSE
   D. OLD WOMAN MAGOUN

50. Ralph Ellison wrote which of the following?

   A. BLACK BOY
   B. INVISIBLE MAN
   C. ARMIES OF THE NIGHT
   D. BELOVED

KEY (CORRECT ANSWERS)

1. B	11. C	21. D	31. D	41. B
2. C	12. A	22. B	32. A	42. C
3. D	13. B	23. D	33. C	43. A
4. A	14. C	24. A	34. B	44. C
5. B	15. D	25. D	35. A	45. B
6. D	16. B	26. B	36. B	46. A
7. A	17. D	27. B	37. D	47. D
8. B	18. C	28. A	38. C	48. C
9. B	19. D	29. B	39. A	49. A
10. A	20. A	30. C	40. D	50. B

TEST 3

DIRECTIONS: Each question or incomplete statement is followed by several suggested answers or completions. Select the one that BEST answers the question or completes the statement. *PRINT THE LETTER OF THE CORRECT ANSWER IN THE SPACE AT THE RIGHT.*

1. Ralph Waldo Emerson is considered the father of

   A. American literature
   C. Transcendentalism
   B. Realism
   D. Romanticism

   1.____

2. Who wrote THE FEDERALIST?

   A. Alexander Hamilton
   C. Thomas Jefferson
   B. Benjamin Franklin
   D. Thomas Paine

   2.____

Questions 3-6.

DIRECTIONS: Questions 3 through 6 are to be answered on the basis of the following passage.

From, CHICKAMAUGA

One sunny autumn afternoon a child strayed away from its rude home in a small field and entered a forest unobserved. (1) It was happy in a new sense of freedom from control -- happy in the opportunity of exploration and adventure; for this child's spirit, in bodies of its ancestors, had for many thousands of years been trained to memorable feats of discovery and conquest -- victories in battles whose critical moments were centuries, whose victors' camps were cities of hewn stone. (2) From the cradle of its race it had conquered its way through two continents, and, passing a great sea, had penetrated a third, there to be born to war and dominion as a heritage. (3)

3. This author of this story is

   A. John Dos Passos
   C. Ambrose Bierce
   B. Stephen Crane
   D. Paul Bowles

   3.____

4. In sentence 2, the clause, *for this child's spirit, in bodies of its ancestors, had for many thousands of years been trained to memorable feats of discovery and conquest,* mainly implies that the

   A. child has been reincarnated
   B. child's behavior has been shaped by centuries of experience
   C. child's behavior is a universal trait
   D. child is just like its parents

   4.____

5. In sentence 2, the clause, *victories in battles whose critical moments were centuries, whose victors' camps were cities of hewn stone,* mainly implies that the child's ancestors

   A. have dominated vast regions for hundreds of years
   B. have disappeared
   C. no longer have any influence in their region
   D. were once powerful, but not any longer

   5.____

149

6. In sentence 3, the clause, *born to war and dominion as a heritage,* mainly implies that the child's future

   A. is as bright with hope as his ancestors' futures once were
   B. is doomed
   C. is predisposed to repeat the patterns of its ancestors
   D. will follow a course dictated by the past

7. While his fiction focused on the difficulties faced by farmers in the Upper Midwest, this writer's autobiography, SON OF THE MIDDLE BORDER, is considered a classic.

   A. William Dean Howells   B. Hamlin Garland
   C. Ambrose Bierce   D. John Milton Oskison

8. Which of the following works by Stephen Crane is best described as a novel which vividly portrays the suffering and poverty of Irish immigrants?

   A. WAR IS KIND
   B. THE RED BADGE OF COURAGE
   C. THE THIRD VIOLET
   D. MAGGIE: A GIRL OF THE STREETS

9. For which of the following writers was the exploration of the effect of Puritan ideals upon the individual and his society a major theme?

   A. Nathaniel Hawthorne   B. Herman Melville
   C. Stephen Crane   D. Henry David Thoreau

10. Which of the following writers is famous for setting his work during the Jazz Age?

    A. John Steinbeck   B. Ernest Hemingway
    C. F. Scott Fitzgerald   D. Langston Hughes

Questions 11-12.

DIRECTIONS: Questions 11 and 12 are to be answered on the basis of the following passage.

These are the times that try men's souls. The summer soldier and the sunshine patriot will, in this crisis, shrink from the service of their country; but he that stands it now, deserves the love and thanks of man and woman. Tyranny, like hell, is not easily conquered; yet we have this consolation with us, that the harder the conflict, the more glorious the triumph. What we obtain too cheap, we esteem too lightly: It is dearness only that gives everything its value.

11. These are the opening lines to THE

    A. CRISIS
    B. DECLARATION OF INDEPENDENCE
    C. HASTY PUDDING
    D. FEDERALIST

12. The phrase, *summer soldier and the sunshine patriot* refers to   12._____

    A. those people who support the cause when it is most dangerous for them to do so
    B. those people who support the cause only when that support is easy
    C. veterans who have served the cause through many years
    D. veterans who have deserted the cause and must now be punished

13. The story, LIFE IN THE IRON MILLS, written by Rebecca Harding Davis, focuses on   13._____

    A. a criticism of the idea that industrialization means social progress
    B. a contrast of men's luxury with working women's poverty
    C. the destruction of artistic creativity by a woman's hard labor in the iron mills
    D. the Pemberton Mills collapse and fire in Lawrence, Massachusetts

14. *A young man named Giovanni Guasconti, came, very long ago, from the more southern*   14._____
    region of Italy, to pursue his studies at the University of Padua. Giovanni, who had but a
    scanty supply of gold ducats in his pocket, took lodgings in a high and gloomy chamber
    of an old edifice, which looked not unworthy to have been the palace of a Paduan noble,
    and which, in fact, exhibited over its entrance the armorial bearings of a family long since
    extinct.
    The lines above open which of the following short stories by Nathaniel Hawthorne?

    A. THE ARTIST OF THE BEAUTIFUL
    B. YOUNG GOODMAN BROWN
    C. THE MAYPOLE OF MERRY MOUNT
    D. RAPPACCINI'S DAUGHTER

15. President Abraham Lincoln referred to this American novelist as *the little woman who*   15._____
    started the big war.

    A. Harriet Beecher Stowe   B. Susan B. Anthony
    C. Charlotte Perkins Gilman   D. Louisa May Alcott

Questions 16-19.

DIRECTIONS: Questions 16 through 19 are to be answered on the basis of the following passage.

From, ODE TO SEQUOYAH

The names of Waitie and Boudinot -
*   The valiant warrior and gifted sage -*
And other Cherokees, may be forgot,
*   But thy name shall descend to every age;*
The mysteries enshrouding Cadmus' name
Cannot obscure they claim to fame.

The people's language cannot perish - nay,
*   When from the face of this great continent*
*   Inevitable doom hath swept away*
The last memorial - the last fragment
*   Of tribes, - some scholar learned shall pore*
Upon they letters, seeking ancient lore.

16. The author of this poem is 16.___

    A. Henry Wadsworth Longfellow
    B. Alexander Posey
    C. Jean-ah Poquelin
    D. Mourning Dove

17. In stanza 1, whose name *shall descend to every age*? 17.___

    A. Waitie and Boudinot's   B. Cadmus'
    C. The poet's   D. Sequoyah's

18. The poem's rhyme scheme depends mainly on 18.___

    A. alliteration   B. internal rhyme
    C. end rhyme   D. assonance

19. The main implication of the second stanza is that 19.___

    A. after all the tribes have disappeared, someone will want to learn about them
    B. the tribes will all be destroyed, leaving no record
    C. the tribes should surrender before they are destroyed
    D. the language of the Cherokee should be forgotten

20. Identified as the *Poet of the American Revolution,* who is the poet whose poems include THE HOUSE OF NIGHT and TO SIR TOBY? 20.___

    A. Royall Tyler   B. Thomas Paine
    C. Philip Freneau   D. Joel Barlow

21. Which of the following writers is known for setting her stories and novels amid many different cultures and political situations? 21.___

    A. Kate Chopin   B. Katherine Anne Porter
    C. Louise Erdrich   D. Flannery O'Connor

22. THE INTERESTING NARRATIVE OF THE LIFE OF ALAUDAH EQUIANO is considered 22.___

    A. one of the first slave narratives
    B. one of the first narratives written by a relocated Native American
    C. the best American slave narrative
    D. the best Native American relocation narrative

23. Henry James' novel, THE BOSTONIANS, tells the story of 23.___

    A. two emotionally aloof young men
    B. a young girl neglected by her divorced parents
    C. a group of young women in post-Civil War America
    D. a young woman who falls victim to her overbearing father and faithless lover

Questions 24-26.

DIRECTIONS: Questions 24 through 26 are to be answered on the basis of the following passage.

Between me and the other world there is ever an unasked question: unasked by some through feelings of delicacy; by others through the difficulty of rightly framing it. All, nevertheless, flutter round it. They approach me in a half-hesitant sort of way, eye me curiously or compassionately, and then, instead of saying directly, How does it feel to be a problem? they say, I known an excellent colored man in my town; or, I fought at Mechanicsville; or, Do not these Southern outrages make your blood boil? At these I smile, or am interested, or reduce the boiling to a simmer, as the occasion may require. To the real question, How does it feel to be a problem? I answer seldom a word.

24. These lines open
    A. THE SOULS OF BLACK FOLK
    B. UP FROM SLAVERY
    C. BLACK BOY
    D. INVISIBLE MAN

25. In the opening sentence of the passage above, when the writer refers to *the other world*, to whom is he referring?
    A. People with a mixed-race heritage
    B. The rich
    C. White people
    D. Affluent black people

26. In the last line of the passage above, what is the *problem* to which the author refers?
    A. His poverty
    B. His African-American identity
    C. The poverty of all African-Americans
    D. His political beliefs

27. The novel, THE STORY OF AVIS, by Elizabeth Stuart Phelps explores the
    A. marriage and divorce of a working-class woman
    B. destruction of artistic creativity by a woman's hard labor in the iron mills
    C. contrast between the luxurious lives of men and the poverty-stricken lives of working-class women
    D. difficulties faced by a typical woman as she tries to explore her creativity while maintaining her domestic responsibilities

28. Who is the African-American writer whose contribution to the New Negro Renaissance included VIOLETS AND OTHER TALES and THE GOODNESS OF ST. ROCQUE?
    A. Alice Dunbar-Nelson
    B. Zora Neale Hurston
    C. Julia Foote
    D. Sojourner Truth

29. Which of the following short stories by Nathaniel Hawthorne is best described as a moral allegory in which a newly married man journeys away from his wife into a mysterious forest?
    A. RAPPACGINI'S DAUGHTER
    B. MY KINSMAN, MAJOR MOLINEUX
    C. THE ARTIST OF THE BEAUTIFUL
    D. YOUNG GOODMAN BROWN

30. Which of the following novels focuses on the experiences of Lena Grove as she searches the South for the father of her unborn child?

   A. A LIGHT IN AUGUST
   B. THE SOUND AND THE FURY
   C. SHIP OF FOOLS
   D. THE AWAKENING

31. Walt Whitman's poem, WHEN LILACS LAST IN THE DOORYARD BLOOM'D is considered a(n)

   A. prose poem
   B. villanelle
   C. elegy
   D. sonnet

32. *At Paris, just after dark one gusty evening in the autumn of 18 --, I was enjoying the twofold luxury of meditation and a meerschaum, in company with my friend C. August Dupin, in his little back library, or book-closet, au troisieme, No. 33 Rue Dunot, Faubourg St. Germain.*

   The lines above open the short story entitled THE

   A. TELL-TALE HEART
   B. CASK OF AMONTILLADO
   C. PURLOINED LETTER
   D. FALL OF THE HOUSE OF USHER

33. Which of the following men was considered one of the most powerful figures in American literature during his lifetime, and who was renowned in his use of realism in novels such as A FOREGONE CONCLUSION?

   A. John Dos Passos
   B. William Dean Howells
   C. T.S. Eliot
   D. Ernest Hemingway

34. The Frank Norris novel, MCTEAGUE, is best described as a(n)

   A. graphic portrayal of greed and degradation
   B. romantic comedy about love between the social classes
   C. adventure-romance between two strong-willed protagonists
   D. exploration of a man's downfall through materialism

35. Willa Cather is commonly described by literary historians as a

   A. colonialist
   B. realist
   C. romantic
   D. modernist

Questions 36-37.

DIRECTIONS: Questions 36 and 37 are to be answered on the basis of the following passage.

Mr. (Booker T.) Washington represents in Negro thought the old attitude of adjustment and submission; but adjustment at such a peculiar time as to make his programme unique. (1) This is an age of unusual economic development, and Mr. Washington's programme naturally takes an economic cast, becoming a gospel of Work and Money to such an extent as apparently almost completely to overshadow the higher aims of life. (2) Moreover, this is an age when the more advanced races are coming in closer contact with the less developed races and the race-feeling is therefore intensified; and Mr. Washington's programme practically accepts the alleged inferiority of the Negro races. (3)

36. Who wrote this criticism of Booker T. Washington?

    A. Paul Laurence Dunbar
    B. W.E.B. DuBois
    C. Julia Foote
    D. Frederick Douglas

37. In sentence 2, the clause, *apparently almost completely to overshadow the higher aims of life*, mainly implies that

    A. Booker T. Washington is not religious enough
    B. the emphasis on work and money is immoral
    C. the emphasis on work and money is well-placed
    D. the emphasis on work and money is too narrow

38. Which of the following novels focuses on the life of an American businessman whose loss of status proves to be his spiritual gain?

    A. A FOREGONE CONCLUSION
    B. THE GREAT GATSBY
    C. THE RISE OF SILAS LAPHAM
    D. BABBITT

39. Which of the following was NOT written by Flannery O'Connor?

    A. SAINT MARIE
    B. GOOD COUNTRY PEOPLE
    C. THE LAME SHALL ENTER FIRST
    D. EVERYTHING THAT RISES MUST CONVERGE

40. In THE GREAT GATSBY, Daisy Buchanan represents which of the following?

    A. Money
    B. Social acceptance
    C. True love
    D. All of the above

41. Which of the following couples exchanged letters during the course of their marriage which are now valued as important documents which shed light on a young country seeking its identity after the Revolutionary War?

    A. Simon and Anne Bradstreet
    B. John and Abigail Adams
    C. Benjamin and Deborah Franklin
    D. Aaron and Elizabeth Ashbridge

42. The novel, CONTENDING FORCES: A ROMANCE ILLUSTRATIVE OF NEGRO LIFE NORTH AND SOUTH, written by Pauline Elizabeth Hopkins, focuses on

    A. a group of African-Americans living in the North who fight for the Union during the Civil War
    B. the life of a large African-American family living in the North before the Civil War
    C. the life of a large African-American family which migrates from the pre-Civil War Caribbean to the American North
    D. a group of slaves living on a Southern plantation before and after the Civil War

43. Who is the African-American poet who wrote LIFT EVERY VOICE AND SING and O BLACK AND UNKNOWN BARDS?

    A. James Weldon Johnson
    B. Langston Hughes
    C. Paul Laurence Dunbar
    D. Charles Wadell Chestnutt

44. Which of the following novels was set in New Orleans just after the Louisiana Purchase and had as its main focus the conflict between old French colonial culture and American culture?

    A. OLD WOMAN MAGOUN
    B. THE LITTLE CONVENT GIRL
    C. THE AWAKENING
    D. JEAN-AH POQUELIN

45. Which of the following poets wrote THE RED WHEELBARROW?

    A. W.H. Auden
    B. William Carlos Williams
    C. T.S. Eliot
    D. Robert Hayden

Questions 46-47.

DIRECTIONS: Questions 46 and 47 are to be answered on the basis of the following passage.

Let us affront and reprimand the smooth mediocrity and squalid contentment of the times, and hurl in the face of custom, and trade, and office, the fact which is the upshot of all history, that there is a great responsible Thinker and Actor moving wherever moves a man: that a true man belongs to no other time or place, but is the center of things.

— Ralph Waldo Emerson

46. The phrase, *the smooth mediocrity and squalid contentment of the times* is used to

    A. explain why society is doomed to repeat the mistakes of history
    B. explain why society has lost sight of its principles
    C. describe a society which has lost sight of its principles
    D. describe a man who has lost sight of his own importance

47. The main purpose of this passage above is to

    A. explain why Americans are so eager to believe in a Christian God
    B. explain why the American experiment in government will fail
    C. comfort those who find themselves out of sync with the beliefs of their time
    D. challenge others to maintain their own moral code, even though it may be out of fashion

48. Which Henry James novel, set in the United States, tells the story of a young woman who falls victim to her overbearing father and faithless lover?

    A. DAISY MILLER
    B. WASHINGTON SQUARE
    C. THE BEAST IN THE JUNGLE
    D. THE TURN OF THE SCREW

49. Which of the following stories, focused on the triumph of small, quick animals over larger, stronger ones, were viewed as metaphors for African-Americans struggling to survive in the ante-bellum South?

    A. UNCLE REMUS: HIS SONGS AND SAYINGS
    B. UNCLE TOM'S CABIN

C. LYRICS OF LOWLY LIFE
D. PO' SANDY

50. Which of the following short stories by Kate Chopin focuses on a sexual affair between a married woman and a man who is not her husband? 50.____

    A. THE STORY OF AN HOUR   B. A RESPECTABLE WOMAN
    C. THE STORM   D. DESIREE'S BABY

KEY (CORRECT ANSWERS)

1. C	11. A	21. B	31. C	41. B
2. A	12. B	22. A	32. C	42. C
3. C	13. C	23. C	33. B	43. A
4. B	14. D	24. A	34. A	44. D
5. A	15. A	25. C	35. D	45. B
6. C	16. B	26. B	36. B	46. C
7. B	17. D	27. D	37. D	47. D
8. D	18. C	28. A	38. C	48. B
9. A	19. A	29. D	39. A	49. A
10. C	20. C	30. A	40. D	50. C

www.ingramcontent.com/pod-product-compliance
Lightning Source LLC
Chambersburg PA
CBHW082039300426
44117CB00015B/2543